.

Daily Might

David Brandt Berg

Acknowledgments

Unless otherwise indicated, all Bible quotations in this book are from the New King James Version, © 1982 Thomas Nelson, Inc. References marked "KJV" are from the King James Version of the Bible. References marked "TLB" are from The Living Bible, © 1971 by Tyndale House Publishers, Inc. References marked NIV are from the New International Version, © 1973 International Bible Society.

ISBN 13: 978-3-03730-299-6

Edited by Keith Phillips
Design by Giselle LeFavre

© 2006–2009 Aurora Production AG, Switzerland
All Rights Reserved. Printed in Taiwan

Visit our Web site at www.auroraproduction.com.

Introduction

The Bible tells us "God is a Spirit" (John 4:24 KJV) and "God is love" (1 John 4:8). Not only is He the all-powerful, everywhere-present, eternal Spirit of love, but He is also our kind and loving heavenly Father who created this beautiful world for us to live in and enjoy.

God is far beyond our human understanding, but because He loves us and wants us to know and love Him, He sent His Son to us in the form of a man, Jesus Christ. Jesus came to show us what God is like and to bring us to Him (John 3:16; 1 Peter 3:18). Jesus talked about love and showed love and *lived* love all the time—and in the end He loved us enough to give His life to save us.

The greatest gift God has for you is eternal life in Heaven—also known as *salvation*, being *saved*, or being *born again*. You receive this gift the instant you believe that Jesus Christ is God's Son and accept Him into your life.

None of us are perfect. We're all sinners by nature, and our sins separate us from God (Isaiah 59:2). The only way we can be reconciled with God is if our sins are atoned for, and only Jesus—who was Himself perfect—could do that. Jesus gave His life "a ransom for many" (Matthew 20:28). Jesus died so *all* could have eternal life, but He would have done it for you alone. God loves you so much that He gave His only Son to die in your place, and Jesus loves you so much that He did that willingly.

God made salvation simple—so simple, in fact, that even a child could understand and receive it. All you have to do is admit that you've made mistakes and need God's forgiveness, accept in childlike faith His explanation that He sent Jesus to pay for your mistakes, and ask for forgiveness.

Would you like to know beyond a shadow of a doubt that Jesus Christ really is the Son of God and the way to salvation? Just try Him! If you haven't yet received Jesus as your Savior, you can do it right now by praying a short prayer like the following:

Dear Jesus, thank You for dying for me so that all my mistakes and wrongs can be forgiven. I now open the door of my heart and ask You to come in. Please forgive me and give me Your free gift of eternal life. Amen.

If you have prayed to receive Jesus, you can be assured that He heard and answered. You've taken the first step into a wonderful new life of love that will never end. (To gain a better understanding of salvation, see the readings listed under "Salvation" in the Index.)

The new you

Once you're saved, you can start enjoying many of the benefits imme-diately. Jesus said, "The kingdom of God is within you" (Luke 17:21). If you have Jesus, the kingdom of God has already entered you. You can begin living in the continual heaven of His love, peace, and joy right here and now.

You can also expect some pretty big changes in yourself. You're a "new creation" (2 Corinthians 5:17). Don't be surprised if you actually feel different, think differently, view the world differently, and are happier than you have ever been before. "I have come that you may have life," Jesus said, "and that you may have it more abundantly" (John 10:10).

You may not be totally different—at least not right away—but you'll soon notice a change in your spirit, your thoughts, and the direction your life is going. As you begin to get your answers and spiritual strength from the Lord and His Word, things you never even dreamed possible will become possible. With His help, you will be able to overcome bad habits and personal weaknesses that you never could before.

You can't expect everything to always be easy or go your way, however. From the day you receive Jesus to the day you arrive in Heaven and see Him face to face, your spiritual life is an ongoing learning, growing, and maturing process. How much you change and how quickly you grow depends largely on how much you *desire* to change, how much you apply yourself to learning more about the Lord and His plan for your life, how far you are willing to go with Him, and how much you ask for His help and depend on Him when troubles come your way.

To help speed the growing process and ease the growing pains, *Daily Might* presents many basic and important principles from the Bible in understandable terms. If you're just getting started in your new life for the Lord, there are a few more things you'll need to know in order to get the most out of this book:

Power up!

You cannot become all you could be or all God wants you to be without His power, and the means of power that He has provided for you is the Holy Spirit.

John the Baptist told those who came to him in search of truth and reconciliation with God that Jesus would "baptize with the Holy Spirit" (Matthew 3:11). Jesus later promised His followers that He would "send the Promise of the Father" upon them, so they would be "endued with power from on high" (Luke 24:49). Acts chapter 2 recounts how they received the Holy Spirit shortly thereafter.

If you have received Jesus as your Savior, you have been "born again of the Spirit" (John 3:3–8) and have already received a little of that Holy Spirit power. But that doesn't mean that you've received the full measure, or "baptism," of the Holy Spirit. This is usually a separate experience that happens later (Acts 8:14–17; 19:2–6).

The Greek word translated as "baptize" in the New Testament is *baptizo*, which means to be fully covered or completely immersed. So to be "baptized in the Holy Spirit" means to be completely filled to overflowing with the Spirit of God. A glass of water makes a good illustration. If the glass has at least some water in it, you could say that it's a glass of water, even though it's not a full glass. Many Christians are like glasses with just a little water, a little bit of God's Spirit. But those who have been baptized with the Holy Spirit are like glasses that have been filled to overflowing. The baptism of the Holy Spirit is such an infilling of power from on high that they cannot contain it all!

The infilling of the Holy Spirit, like salvation, is a gift of God. All you have to do to receive it is believe that it's there for you and ask for it. "Your heavenly Father [will] give the Holy Spirit to those who ask Him" (Luke 11:13).

Soul food—Nourishment and growth

After being "born again" you are similar spiritually to what a newborn baby is like physically. You have a lot to learn and a lot of growing to do, so don't be discouraged if you don't understand everything all at once. The way to mature in faith and understanding of God's ways and plan for your life is to "desire the pure milk of the Word [of God], that you may grow thereby" (1 Peter 2:2). Reading the Bible, *Daily Might*, and other Christian publications can help keep you healthy and strong spiritually and accelerate your spiritual growth.

Spiritual warfare

A fierce, continual battle is taking place in the unseen spiritual realm that surrounds us. It's a spiritual battle of good against evil, a battle for our hearts and minds, which control our actions and destinies. God and His heavenly forces are fighting and defeating the Devil and his demons.

The battle carries over into our physical realm and involves us. "We do not wrestle against flesh and blood, but against principalities, against powers, against the rulers of the darkness of this age, against spiritual hosts of wickedness in the heavenly places" (Ephesians 6:12). The Devil is especially out to get Christians. If he can't stop you from being a Christian, he will try to stop you from being an active, effective Christian. He will do everything he can to interfere with your relationship with Jesus, stunt your spiritual growth, and hinder anything you try to do that would further the kingdom of God.

The Bible admonishes us to "fight the good fight of faith" (1 Timothy 6:12) and to not be ignorant of the Devil's tactics (2 Corinthians 2:11). A number of the daily readings in *Daily Might* are devoted to helping you learn to recognize the Devil's attacks so you can fight back and overcome them. You won't be able to win every skirmish, but you're on the winning side, and if you will stay close to your Commander in Chief and follow His instructions, you'll have many more victories than losses.

Heavenly communication *—Conversing with God*

God loves you so much that He not only wants to communicate with you through His written Word, but also directly. Like the loving Father He is, He takes a personal interest in you and wants to be involved in your daily life. He knows that you have questions and problems, and He wants to give you the answers and solutions. He wants to speak personal words of love and encouragement to you that will boost your faith and get you through the rough times. Most of all, He wants you to know how much He loves you. So He created a means of two-way communication, a channel between Him and you, so that you can talk to Him in prayer and, in reply, hear words He gives especially for you. *Daily Might* will help you establish and maintain that line of two-way communication.

Spread the good news

Telling others about God's love and Jesus is known as "witness-ing." Just as children grow up and have children of their own, the born-again child of God should grow up to bear spiritual children, more saved souls for God's kingdom. This is the most important and satisfying job in the whole world—what has come to be known as the Great Commission: "Go into all the world and preach the Gospel [good news] to every creature" (Mark 16:15). Twenty-eight of the 366 daily readings in this book are devoted to helping you understand and fulfill that commission. (See "Witnessing" in the Index.)

The secret to sustained spiritual growth is spending time with Jesus every day, communicating with Him through prayer and learning from Him through the Word. May *Daily Might* help you toward that end and daily draw you closer to Him!

We're in the best of hands.

"I SAID TO THE MAN WHO STOOD AT THE GATE OF THE YEAR: 'Give me a light that I may tread safely into the unknown.' And he replied: 'Go out into the darkness and put your hand into the hand of God. That shall be to you better than light and safer than a known way.'"[1]

We don't know what the future holds, but we know who holds the future. The things we need to know, the Lord tells us, and sometimes the things we *want* to know, He tells us, but most of the time He throws a veil over the future so it is known only to Him—and that really keeps us close to the Lord.

He's promised to never leave or forsake us (Hebrews 13:5). "I am with you alway, even unto the end of the world" (Matthew 28:20 KJV). He's also given us the torch of His Word to show us where our path is going. "Your Word is a lamp to my feet and a light to my path" (Psalm 119:105).

> I don't worry o'er the future,
> For I know what Jesus said;
> And today I'll walk beside Him,
> For He knows what lies ahead.
>
> Many things about tomorrow,
> I don't seem to understand,
> But I know who holds tomorrow,
> And I know who holds my hand![2]

[1] Minnie Louise Haskins (1875–1957).
[2] Ira Stanphill (1914–1994).

The best is yet to come!

JESUS PROMISED HIS FOLLOWERS THAT THEY WOULD GO BEYOND WHAT EVEN HE HAD DONE. "He who believes in Me, the works that I do he will do also; and *greater* works than these he will do" (John 14:12). And they did! Those He was speaking to at the time carried the Gospel much further than Jesus had been able to during His brief public ministry, and those they reached carried it even further—and it hasn't stopped yet!

Why shouldn't we also do "greater things"? The world population is greater, the need is greater, the opportunities are greater, and the means are far greater with the printed word, radio, television, air travel, the postal system, the Internet, and much, much more. We've got the greatest opportunities in history and all the means at our disposal. If we will stay close to Jesus, He will help us surmount whatever obstacles we may encounter, win victories, and accomplish His purposes in the coming year and always.

Of course, we should give all the credit and praise to Jesus because *He* will have done those great things through us. "May the God of peace … make you complete in every good work to do His will, working in you what is well pleasing in His sight, through Jesus Christ, to whom be glory forever and ever" (Hebrews 13:20–21).

"Heaven and earth will pass away, but God's words will by no means pass away" (Matthew 24:35).

IN ESPECIALLY TRYING TIMES, WE NEED TO LIVE MORE IN THE WORD. We must put our faith in the Word. Then it wouldn't matter if everybody in the whole world lost faith, or the whole world went haywire, or the heavens and earth passed away. We will keep going for God as long as our faith is in the Word. No matter what happens, we will still stand if our feet are planted on the firm foundation of God's Word. I can fail, you can fail, the whole world can fail, but God's Word will never fail!

Often if it weren't for that tiny spark of faith, we would just flicker out. But when we tank up on God's Word, we get re-inspired. God blows on our little ember of faith and brings it back to life again. It comes so much through taking in the Word. "Faith comes by hearing, and hearing by the Word of God" (Romans 10:17). His Word is always an encouragement, even when everything seems to be going wrong.

> The Bible stands though the hills may tumble,
> It will firmly stand when the earth shall crumble;
> I will plant my feet on its firm foundation,
> For the Bible stands.[1]

[1] Haldor Lillenas (1885–1959).

God is the only One who can give real meaning to living.

So MANY PEOPLE TODAY DON'T KNOW WHAT TO BELIEVE. They don't know where they came from, who they are, or where they're going. They're in absolute confusion because they've lost touch with the only concrete frame of reference, and that's God and His plan for their life as explained in the Bible. They've either never had or lost faith in God, so therefore they lose faith in love and life and people—in everything!

But we who have found God's love in Jesus have found a God that cannot fail and a love that lasts forever. We know Him, whom to know is life eternal (John 17:3). We've been born again and now have an entirely new outlook on life. His coming into our lives not only purifies and regenerates our spirits, but also renews our minds, breaking old connections and reflexes and gradually rebuilding and rewiring it into a whole new computer system with new reactions to nearly everything around us.

Besides the wonderful happiness, life, and love that Jesus gives us, we've also found a real purpose in living and Someone to live for. We now find a thrill in our newfound faith, the greatest of satisfaction in our work for Jesus, and pleasure in the fellowship of our spiritual family.

The Word of God is like a map to help you find your way through life.

WHILE TRAVELING ALONG A ROAD, you can only see what's ahead of you moment by moment. But if you'll look at the map and have faith in it, you can also see where the road came from, regardless of where you started out yourself. And even if you've never been to your final destination or traveled that road before, you can also know where the road ends. But if you don't take time to study the map, you could waste an awful lot of time or ruin your chances of getting to your destination at all.

You should no more try to find your own way through life than you should take a trip without a map. God can see it all. He not only knows where you are right now and where you came from, your present and your past, but He also knows the safest, surest, and most pleasant route to get you where you're going. Consult and follow the "Map Book," the Bible, and you will know too. Just as you must look at the map, believe that it's true, and follow it to get where you're going, if you will read God's Word, believe it, and follow it, you'll come out at Heaven. Absolutely! Without fail!

If you sometimes feel like nothing, cheer up! God can use you.

LITTLE IS MUCH IF GOD IS IN IT. In fact, God doesn't have to have *anything* to begin with. He made the world out of nothing (Hebrews 11:3). Pretty good old world, isn't it? He hung it on nothing (Job 26:7). Hangs pretty good, doesn't it? And He can make something out of nothing—even you—if you will let Him.

God doesn't go very much for bigness after the manner of this world. In fact, He specializes in using people who seem most likely *not* to succeed; yet by the miraculous power and grace of God they become shining lights to others. God only makes great people out of little people, to show *His* greatness (1 Corinthians 1:26–29).

Dare to trust Him in spite of yourself, and give Him all the credit when He does the miracle—what you couldn't do. If you can believe in God, everything is possible, because He makes everything out of nothing. We're all nothing and can do nothing good of ourselves (Galatians 6:3; John 15:5). God is like the circle around the nothing that makes it something. With God all around you, even your nothing can be something. In fact, you can be almost anything!

You don't have to understand God in order to love Him.

No ONE CAN EVER FULLY UNDERSTAND GOD. It's impossible because, as He says, His ways are far above our own. "As the heavens are higher than the earth, so are My ways higher than your ways, and My thoughts than your thoughts" (Isaiah 55:9). Forget trying to figure out God! Just accept His love by faith.

Jesus tried to make it simple. He said, "Unless you are converted and become as little children, you will by no means enter the kingdom of Heaven" (Matthew 18:3). What baby or little child understands all about his mother or father, or how he was born, or all about life? Yet he is instinctively attuned to the most profound thing in the world—love. He feels his parents' love and receives it and responds with love.

The Bible tells us that "God is Spirit" (John 4:24) and "God is love" (1 John 4:8). He's the very Spirit of love in your heart. It's impossible to fully understand God and His love, but it is possible to receive His love and to love Him in return. Making a personal connection with the God of love is so simple that many people can't believe it. It's just a matter of asking in faith and receiving.

Put God to the test.
Prove He exists!

A LOT OF PEOPLE WHO SAY THEY DON'T BELIEVE IN GOD AREN'T REALLY ATHEISTS. Maybe they simply haven't made a final decision because they haven't had a chance to know the truth. But even if they have doubts or questions that need answering before they will be convinced, if they're sincere and really want the answers, if they really want to know, God will show them.

So even if you don't believe in God or the Bible or anything else, you can put God in a test tube and prove He exists—and *you* are the test tube! You just need to put God inside of you and see what happens. If you will sincerely pray, "God, if there *is* a God out there somewhere, show me. Reveal Yourself," He will! Once you admit the possibility by doing that, then you're giving God a chance. There's a tiny spark of faith, and God will honor that faith by letting you see and feel and know the proof. He may not do it immediately or in the way you expect, but sooner or later in some way He will.

God loves faith. He loves us because we believe Him. Once you begin to believe, then God will prove Himself in many ways—by answers to prayers and miracles, and by changes in your life.

Faith and obedience come first, then God answers prayer.

THROUGHOUT HIS WORD, God commanded people to do something first before He answered their prayers. God told Moses to strike the rock, and then He would bring forth water (Exodus 17:6). Before Jesus raised Lazarus from the dead, He told the mourners to first take away the stone that covered the entrance of Lazarus' tomb; then He brought Lazarus back to life (John 11:39–44). Jesus told the blind man to go wash in the Pool of Siloam (John 9:1–7) and the ten lepers to go show themselves to the priests (Luke 17:12–14). They manifested their faith by obedience, and *then* God did the miracle.

"We walk by faith, not by sight" (2 Corinthians 5:7). God likes to test our faith. He likes to see how much we really believe, and He often will not answer our prayers or let us see where He's leading us until we obey what He's already told us or showed us. Many times we just have to step out by faith, even if we can't see the ground we're going to put our foot on. We have to take that first step by faith in order to receive His blessings. But if we take that step of faith and it's God's will, He will do the humanly impossible! Step by step, as we follow Him, He will lead and guide and reward our faith with more and more answers to our prayers.

Have you found the greatest doctor in the universe?

HEALING HAS ALWAYS BEEN ONE OF OUR MOST DESPERATE PHYSICAL NEEDS. Jesus healed all that came to Him—anybody and everybody—as long as they had faith that He could heal them. Their most immediate need was healing of their bodies, even before they could understand salvation, and He often healed them before He ministered to their spiritual needs.

The day of miracles is not past! God is still in the business of transforming bodies that need it. He's still the Great Physician. He still says, "I am the Lord who heals you" (Exodus 15:26). He "forgives all your iniquities … heals all your diseases" (Psalm 103:3).—Not just some or a few or many or most, but *all* of them. God can heal anything!

He's your heavenly Father. He loves you and He answers prayer. God not only can do it, He *wants* to do it. Healing is there! He will heal if you will believe. All He asks is that you honor Him with faith by believing the promises in His Word. It's just that simple!

> Power, all power, surely is Thine!
> Touch me and heal me, Savior divine.[1]

[1] Adelaide Addison Pollard (1862–1934).

The best way to find God's will is to say, "I will" to God.

GOD MAY GIVE YOU YOUR CHOICE, but He alone knows what is best, so you'd better ask Him what that is. How do you find God's best? The first requirement is having no will of your own. According to the Scripture, you need to surrender your life, your mind, and your will, and not be conformed to this world:

"I beseech you therefore, brethren, by the mercies of God, that you present your bodies a living sacrifice, holy, acceptable to God, which is your reasonable service. And do not be conformed to this world, but be transformed by the renewing of your mind, that you may prove what is that good and acceptable and perfect will of God" (Romans 12:1–2).

Ask God to lead and guide you. Ask Him to open your heart and mind to His truth. Ask Him to help you to understand it and follow it. Be willing to yield to His will, whatever it may be, and then you'll find out—you'll know—because then you're in a position for God to show you. If you're His child and you're letting Him do the choosing, what's He going to choose for you? He's going to choose that which is the best for you.

He knows, He loves, He cares,
Nothing this truth can dim.
He gives His very best to those
Who leave the choice with Him.[1]

Our salvation is only by grace, never by works.

WE CANNOT SAVE OURSELVES BY OUR OWN GOODNESS or attempts to keep God's laws. We cannot be good enough to earn, merit, or deserve the heavenly perfection of His salvation. It is impossible for anyone to be saved without the miracle-working power of God. It only comes by His grace, His love, and His mercy.

Salvation is free; it is the gift of God. You can't work for it. You can't earn a gift or else it wouldn't be a gift. God's Word says, "For by grace you have been saved through faith, and that not of yourselves; it is the gift of God, not of works, lest anyone should boast" (Ephesians 2:8–9).

God's idea of righteousness is a self-confessed sinner who knows he needs God and depends on Him for salvation. God's idea of saintliness is not self-righteousness and sinless perfection; it's a sinner saved by grace, a sinner who has no perfection, no righteousness of his own, but is totally dependent on the grace and the love and the mercy of God. Those are the only saints there are; there are no others. You haven't got anybody's righteousness except Christ's, and He's the only One that can give it to you (Philippians 3:9).

You can't keep the birds from flying over your head, but you can keep them from building a nest in your hair.

THE DEVIL IS ALWAYS ON THE JOB, tempting us to disobey God. And though nobody can keep temptation from coming, we don't have to yield to temptation. God gives us enough sense by His Spirit to know the difference between what's right and what's wrong, what's good and what's bad, then He lets us choose. The Devil cannot prevent us from choosing. That's the one thing we can do no matter what the Devil does. We each have a will, and we can choose to ignore the Devil and resist his temptations. "Therefore submit to God. Resist the Devil and he will flee from you" (James 4:7).

It is impossible for the Devil to win over you unless you give in to him, for "He who is in you [Jesus] is greater than he who is in the world [Satan]" (1 John 4:4). The only way the Devil can win is if you quit, give up, give in, surrender, or stop fighting. As long as you keep fighting, you keep winning! So when the Devil tempts you to get down and discouraged—fight back! Put on the armor of God, that you may be able to withstand the Devil's attacks (Ephesians 6:10–17). Don't even listen to him, much less surrender!

"The fool has said in his heart, 'There is no God'" (Psalm 14:1).

JUST BY LOOKING AT CREATION, you know that there is a Creator. Just logically and reasonably, it's obvious that there's a God. Only a fool could really believe that it all happened by accident. Just look at the trees and the birds and you know that it wasn't an accident; too much planning went into it all. God's entire glorious creation is a constant testimony to the existence of a divine designer. "Since the creation of the world His invisible attributes are clearly seen, being understood by the things that are made" (Romans 1:20).

Although the whole creation testifies of the existence of the invisible God, many people today refuse to receive the testimony because they choose to be ignorant. They don't want to confess that He exists. They would like to get rid of Him, but in order to do that they need some other explanation for how all this got here, so the Devil helped them cook up the idiotic scheme of evolution. "As they did not like to retain God in their knowledge, God gave them over to a debased mind" (Romans 1:28).

But we who believe marvel at the work of God's hands. We see Him in His handiwork. We come to understand Him better through the things that He made, and we glorify Him and are thankful.

God's delays are not denials.

GOD ANSWERS PRAYER, but not always the way we want or expect Him to. He is rarely in a hurry, as is evident in His creation. It takes Him time to make a baby, a flower, a tree, a sunset, or even a blade of grass. We can't rush God. We've got to wait till it's His time.

Perhaps He is waiting for the circumstances to be right to ensure the result He wants to bring. Take, for example, the man in the Bible who was blind from birth. He had had to be blind all his life so that everybody would know it and so that when Jesus came along one day and marvelously healed him, God would be glorified (John chapter 9). It may sometimes take years before you know why God didn't answer prayer as you thought He should, or right when you asked Him to, but the time will come and you'll know God was right.

The greatest darkness is just before dawn; the greatest desperation is just before salvation; the greatest hopelessness attacks just before rescue. So never doubt for a moment that God is going to answer. He will! Trust Him and thank Him for the answer, even if you don't see it immediately. You'll be glad you trusted Him tomorrow!

God's creation is His love manifested toward you.

DOES GOD LOVE YOU? You can see it and feel it in the beautiful world He's given you to live in. Just look around you at God's beautiful creation and you'll know that God loves you. His love is obvious from all that He's made for you to enjoy (Romans 1:20).

Look at the patience and mercy of God. To every man ever born He has at some time sent His light to enlighten his darkened heart with the love of God, to show him His love (John 1:9). He showers all this beauty and blessing not only on the just, but even upon the unjust who really don't deserve His love and mercy. He still sends them sunshine almost every day, rain to make the flowers grow, the beautiful trees, the grass, the sky, the clouds, the heavens, the sun, the moon, the stars, and all the rest of God's wonderful creation (Matthew 5:45).

If you don't believe God loves you, just look around at His blessings. What more can He say? He didn't have to make life so wonderful or the world so beautiful, but He did—and He did it just for you!

Let others see Jesus in you.

So MANY PEOPLE TODAY ARE LOST, lonely, downtrodden, weak and weary, poor and persecuted, victims of war and crime and exploitation. They are the ones nobody wants, the ones who have so little and seem to count so little in man's scheme of things.

Then there are those who are well off materially and appear to "have it together," but are lost and lonely prisoners of their own selfish desires and misplaced priorities. They are weary and heavy laden with problems, stress, fears, and phobias. They wear smiles but ache inside. They fear the future. They are engulfed in emptiness, pain, guilt, bitterness, condemnation, and remorse.

There are so many lost and desperate folks in the world today! It's like the question in that old Beatles song, "All the lonely people, where do they all come from?" Well, I'll tell you where they come from. They come from a world that has selfishly turned from the light of God's love and is being swallowed up by the darkness.

There is a great need for His love to shine through. Hold it up for all to see. Shine the light of God's love on people, and He will do the rest. He'll cause it to accomplish His purpose in their lives (John 12:32). Let others see Jesus in you!

All you have to do is follow Jesus!

JESUS ALWAYS KNOWS BEST, even when we don't know what we're doing. As long as we're obeying and following Him, He'll lead the way and we'll soon see where we're going, just like sheep with their shepherd. Jesus said when a good shepherd takes his sheep to pasture, he goes before them and the sheep follow him (John 10:4). Jesus is the Good Shepherd, and He knows what's ahead. He knows where the green pastures and the mountain passes are. He knows where the cool waters flow. He knows where the sheepfolds are, where you'll be safe and secure. He also knows the danger spots, so you'd better stay close to Him.

You should always follow the guidance of the hand of God. You cannot go by your own understanding of the situation. You dare not rely on your own experience or wisdom. You must look for the Lord's supernatural, miraculous, powerful leading. You must be guided by the hand of God. If you follow Jesus, you'll never go wrong! He's right out there with you, and He knows exactly what to do. Don't try to rush ahead of Him or show Him the way you think you should go. He's the One who has got to lead, because only He can.

May your prayer always be: "Lord, I will follow. Show me the way."

The baptism of the Holy Spirit is a baptism of love.

WHAT IS THE BAPTISM OF THE HOLY SPIRIT? It's a baptism of *love* most of all—love for God and love for others. Everybody who is saved has a measure of the Holy Spirit, like having a little bit of water in the bottom of a glass, but being baptized with the Holy Spirit is like filling the glass to running over. Jesus said of the Holy Spirit: "He who believes in Me … out of his heart will flow rivers of living water" (John 7:38). God pours in His Holy Spirit and fills us from bottom to top until we have a mighty tide of love and happiness that not only satisfies our own souls, but also overflows on others so they can find and be filled with God's love too.

We're not just filled with the Holy Spirit once, but we're refilled every day as we read the Word and ask Him for more love. The more of His love we receive from Him, the more our hearts are filled to running over, till we aren't able to contain it. Then as we overflow on others, they also are filled with His love and grow and blossom spiritually.

Faith is doing what God tells you to do today, and trusting Him to take care of tomorrow.

It's TODAY THAT YOU HAVE TO HAVE FAITH FOR. It's today that God has provided the strength for. "As your days, so shall your strength be" (Deuteronomy 33:25). God gives you power for the hour, grace for the trial, at the hour and when it comes, not before. You don't have to have faith for tomorrow today. Trust God! Your heavenly Father loves you and is going to take care of you tomorrow, just like He's taking care of you today.

Jesus said, "Do not worry about tomorrow, for tomorrow will worry about its own things. Sufficient for the day is its own trouble" (Matthew 6:34). Quit worrying about tomorrow! That's a commandment! It's not optional. It's not something that's just good advice. It's an order! When tomorrow comes, God will take care of it.

> I have nothing to do with tomorrow.
> My Savior has made that His care.
> Its grace and its strength I can't borrow,
> So why should I borrow its care?[1]

[1] Author Unknown.

The Word of God is the most powerful truth on earth!

THE PEN IS MIGHTIER THAN THE SWORD. Men and women of God have seldom ruled empires, but they have won worlds of men and women with their words, faith, and ideals. The words of God's prophets and messengers have crossed the ages, swept around the earth, and changed the course of nations. Their words have captured hearts and minds, and set multitudes forever free. Their message of life and love through Jesus has won countless millions to God's eternal kingdom—a kingdom far greater, longer lasting, and happier than man's mere worldly empires of the sword. Their words have saved millions from hopeless, Christless tombs, and given the love of God to a world dying for His love.

The Word of God is far greater than anything man can muster. It can change hearts; no atom bomb can do that. It can change minds; no number of bullets has ever done that. It can fill people's lives with love and genuine purpose; no conquering army has ever managed to do that. God's words are spirit and life (John 6:63); who else can claim that? That's how powerful God's Word is!

You can know your future!

Do you, like so many people today, sense that we're living on borrowed time? Are you worried about the future of the world and what is going to happen to us all? Well, you can know what's going to happen!

How can this be? By what means can mortal man transcend the bounds of time and peer into the future?—By tuning into God and His wonderful Word! In the spirit, where God dwells, the past, present, and future are all one. It all looks the same to Him, and He can easily reveal to His prophets and seers the mysteries of the future.

You'll be amazed at how specific and clear God's Word is about many soon coming events. It may not tell you every detail, but through it you can know what major events to expect. In some cases it even describes the characters in these events, and tells us where and when these events are going to take place.

Why does God tell us these things in advance?—Because He doesn't want us to worry about or fear the future. To be forewarned is to be forearmed. To understand what's going to occur is to be prepared to face it and take it as it comes, trusting in Him and His unfailing love and concern.

"Neither shall they learn war anymore" (Isaiah 2:4).

ONE OF THESE DAYS VERY SOON, the King of kings is going to come back to claim His kingdom. "He shall judge between the nations, and rebuke many people; they shall beat their swords into plowshares, and their spears into pruning hooks" (Isaiah 2:4). There will be the world's first complete and lasting disarmament—turning their weapons of destruction into instruments of peace!

At last there will be peace on earth, under the reign of Jesus Christ, the Son of God and Prince of Peace Himself. Today's wicked and vengeful men of war will be stopped. There'll be no more big powers and oppressed poor. He's going to put an end to all this war business. "He makes wars cease to the end of the earth; He breaks the bow and cuts the spear in two; He burns the chariot in the fire" (Psalm 46:9). All those warplanes and tanks and missiles are going to be burned up, thank God!

Then and only then, under the supreme and powerful rule and reign of the Prince of Peace and His men and women of peace, will all wars finally cease. Then and only then will the world at last be governed fairly and well with true justice, liberty, peace, plenty, and happiness for all. Hallelujah! What a day that will be!

"First apostles"
(1 Corinthians 12:28).

WE ALL WANT TO BE HUMBLE, but we don't like to be humbled—and talking with others about our faith can be a humbling experience, especially at first. It's like the story of the woman who said, "Oh, this just kills me!" when she was asked to go witnessing. It kills our pride, and that's exactly what it *should* do. The more God can get us and our egos out of the way, the more He and His love are able to shine through.

When you're out witnessing and begin to feel self-conscious or like people are looking down at you, it helps to remember that God is proud of you and you have every reason to be proud of Him and proud to be His messenger. The Greek word that is translated "apostle" in the New Testament is *apostolos*, literally "somebody sent out," and in 1 Corinthians chapter 12, where Paul lists the jobs and offices of the Church, God puts His apostles at the top of His list. "First apostles." You may be on the bottom of some people's list, but you're on the top of God's list! We're not to be proud of ourselves, as though we are something great ourselves, but we can be proud to be servants of the Almighty God, the Most High, His faithful messengers bearing His words to the people.

"Many are the afflictions of the righteous" (Psalm 34:19).

MANY ARE THE AFFLICTIONS OF WHOM?— Even the righteous suffer afflictions, "but the Lord delivers them out of them all." The Lord allows such things as sickness, troubles, and problems to test and strengthen our faith, and to help us get even greater victories out of seeming defeat. Sometimes "bad" things happen just to keep us close to the Lord. Sometimes they happen to draw us closer to each other. Sometimes they happen to keep us humble. Sometimes they happen to make us pray. So even troubles and tribulations are good for us if we let them accomplish God's purpose.

It's important to remember that whatever God does, He does it in love. "*All* things work together for good to those who love God" (Romans 8:28). God is not going to let anything happen to you, His child who loves Him, except what is for your ultimate good. So even though "many are the afflictions of the righteous," the Lord is going to deliver you out of them all, no matter how many or what. A-L-L, all! Not just some or a few or most or many, but *all* of them! So the next time you're afflicted with sickness or other troubles, expect God to deliver you, just as He has promised to in His Word.

One of the greatest healing factors is faith.

YOUR PHYSICAL STATE OF HEALTH is definitely dependent on your emotional state of health, and your emotional health is largely dependent on your spiritual condition. In fact, some doctors estimate that emotional causes contribute to as much as 90 percent of all illnesses.

Fear, tension, and hatred all produce various psychological and nervous diseases. Many physiological diseases like heart trouble, arthritis, and stomach ulcers can also be caused by worry, fear, bitterness, hatred, or a negative attitude toward life. Science has proved that all of these negative attitudes and feelings can cause an actual buildup of poisons in the body that in turn cause illnesses. In other words, the wrong state of mind can actually poison your body!

That is why faith is such a marvelous cure. Knowing that your heavenly Father loves you and is going to take care of you and yours—your health, your family, your future, your job, everything—eliminates fear and gives you peace of mind, contentment of heart, and a feeling of spiritual well-being that brings rest to your vital organs, and that in turn actually causes the elimination of poisons from your body. Simple faith in God's love is the best medicine there is!

Winners never quit, but quitters never win.

WHEN THINGS GET TOUGH, you've got to fight all the harder in the spirit. If you'll do that and not give up, you'll win greater victories.

Take a lesson from the 18th-century, Scottish-born U.S. naval commander John Paul Jones (1747–1792). In one battle his ship had been hit and was sinking. Half his men had been killed, and many others had been wounded, including Jones himself. When the enemy captain asked Jones if he was ready to surrender, Jones screamed back, "Surrender? Hell no! We haven't even *begun* to fight!" Jones kept on fighting, and eventually won the battle!

Maybe you haven't even begun to fight the ol' Devil yet. Maybe "you have not yet resisted to bloodshed, striving against sin" (Hebrews 12:4), like Jesus did. Even though it killed Him, only three days later He rose in triumph from the tomb!

So don't be weary in well doing, for in due season you will reap if you don't give up (Galatians 6:9). "You therefore must endure hardship as a good soldier of Jesus Christ ... that you may please Him who enlisted you as a soldier" (2 Timothy 2:3–4). Fight the good fight, keep the faith, finish the course, and Jesus will give you a crown of life (1 Timothy 6:12; 2 Timothy 4:7–8; Revelation 2:10).

Days filled with sharing, years filled with caring, there's just no comparing a life filled with love.

OLD AGE SHOULD BE THE GREATEST TIME OF LIFE. If you've filled your days with love, lived a good life, and done your best to please God, it's a time when you can see the good fruit of your labors. That should give you a feeling of genuine permanent accomplishment, and you can look forward to eternal rewards.

It's really sad that so many people view old age as a terrible time of life, when really things should be getting better and better. Old age only becomes a disappointment if we find ourselves growing older in years without growing closer to God. That's like walking in a circle; it's motion without progress. But God didn't give us the gift of life intending the first half to be the best. What God begins, He completes and brings to perfection (Psalm 138:8; Philippians 1:6). So neither fear old age nor fight it, but take hold of this stage of life and make something beautiful out of it.

Age is opportunity no less,
Than youth itself, though in another dress;
And as the evening twilight fades away,
The sky is filled with stars, invisible by day.[1]

[1] Henry Wadsworth Longfellow (1807–1882).

The secret of success: Choose and yield to God's will.

GOD HAS GIVEN US A FREE WILL, but to be successful for Him or even as happy as He would like to make us, we have to continually yield that will to Him. We have to find out from Him what His will for us is—what He knows is best for others and us—and then choose that.

Once you have found and chosen God's will, He will reach down and take ahold of you and move you where He wants you to go. Everybody has their place and job for the Lord, like the pieces on a chessboard. Chesspieces have no will of their own. When a player picks up a chesspiece and moves it to another square, the chesspiece doesn't protest; it yields and goes where it's sent, right? Well, you're in the hands of the Master Player and He's going to put you wherever He wants you, so trust the Lord.

You don't have to make all the decisions; you only have to be yielded to His moves and let Him do the thinking and the choosing. You've got very limited vision, but He can see the whole game, the whole chessboard and all the pieces. It's wonderful to let God decide, because He always has our best interests at heart and He knows what's best.

Deliver us, Jesus, from the spirit of "busyness"—too busy for You and too busy for Your Word.

To learn from Jesus, you have to stop and look and listen. If you don't, instead of running over with His truth, His love, and His joy, you'll get run over by all the cares of this life. If you drive yourself too hard and too fast, you may never get there! You'll get out of touch with Jesus and our heavenly headquarters. Like the little girl said about her new kitten, "Oh Mama, the kitty's gone to sleep and left its engine running," you may be running around but still be asleep spiritually. You may be busy but not be getting anywhere, "as one who beats the air" (1 Corinthians 9:26).

You cannot do the Master's work without the Master's power, and to get it, you must spend time with the Master. Jesus said that only one thing is needful: to sit at His feet and learn of Him. Those who have chosen this good part, it shall never be taken away from them (Luke 10:39–42). If you're too busy to get alone with Jesus and pray, you're too busy!

So take time to be holy—wholly His. He says, "Be still, and know that I am God. In quietness and in confidence shall be your strength" (Psalm 46:10; Isaiah 30:15).

Christ stands at the heart's door and asks to come in.

JESUS IS THE VERY PICTURE OF PATIENCE, calmness, love, gentleness, and longsuffering. He's the picture of tenderness, gently wooing like a dove. He goes where there are open, receptive, hungry hearts. He seeks out the humble and contrite hearts, but resists the proud. He waits lovingly and meekly at your heart's door, not forcing Himself on you, not pushing the door open, but waiting for you to simply open your heart and invite Him to come in.

Jesus promised, "Behold, I stand at the door and knock. If anyone hears My voice and opens the door, I will come in to him" (Revelation 3:20). When you open your heart's door to Jesus, He always comes in. He likes to fill every place that's made for Him. If you will just open your heart, His Spirit of love will flow in.

If you haven't yet received Jesus as your Savior, you can right this minute by asking Him to come into your heart with His love, life, liberty, truth, peace, plenty, and happiness here, now, and forever. Simply pray: "Jesus, come into my heart. I believe You are the Son of God. Please forgive me for my sins. Help me to love You and others, and help me to tell them about You. Amen."

We don't need to fear the Devil or his demons. Jesus is with us!

JUST AS THE FEAR OF GOD LEADS TO LIFE (Proverbs 19:23), fear of Satan leads to death. Fearing God is a form of worshiping God. It's giving Him the reverence He deserves. But to fear the Enemy, to fear Satan, is giving him just the kind of worship he wants. It's really worshiping the Devil, so don't do it—not for a fraction of a second!

Satan's powers are not to be feared, much less worshiped. They are to be resisted and rebuked and gotten rid of! You have to fight fear like you have to fight the Devil. Resist it with faith and the Word of God. "For God has not given us a spirit of fear, but of power and of love and of a sound mind" (2 Timothy 1:7). Give God due respect by putting your faith in Him, and all fear will disappear.

> Although this world, with devils filled,
> Should threaten to undo us,
> We will not fear, for God hath willed,
> His truth to triumph through us!
> The Prince of Darkness grim,
> We tremble not for him!
> His rage we can endure,
> For lo, his doom is sure!
> One little word [Jesus] shall fell him![1]

[1] Martin Luther (1483–1546).

Don't trade the best for something merely good.

A LOT OF PEOPLE TRY TO GET AWAY WITH WHAT THEY CALL "GOD'S SECOND BEST." They desert God's highest calling because they aren't willing to pay the price.

But we shouldn't even consider second best because as far as God is concerned, there's only one best—the "high calling of God in Christ Jesus" (Philippians 3:14 KJV). If we take second best, it's not really *His* second best; it's *our* best.

What is sin? It's missing the mark, missing the target, missing the bull's eye. It's not really doing the most important thing that God wants us to do. So "let us lay aside the weights and the sins" (Hebrews 12:1)—anything that keeps us from doing God's highest and His best, anything that keeps us from being where He knows we'll be of most use to Him and the biggest blessing to others.

(Prayer:) Lord, bless and keep us all in the center of Your will. Keep us single-minded, single in purpose. We have no idea how great Your purpose is, but we've answered Your call. Do help us to do *Your* best—the best we can, and nothing less.

Living by faith means putting faith into action.

SOME PEOPLE SEEM TO HAVE THE IDEA that living by faith means living by nothing or living for nothing or with nothing. Well, they're mistaken. Living by faith means putting feet to your prayers. It means doing everything you can possibly do. It means praying as though everything depended on prayer, and doing as though everything depended on doing. Real faith is not a passive thing. It puts into action what it believes.

It's been said that God helps those who help themselves, and that's true. He also helps those who *can't* help themselves, but He seldom helps those who can help themselves but won't. He works on the principle of "whatever a man sows, that he will also reap" (Galatians 6:7). Nothing succeeds like success, and God blesses those who are fruitful, diligent, hard working, truly trusting, and genuinely obeying. He will always reward hard work, diligence, and faithfulness. If we do our best, God will do His best to help us.

So whatever you do, don't have a do-nothing religion. Have a do-something religion—whatever the Lord tells you to do. Have a do-it-together religion. Do what you can do, and God will do the rest.

Be a faithful operator—pray.

WHEN GOD PUTS A THOUGHT IN YOUR MIND ABOUT A CERTAIN PERSON, that's a message from Him. He's putting in a phone call to them, and He wants you to act like one of those old-time telephone operators and connect the call.

God initiates the call, and you are like the telephone operator who transfers the call. If you do your part, which is to pray for that person, you can put God through to whomever He's trying to reach. Your faith is the hand that flips the switch that makes the connection so they can receive God's message. You are the link between God and them, so if you fail to pass the call on, they will never get the message.

Of course, the person on the other end of the line has to pick up the phone when it rings, and they have to listen and receive the call. You can't make them answer the phone. That's their responsibility. There are a number of reasons why you, the operator, sometimes can't get through, but you have to keep trying.

You're the operator, and it's your responsibility to pass on the message. So be faithful to pray for the person that comes into your thoughts. Please don't fail, or someone will miss God's important call.

To truly give is to give cheerfully.

GOD LIKES CHEERFUL GIVERS—those who give voluntarily because they know it pleases Him and they're helping others, expecting nothing in return. That kind of giving can be the greatest of all pleasures, because as the purse is emptied, the heart is filled. "The generous soul will be made rich, and he who waters will also be watered himself" (Proverbs 11:25). "It is more blessed to give than to receive" (Acts 20:35).

But when we don't give cheerfully, we're not really giving. It's like the story of the rich man who thought he was throwing a copper penny into the church offering, but noticed as it left his fingers that it was a gold sovereign. When he saw what he was losing, he tried to snatch it back, but the usher put his hand over the bag and said, "Sorry! Once in, forever in."

So the rich man said, "Well, at least I'll get credit for the sovereign in Heaven."

"No you won't," said the usher. "You'll only get credit for the penny."

"God loves a cheerful giver" (2 Corinthians 9:7). We must give willingly and in love if we want our giving to do any good and if we expect any credit for it from the Lord.

Do you feed your body but starve your soul?

YOU COULD FEED YOUR BODY AND LOSE YOUR SOUL, like the man in the Bible who stuffed his barns full of grain, only to have God say to him, "You fool! This very night your life will be demanded from you. Then who will get what you have prepared for yourself?" (Luke 12:16–21 NIV).

Having a full stomach and a full purse and a full head cannot give you a full heart. If you put the desires of the flesh above the needs of your spirit, then you will find that nothing ever satisfies. You will become as the world-famed British poet Lord Byron (1788–1824) when he said at the height of his fame, "I've drunk of every fount of pleasure and quaffed every cup of fame, yet, alas. I die of thirst!"

Just like you have to eat in order to have physical strength, you have to feed from God's Word to have spiritual strength. You've got to feed your soul or you will never fully develop or mature spiritually. If you really want to grow in spirit, you will feed from the Word every day.

"Even though our outward man is perishing, yet the inward man is being renewed day by day" with the life-giving nourishment of His Words (2 Corinthians 4:16).

We are citizens of the world by birth, but citizens of Heaven by rebirth.

WHEN WE RECEIVED JESUS, the King of kings, into our hearts, we automatically and instantly became citizens of God's great heavenly kingdom.

Jesus said, "My kingdom is not of this world" (John 18:36), and the Bible tells us, "His kingdom is an everlasting kingdom" (Daniel 4:3). "Of the increase of His government and peace there will be no end ... to order it and establish it with judgment and justice from that time forward, even forever" (Isaiah 9:7).

We are no longer citizens of this temporal world only, but citizens of a new and everlasting world of love and life and truth and justice and happiness in Jesus. Ours is the only country that never did a wrong thing or fought a wrong war or persecuted the poor or oppressed the weak or polluted the earth. Our country's trying to save the world, stop the wars, relieve the poor, feed the hungry, heal the sick, and liberate the captives who are bound. We're citizens of the only truly righteous nation in the universe, the kingdom of Jesus Christ. That's our country, and Heaven is our home.

Are you a citizen of Heaven? Have you received your passport? Are you claiming your citizenship papers? Your passport is Jesus, and your citizenship papers are the promises of God for your salvation.

"Our struggle is not against flesh and blood, but against ... the spiritual forces of evil in the heavenly realms" (Ephesians 6:12 NIV).

WE ARE FIGHTING IN A WAR, not against carnal man, but against spiritual forces. That war is going on all the time in the unseen realm of the spirit that is all around us and even in us. It is a war between God and the Devil, between the forces of good and the forces of evil, between the angels of Heaven and the demons of Hell, between the people of God and the Devil's agents on earth.

"The weapons of our warfare are not carnal but mighty in God for pulling down strongholds" (2 Corinthians 10:4). We need a lot more than mere physical weapons to fight and win this war. To tear down the spiritual strongholds of the evil forces that oppose God and His people and His purposes, we need to wield the powerful spiritual weapons of God's love and Word.

It's serious business fighting the Devil, but it's a fight that we're destined to win. As long as we stay on guard spiritually, as long as we stay close to Jesus and His Word, we can't be beaten. How can we be so sure?—Because He who is in us—Jesus—is greater than he who is in the world—the Devil (1 John 4:4).

Nothing happens without God's will, especially to His child whom He loves.

Nothing "bad" happens to a Christian without some good reason. "All things come of God" (2 Corinthians 5:18), and "all things work together for good to those who love God" (Romans 8:28). Don't worry about the times of testing and weakness, thinking that you must have done something terribly wrong, so God must be finished with you. What you feel is God's tender hand upon you, making you into the person He knows you can be. As hard as it is, these breakings and remakings are inevitable. He must make you weak in yourself so you will depend on His strength. He must make you humble. He must make you desperate for Him and His help.

You're in His hands and He will perfect that which concerns you (Psalm 138:8). So don't be angry or bitter at God for these testings. They are only for a time. You will rejoice and be grateful when you look back and see how this was necessary for Him to accomplish His good purpose.

> Things don't just happen to children of God,
> They're part of a wonderful plan.
> The troubles, reverses, the sorrows, the rod
> Are strokes of the Great Sculptor's hand.[1]

[1] Alice Reynolds Flower (1890–1991), "It Didn't Just Happen."

John 3:36 ends all our worries: "He who believes in the Son *has* everlasting life."

You don't need to worry about whether or not you are going to lose your salvation or how you are going to manage to *stay* saved, because eternal salvation by grace means once saved, always saved. Once you've received Jesus Christ as your Savior, there are no ifs, ands, or buts about it—you are a saved child of God! "He who believes in the Son *has* everlasting life" (John 3:36). That one verse should be enough to end all your worries. You *have* eternal life right now, and you can't lose it.

Besides, you can't keep yourself saved any more than you could save yourself in the first place. Even though you're not perfect and you're bound to make mistakes, God is going to save you anyway. Once you've received Jesus, you are completely purified and redeemed in the eyes of God by the sacrifice of Christ on Calvary. You're saved right now because God has promised it and His Word is true. He cannot go back on His Word!

Salvation is forever. He's already given it to you, and He's not going to take it back. It's yours!

It's wise to be simple!

MANY PEOPLE STRIVE TO GAIN MORE AND MORE KNOWLEDGE, but they'd be wiser if they just stayed simple. Jesus has to get by people's head knowledge to get to their hearts. The Bible warns us to beware of being corrupted from the simplicity that is in Christ (2 Corinthians 11:3), and Jesus Himself said, "Unless you are converted and become as little children, you will by no means enter the kingdom of Heaven" (Matthew 18:3). If we'll recognize that in the Lord's eyes we're just like little children that don't know anything and that He is the only One who knows what He's doing, that's being really smart!

The newborn babe doesn't try to analyze his mother and father and brothers and sisters and the new world and life around him. He just accepts and enjoys them and starts learning how to live and enjoy life. You don't have to personally know all the answers or be able to explain everything; just know Him. He brings you love, He makes your life, and He gives you happiness and all you ever wanted and more. What else matters?

> Jesus loves me, this I know.
> For the Bible tells me so.
> Little ones to Him belong,
> We are weak, but He is strong![1]

[1] Anna Bartlett Warner (1827–1915).

Don't worry, God will supply.

GOD IS VERY GOOD TO US when we love Him and try our best to serve and please Him. In fact, He tries to be as good to us as possible. He will give us "exceeding abundantly above all that we ask or think" (Ephesians 3:20). "No good thing will He withhold from those who walk uprightly" (Psalm 84:11). "Delight yourself also in the Lord, and He shall give you the desires of your heart" (Psalm 37:4). "And my God shall supply all your need according to His riches in glory by Christ Jesus" (Philippians 4:19).

He will solve every problem, He will meet every need, He will even give us our heart's desires if we please Him. He's promised it. He'll give us what we ask for and have the faith for. Our God is a God of miracles, and He can supply from some of the most unexpected sources. When we please Him, He not only gives us everything we need, but even many of the things we want.

If you will be faithful to God and stay in the center of His will, He will be faithful to take care of you.

"Every Bible should be bound in shoe leather."[1]

MANY PEOPLE WON'T READ THE BIBLE, but they will "read" a Christian. The only love of God that many people can see is the love they see in us, and if we don't show them a love they can see and feel, they're going to have a hard time believing that there is Someone up there whom they don't know, and that He really loves them.

In winning people, you often have to inspire their faith in you before they can believe God. They may not understand or believe what you have to say about God unless you show them His love by some visible, tangible work that puts your words into action and your faith into effect and makes it fact and not fiction, a sample, not just a sermon. Show them His real love, and manifest it by genuine proving action.

The only way that others will ever find God's joy and peace and love and happiness and Heaven is through you. So in everything you do, remember that God wants you to show this world how wonderful it is to belong to Him (Matthew 5:16).

[1] Dwight Lyman Moody (1837–1899).

Love is...

Love is believing, trusting, helping, encouraging, confiding, sharing, understanding, feeling, touching, caring, praying, giving. Love is communication. Love is an emotion. Love is passionate, alive, vibrant, and warm. Love is something that gets better all the time!

Love is the greatest need of mankind, so love is the greatest service to mankind. Love is spiritual, but is manifested in the physical. Love is seen as it is put into action. Love is thoughtfulness. Love is always. Love knows no hours or days. Love is always finding a way. Love is giving all. Love is rare—the unselfish kind. Love is priceless. Love is its own reward.

Love is sacrificial. Love is preferring the happiness of others to our own. Love is patient. Love is kind. Love is merciful. Love can overcome any obstacle, heal any wound. Love is quick to forgive. Love is humble.

Love is never lost.—It always has its effect sooner or later. Love is forever.

Love is the name of God. Love is the power of God. Love is God, for God *is* love! God's ultimate love is Jesus (1 John 4:8–9).

If you want to drive away the Devil and his doubts, start praising the Lord no matter what's happening.

THE DEVIL CAN TELL YOU A LOT OF TRUTH ABOUT YOURSELF THAT'S HORRIBLE, not to speak of the lies he tells you. One of his favorite tactics is to try to persuade you to quit by hitting you with a barrage of doubt, discouragement, and self-pity. If you don't keep your eyes on the Lord and your mind on His Word when that happens, you're doomed to defeat, doubt, discouragement, and final failure.

When you're discouraged, the Devil tries to make you mad at the truth because he's afraid of being defeated by it. If you listen to the Devil's lies, you'll forget the words of God. If you spend your time listening to the Devil's doubts and singing his dirges, you'll forget God's praises.

So rebuke the Enemy in Jesus' name when he tempts you with negative thoughts. Start praising the Lord and you'll often praise your way right out of the pit into which the Devil is trying to cast you. When he comes around with his doubts, lies, and fears, don't just stand there—do something! Sing, shout, praise the Lord, quote Scriptures! Sock it to him with the Word! The Devil can't take the Word. He'll turn tail and run every time!

For God's sake, don't praise man, praise God! Give Him all the glory.

AT THE TOWER OF BABEL, the people said, "Now we're going to make a name for ourselves. Look how big and powerful we are! Look how great we are!" Instead of giving God the credit, they tried to take it for themselves, so God came down and scattered them and laid waste to their tower (Genesis 11:1–9).

One of the biggest dangers you have is to begin thinking too highly of yourself. The minute you start patting yourself on the back, God will see to it that you're humbled (Romans 12:3; 1 Corinthians 10:12; James 4:6). He's a jealous God, and He wants and deserves all the glory (Exodus 20:5; Isaiah 42:8).

Whatever you do in word or in deed, you are to do all to the glory of God (1 Corinthians 10:31; Colossians 3:17). So make that your prayer—that you will please the Lord by doing all things to His glory. "God forbid that I should boast except in the cross of our Lord Jesus Christ" (Galatians 6:14). To Him be the glory forever and ever!

The perfect synchronization of this great universe is proof of its divine architect.

THE MARVELOUS WONDERS OF OUR UNIVERSE, the bodies of our solar system such as the Sun, Earth, Moon, and the other planets and their moons, as well as the stars of every galaxy, all work in perfect unison. Each stays where it belongs and only orbits where it's supposed to, in the path it's supposed to follow and at the speed it's supposed to travel, so that they don't collide and their courses can be calculated with astounding accuracy.

How could anybody say it all happened by accident? If you have a reasoning mind at all, all you have to do is just look at the creation to know somebody had to design and put it together. Someone had to design the pattern and make it work like that.

In what has since become a widely used metaphor, British theologian and philosopher William Paley (1743–1805) likened the origin of the universe to that of a watch: "When we come to inspect the watch, we perceive that its several parts are framed and put together for a purpose. The inference we think is inevitable, that the watch must have had a maker. The universe must have had a designer. That designer must have been a person. That person is God."[1]

[1] *Natural Theology* (1802).

"Lovest thou Me? ... Feed My sheep."

ONE OF JESUS' LAST MESSAGES TO HIS DISCIPLES WAS "FEED MY SHEEP" (John 21:16 KJV). What He meant by that, of course, is that He wants us to have real love for the lost, to tell others about His love, and to feed them spiritually with His Word.

The most wonderful experience you can ever have is to find the love of God in Jesus, and then pass it on to your children, your mate, your loved ones, your friends, and even strangers. Jesus alone can save you, but He can't save you alone. If you're really saved and you really love Jesus, you're going to share His love; you're going to tell others.

What can you do for Jesus?—You can reach the lost, you can feed His sheep, you can share His love with others. That's what He wants you to do. This is the greatest work in the world: to feed His sheep, to witness the Word of God, to preach the Gospel, to tell others about God's great love, to show them the love of Jesus. So keep on loving Jesus and continue to search out His dear little sheep and love them into His fold till the Great Shepherd returns for His own (Isaiah 40:10–11; 1 Peter 5:2–4).

Live in the Word.

THE BIBLE IS A VERY DEEP BOOK. Read it and you will find a continual revelation of more and greater truth. In fact, you'll find that the Bible is such an enormous study and so fascinating and so deep and so broad that it is, as the prophet Ezekiel said, "waters to swim in" (Ezekiel 47:5 KJV). So, dive in and swim! Revel in the depths of His Word—the refreshing water of the Word that will feed your soul, strengthen your body, renew your mind, lift your spirit, encourage your heart, and purify your whole being.

You should hunger for the pure milk of the Word, just like a newborn baby hungers for his mother's milk (1 Peter 2:2). There is a saying about health: "You *are* what you *eat*." That's just as true of your spirit: You are spiritually what you read or take in by other means. So be sure you're getting the right spiritual food—the good, wholesome, nourishing, uplifting, encouraging, inspiring, feeding truth of the Word of God. God will bless you as you take in His Word.

(Prayer:) Help us, Jesus, to remember what King David said about Your Word: The secret to being blessed in all we do is living in Your Word night and day (Psalm 1:2–3). Help us to do that. Amen.

If you don't get the credit here, you'll get it in Heaven.

WHAT A SURPRISE WE'RE GOING TO GET WHEN JESUS HANDS OUT THE REWARDS, as to who was really greatest. Some people serve unselfishly, sacrificially, utterly giving themselves to the utmost, yet they never seem to get any credit for it and are virtually unknown. But God has a great big book, and it's known to Him. He's writing it all down and will reward everyone accordingly. "For God is not unjust to forget your work and labor of love which you have shown toward His name, in that you have ministered to the saints, and do minister" (Hebrews 6:10). "For we must all appear before the judgment seat of Christ, that each one may receive the things done in the body, according to what he has done, whether good or bad" (2 Corinthians 5:10).

Salvation is free, but rewards are earned. At the judgment seat of Christ during the marriage supper of the Lamb, Jesus will greatly reward all those who had the faith and perseverance to stay in His school till class was dismissed (Revelation 19:6–9; 20:4; 2:26–28). Be faithful to the end so when that time comes you will know you have done your job the best you can. Then you will "rejoice and be exceeding glad, for great is your reward in Heaven" (Matthew 5:12).—Not always here, but always there!

"Blessed are those who are persecuted for righteousness' sake" (Matthew 5:10).

"ALL WHO WILL LIVE GODLY IN CHRIST JESUS SHALL SUFFER PERSECUTION" (2 Timothy 3:12 KJV). Persecution shows we're hitting the Devil where it hurts. Jesus was terribly persecuted and finally crucified for telling the truth and showing God's love to the world, and He warns us to expect the same: "A servant is not greater than his master. If they persecuted Me, they will also persecute you" (John 15:20). But He also tells us: "Rejoice and be exceeding glad, for great is your reward in Heaven, for so they persecuted the prophets which were before you" (Matthew 5:12). "If we suffer for Jesus' sake and the Gospel's, we shall also reign with Him" (2 Timothy 2:12).

We owe the message of God's love to all, but especially to those who will believe and receive it. We're not to fear persecution, but neither are we to cause ourselves unnecessary trouble by giving the message to people who we know won't receive it and will possibly even persecute us for it. The whole purpose of witnessing is to win others with God's love, not antagonize or offend. The Lord expects us to exercise wisdom. "Behold, I send you out as sheep in the midst of wolves," Jesus says. "Therefore be wise as serpents and harmless as doves" (Matthew 10:16).

The most important job you have is listening to the King.

IT'S NOT UP TO THE KING TO GO CHASING AFTER HIS SUBJECTS, screaming and hollering at them to try to get them to follow his instructions. Rather, his subjects should come to the king with quietness and respect, present their petitions, and then wait silently for the king's answer. You need to treat Jesus like the King He is.

If you're in a room full of people and the TV is on, if they keep raising their voices and drowning out the TV, no matter how loud the volume is, you won't get what it has to say. Jesus, unlike the TV, will just shut up if you don't listen. When Israel stopped listening and ceased to believe and obey what God had to say, He just stopped talking to them for nearly four hundred years between the Old and New Testaments. The Lord does not like to talk to deaf, unbelieving, or unheeding ears, so He just shuts up.

But if you seek the Lord and want to hear from Him, He will speak to you and lead you step by step. He says, "Call unto Me, and I will answer you, and show you great and mighty things, which you do not know" (Jeremiah 33:3).

God's idea of perfection is love.

GOD'S IDEA OF PERFECTION IS OFTEN QUITE DIFFERENT FROM OURS. God took a man who persecuted many of the first Christians and made him the apostle Paul. Jesus took a woman who was one of the most notorious harlots in town and made her one of His favorite followers, Mary Magdalene. King David had one of his soldiers killed so he could take the man's wife for himself, but David also became one of the Bible's greatest heroes because he had a great repentance.

God's idea of saintliness is not sinless perfection; it's a sinner who has no perfection, no righteousness of his own at all, but is totally dependent on the love and mercy of God. These are the only saints there are; there are no others.

When we feel so righteous and good, it's really because we are *self*-righteous. We're not closer to God, but closer to ourselves. So let's forget about trying to be perfect, because we never will be. Let's just follow God and do the best we can for Him and others.

The only standard of righteousness or perfection is this: Do you depend totally on God and trust only in Him and His love and His mercy? True righteousness is being full of the Lord and His love, for only He is always right about all things.

"I will not doubt though all my ships at sea come drifting home with broken masts and sails."[1]

WHEN EVERYTHING GOES WRONG and seems contrary to the Word of God and the usual, only those with great faith can say with Job, "Though He slay me, yet will I trust Him" (Job 13:15). Even though God let the Devil nearly destroy him, Job still didn't say "uncle" to the Devil. He kept on believing and obeying, and he came out doubly blessed.

But a lot of people give up on the way to victory. They get weak and tired and quit. They suffer so many things in vain (Galatians 3:4). They go through so much, and then miss the victory. Like Esau, they give up too easily. Esau despised his birthright and settled for something he could see and easily believe in, rather than something he couldn't see and had to have great faith for (Genesis 25:33–34).

So when things look darkest, don't look down, look up! Be not fearful, but believing. Keep believing and obeying no matter what happens. Don't get down in the mouth, but praise God and thank Him for the glorious victories of the future, even if you can't see them now and have to take them by faith. You'll be glad you trusted Him tomorrow!

---

[1] Ella Wheeler Wilcox (1850–1919), "Faith."

"It is no longer I who burn, but Christ burns in me."

WHEN A CANDLE BURNS, it's mostly the wax, not the wick, that's burning. An oil lamp is the same; it must be the oil that burns, and not the wick. If the wick burns without oil, it will be consumed quickly. Most of the wick must be deeply immersed in the oil, so only a small part of the wick is exposed to the air and flame. That way, it's mostly the oil that burns and very little of the wick—almost none. The oil flows freely through a wick that is deeply soaked in the oil, and as the oil burns, it gives a bright, clear light.

Sometimes we work too hard, trying to do everything ourselves when we need to let Jesus do it through us. When *we* do the burning, we give off smoke and soot and burn out fast, but when we let the Lord's oil, the Holy Spirit, flow through us and do the burning, we last a long time.

"It is no longer I who burn, but Christ burns in me" (Galatians 2:20, paraphrased). "Let your light so shine before men, that they may see your good works and glorify your Father in Heaven" (Matthew 5:16).

The secret of calm and peace and rest and patience and love is resting in the Lord.

JESUS SAID, "Come to Me, all you who labor and are heavy laden, and I will give you rest. Take My yoke upon you and learn from Me, for I am gentle and lowly in heart, and you will find rest for your souls. For My yoke is easy and My burden is light" (Matthew 11:28–30).

Jesus promises that His yoke will be easy and His burden light, but there's one condition: "Come to Me." When you are wearied with the strain of it all, you can fly to Jesus on the wings of prayer and faith and get the relief that He alone can give you. He knows what you need most of all: rest and peace and fellowship with Him, and feeding on His Word.

"And you will find rest for your souls." Not many people understand that a soul is both body and spirit. If you don't rest in the Spirit, you are going to wear out your body.

Take His yoke on you—not the yoke of this world or your own yoke, but the yoke of Jesus' own love and His burden of love for others.

Let the Lord do the worrying!

THE TWO GREATEST SOURCES OF FEAR AND WORRY ARE THE PAST AND THE FUTURE—remorse over the past, and fear of the future—and God's Word forbids us to worry about either. If you know the Lord, then you're His child, and you don't have anything to worry about.

Worry is a sign of fear, and fear is not faith. Lack of faith can be a terrible, frightening thing because fear has torment (1 John 4:18). But faith in God, trust in God, gives you a feeling of rest of body, peace of mind, contentment of heart, and spiritual well-being. It's faith that keeps you from worry. It's faith that keeps out fear. Jesus said, "Let not your heart be troubled; you believe in God, believe also in Me" (John 14:1). The beginning of faith is the end of worry. When you trust the Lord, you know He's going to take care of you and you don't have to worry about anything.

"God has not given us the spirit of fear, but of power, and of love, and of a sound mind" (2 Timothy 1:7). So commit your way, your life, your mind, your thoughts, your time, your everything to the Lord. "Cast your burden upon the Lord and He shall sustain you" (Psalm 55:22). His shoulders are broad enough to carry any load!

God wants you to be happy!

GOD IS NOT A SAD GOD; He's a happy God who wants you to be happy too! The Bible says, "Happy are the people whose God is the Lord" (Psalm 144:15). This is the whole point of salvation, to relieve us of the suffering, pain, death, and tears brought into the world by the Devil and the sins of man. God is not a monster who's trying to deny you everything and make you miserable. He loves life and created it for you to enjoy. He made this beautiful world as a home for you to live in and enjoy, and He gave you a wonderful body, mind, and heart with which to enjoy it. He even promises you the desires of your heart when you delight yourself in Him (Psalm 37:4).

But God's pretty smart and He knows that the happier you are, the more you'll love Him, the more obedient you'll be out of pure love, and the better job you'll do for Him in sharing Him and His love with others. He wants to make you happy with His love, and He wants to help you make others happy, too, with both His love and your love. Our main purpose in life, as Martin Luther (1483–1546) said, is to love God and enjoy Him forever—and I might add, to try to help others to do the same.

For our witness to go as far as it can, we must teach others to teach others to teach others.

As active Christians and witnesses for Jesus, our object is to preach the Gospel to everyone, everywhere (Mark 16:15). But if we're going to accomplish that task, we can't try to do it all ourselves. We must teach others to teach others. That's the way to multiply our efforts and results.

The apostle Paul wrote, "The things that you have heard from me among many witnesses, commit these to faithful men who will be able to teach others also" (2 Timothy 2:2). To be productive and self-propagating, we must not only witness and win souls, but we must make disciples of those souls—disciples who can teach others to teach others to teach others in an endless chain reaction of preaching the Gospel. That's how Jesus meant for it to spread.

Jesus didn't reach millions Himself. He spent most of His time teaching and training His disciples to carry on. He preached most of His sermons to them and a few others, until by the time He was ready to leave them behind, they were well able to carry on with the inspiration of the Holy Spirit—and they did a terrific job!

So each one teach one—the name of the game being multiplication of citizens for the kingdom of God.

We must learn to live in Jesus' strength; we cannot live in our own.

IF WE TRY TO DO THE MASTER'S WORK WITHOUT THE MASTER'S POWER, we're tackling an impossible task. We cannot strive in our own strength. Unless we look to Jesus in very earnest prayer for the strength and spirit and inspiration to help us through, we're apt to wear ourselves out.

It's like the story about a small boy who was trying very hard to lift a heavy object. The boy's father came into the room and asked him, "Are you using all your strength?"

"Yes, of course I am," the boy impatiently exclaimed.

"No, you're not," the father answered. "You haven't asked me to help you!"

So it is with Jesus and us. Aren't we so often like that little boy? But a little help from Jesus is the biggest help we can get, and that's all the help we need. Just a little help from Jesus will make it right. Without Him we're nothing, but with Him we can do anything (John 15:5; Philippians 4:13).

"Give me a task too big, too hard for human hands, then shall I come at length to lean on Thee, and leaning find my strength."[1]

God said, "It is not good that man should be alone" (Genesis 2:18).

ALTHOUGH ADAM HAD GOD and the whole world to himself in the Garden of Eden, he wasn't truly happy or satisfied. He looked each of the animals over trying to decide not only their names, but also which one could be his companion. But none of them fully met his needs, so God created a very lovely helpmeet for him, which was His intention all along, of course. Apparently God needed to let Adam go through all that so he would really appreciate Eve when she arrived.

God put Adam to sleep, took out one of his ribs, and made a woman out of it. Why didn't God take a bone out of his head?— If he had, she might have tried to be the head of the house. Why didn't He take a bone out of his foot?—Adam might have wanted to walk all over her then. He took a piece of Adam that was close to his heart, so Eve would always be close to his heart.

God knows we all need companionship and a helper to stand by us, and if we'll just wait and be patient, God will always bring along the right mate—and by that time we'll really appreciate them.

Wait for God to work!

IF YOU DON'T KNOW WHAT TO DO, stop everything. The worst thing in the world you can do is to keep on going when you don't know what to do. That was King Saul's mistake and it cost him his kingdom.

Giving God time to work solves so many problems. A few minutes, a few hours, a few days, and we find that God has taken care of things without our help. Give God a chance. Give Him time. Wait on the Lord (Psalm 27:14). Take time to hear from God, and He'll take the time to straighten out the problem (Jeremiah 33:3). If you stop and look to Him before you leap, you may not have to leap at all.

When you don't know where to go, sit still. When you're driving your car through a fog and it becomes so dense you can't see, you shouldn't just keep on driving; you should find a place where you can pull off a safe distance from the road and wait. Sit still until the fog lifts and you can clearly see your way.

Slow down! Trying to force the situation and push your way through just won't work. He says, "Be still and know that I am God" (Psalm 46:10). "In all your ways acknowledge Him, and He shall direct your paths" (Proverbs 3:6).

You'll never know the true power of love until you learn the power of surrender to God.

WE CAN ONLY FIND FULLNESS OF FAITH WHEN WE ARE WILLING TO YIELD OUR PRIDE AND OUR OWN WILL TO GOD. Jesus prayed in the Garden of Gethsemane, "O My Father, if it is possible, let this cup pass from Me; nevertheless, not as I will, but as You will" (Matthew 26:39), and that should be our prayer. God has to have our cooperation. Submission is the first step. If we are unwilling to take that step, we won't be able to go to other steps. The Lord will do everything else for us—give us strength, wisdom, guidance, and love—but we have to make the decision. All that He asks is for us to commit ourselves. He likes for us to freely choose and yield to Him because we love Him.

Total love gives all. But if we give our all to the Lord, He gives His all to us. You can have peace and power that you've never known before, through Jesus, if you'll just let Him control your life.

> Deep abiding joy fills all my life today.
> There is a secret reason why I love to pray.
> There is an inner wellspring deep within my soul:
> Jesus, precious Jesus, has at last complete control![1]

[1] Author unknown.

Fulfilled Bible prophecy proves that the Bible is the inspired Word of God.

Jesus said, "I have told you before it comes, that when it does come to pass, you may believe" (John 14:29).

"Search from the book of the Lord, and read: not one of these shall fail; not one shall lack her mate. For My mouth has commanded it" (Isaiah 34:16). The mate of every prophecy is its fulfillment. Hundreds of prophecies given in the Bible—sometimes hundreds and even thousands of years in advance—have been fulfilled down to the most intricate detail, and the ones that are yet to come will be fulfilled just as surely. What God has determined and said will happen, He's going to do. God will make sure that every single prophecy is fulfilled!

It's thrilling to study fulfilled prophecies because it encourages your faith to know that other prophecies regarding the future will also be fulfilled just as accurately and just as surely. "God is not a man, that He should lie, nor a son of man, that He should repent. Has He said, and will He not do? Or has He spoken, and will He not make it good?" (Numbers 23:19). "Till heaven and earth pass away, one jot or one tittle will by no means pass from the Word till all is fulfilled" (Matthew 5:18).

God offers us a pardon.

W<small>E ALL STAND ACCUSED OF WRONGDOING,</small>
and we're all guilty; we're all sinners (Romans 3:23). God is the
judge, and the Devil is the prosecuting attorney who demands
the execution of the law—and of us (Job 1:6–12; Revelation
12:10). But Jesus is our defense attorney and He already paid the
price of our pardon, so God can set us free.

When the Devil reminds God of all your sins, all you have to do
is look to your defense attorney, Jesus (1 John 2:1). Jesus will
then look to the Father and say, "Father, forgive this man. This
is another one of Mine who has received Me and believed in Me
as his lawyer, as his defense attorney, as his advocate. He has
received My defense; he has received My sacrifice in his place,
and he believes that I took his punishment for him. Therefore,
You can hand him one of those pardons." And God hands down
the pardon, and Jesus hands it to you, and the Devil slinks away
with his tail between his legs, defeated again!

You've got a pardon from God, no matter what you've done,
because Jesus took your punishment on the cross. "The blood of
Jesus Christ His Son cleanses us from all sin" (1 John 1:7).

If you want to read a marvelous book, read the Bible.

THE BIBLE IS AN ABSOLUTELY INEXHAUSTIBLE SOURCE OF WISDOM AND KNOWLEDGE, in which you can constantly find treasures new and old (Matthew 13:52).

If you love beautiful poetry and oratory, read the Psalms and the Prophets. If you like philosophical arguments, you'll enjoy the book of Job. The Song of Solomon is romantic. Science fiction? It's got nothing on the future as foretold in the books of Daniel, Ezekiel, and Revelation. The Bible is more fascinating and amazing than Greek and Roman mythology and all the legends and fairy tales and made-up stories of man put together. If you want to read about miraculous and supernatural happenings, just read the Bible. It's more thrilling and more wonderful than any other book ever written—and it's true! It tells stories, but it doesn't tell lies. Every single passage is the truth of God!

And the most wonderful thing about the Bible is that through its life-giving words, especially those found in the four Gospels, we can personally know its divine author, who alone can guarantee life and love and happiness and Heaven forever through simply reading and believing these words of love from Him to us (John 20:31).

Even though war and confusion are all around you, you can have peace in your heart through the Prince of Peace, Jesus.

No matter what is happening on the outside, you can have peace on the inside. You never have to worry! Jesus is able to keep you safe, even if you're right in the middle of trouble or chaos (Psalm 91). He never sleeps. He watches all the time. He knows every hair of your head, and everything is in His hands, as the old hymn says:

He hideth my soul in the cleft of the rock
That shadows a dry, thirsty land;
He hideth my life with the depths of His love,
And covers me there with His hand.[1]

Jesus is able to keep you no matter where you are, but if He knows it would be better to take you home to Heaven, either way you've got it made. "Your life is hidden with Christ in God" (Colossians 3:3), and Jesus will keep you in perfect peace as you keep your mind stayed on Him, because you trust in Him (Isaiah 26:3).

Safe in the arms of Jesus,
Safe on His gentle breast!
There shall thy heart be happy,
There thou shalt find sweet rest![2]

[1,2] Fanny Crosby (1820–1915).

Life is in the seed, not the sower.

WINNING PEOPLE TO JESUS IS LIKE FARMING: We plant little seeds of truth in the earth of people's hearts, and the great warm sunshine of His love and the water of His Word will cause some of those seeds to burst forth in the miracle of new life.

Of course, we hope to win many others to faith in Christ, but that's really God's job and the work of the Holy Spirit. We can only give people the truth and show them the Lord's love; we can't force results or make the decision for them. Whether or not they choose to believe and receive and follow that truth is between each individual and God.

One person sows the seed, another may water it, but it is God that gives the increase (1 Corinthians 3:6). We can only try to prepare the ground, soften it with our prayers, and sow the seed. It's up to the individual to receive it, and only God can make it take root and grow and produce fruit.

Our job is simply to go forth bearing precious seed and to plant it in fertile, fruitful, receptive hearts. We may not always see the harvest ourselves, but as long as we have faithfully done our part, we can leave the rest up to God.

God can give you the solutions to your problems that will make the mountains melt away.

You WILL GET A LOT MORE DONE IF YOU WILL SPEND MORE TIME IN PRAYER, alone with God. You will get more instruction, insight, and inspiration from the Lord when you are alone and quiet than at any other time because He has your full attention and you can give Him the reverence that is His due. Even Jesus had to get up at the break of day, before His disciples, and find a quiet place to get alone with and hear from His Father (Mark 1:35).

You're going to have to get quiet by yourself—somewhere, some-how, sometime—if you're going to hear from the Lord. You can't solve your problems on your own. You've got to be desperate for God's solutions, and then you've got to stop everything else and listen.

(Prayer:) Help us, Jesus, to remember that we can't go on without the heavenly vision that You give. We all need more quiet time alone with You, to nestle in Your arms and be refreshed and strengthened by Your Spirit, to have You and You alone to think about and pray about and to get close to, without any other distractions.

The Devil flees when he sees the weakest saint upon his knees!

Y<small>OU'RE NOT STRONGER THAN THE DEVIL,</small> but God is (1 John 4:4). With God on your side, you're more than a match for the Devil. So when the Devil tries to fight you or what you're doing, pray and ask God to deliver you from his clutches.

The Devil has no power over you when you pray and claim God's promises. The Devil can't stand the Word or the name of Jesus; he turns tail and runs! Remember, Jonah got out of the belly of the whale when he exclaimed, "Salvation is of the Lord!" (Jonah 2:9).

"Fear not, for I am with you; be not dismayed, for I am your God. I will strengthen you, yes, I will help you, I will uphold you with My righteous right hand" (Isaiah 41:10). Don't in any way be terrified by your adversaries (Philippians 1:28). "Resist the Devil and he will flee from you" (James 4:7).

When you pray, you just can't lose for winning and the Devil just can't win for losing, because God is with you. God has given you the power to call in the forces of Heaven to assist you and to overpower all the forces of evil—the Devil and his minions—so use it.

Grace plus faith plus nothing— that's salvation!

JESUS, GOD'S GIFT OF LOVE TO US, is just that, a gift. We just have to receive Him humbly. We can't possibly pay enough to buy our way into Heaven, to buy eternal life, to buy the happiness that Jesus brings. Accepting salvation through His Word is a work of God's grace. "For by grace have you been saved through faith, and that not of yourselves, it is the gift of God" (Ephesians 2:8). You can't earn a gift or else it wouldn't be a gift.

Salvation is not a reward, it's not pay, it's not wages; it is a gift that you can't earn by faithfulness or by any kind of works of your own. Your good works can't save you and your bad works can't damn you. We're saved purely by faith in Jesus, the gift of God, by His grace. The worst sinner can go to Heaven by faith, and the "best" person can go to Hell because of unbelief. Heaven is full of sinners, saved by grace through faith.

Do you depend totally on God's grace and His mercy? Do you give Him all the glory and all the credit? It's wonderful when you realize that *you* don't have to do it. Jesus has done it for us!

To be "faithful unto death," just be faithful today.

THE BEST THING THAT WE COULD POSSIBLY ASK OF THE LORD for ourselves is that we will be faithful. "Be faithful unto death," He says, "and I will give you a crown of life" (Revelation 2:10 KJV).

When you think about trying to be faithful for the rest of your life, that seems impossible. That's just too big; you'll never make it. But what about today? You may have had your trials and tests, you may have gotten discouraged, you may have made mistakes, but have you still got your faith today?—Then you're full of faith. You've been faithful today.

You can only live one day at a time, so you can only be faithful one day at a time. Don't worry about when you weren't faithful yesterday or whether you're going to be faithful tomorrow, but do your best to be faithful today. Just be faithful one day at a time. You don't even have to have faith for a whole day. The only faith you need is what you've got right now. Just have faith for this moment, right now, one moment at a time. Just be faithful for one moment, one hour, one day at a time, and you will inherit an eternal crown of life.

To learn all the lessons God has for us, we need to ask Him what He's trying to teach us.

WE CAN GO THROUGH LIFE AND MISS MANY OF THE THINGS THAT GOD IS TRYING TO TEACH US. Some things are obvious, but others aren't, and we can miss the point if we don't ask Him or don't open our eyes to what He's trying to show us through them.

Many things happen that God would like to speak to us through, but if we don't look at them as messages from Him, then they just pass and we don't get it; we don't learn from it and it's wasted. What God wants to be a lesson may not be a lesson if we don't take the time to ask Him, "What are You trying to show me?"

The more we pray about things beforehand, the more the Lord is able to help us and the better things will turn out. But it's just as important to pray about the outcome, especially when things don't go the way we expect or want them to. If we take time to think about it and ask the Lord, He can help us learn from every experience. The lesson is there if we will ask for it, but by the same token, if we don't ask, a lot of times we don't receive (Matthew 7:7; James 4:2).

Why does God allow the Devil to test us?

GOD PROTECTS HIS CHILDREN, but has anything bad ever happened to you since you've been saved? Has God ever let the Devil touch you in some way through an accident, affliction, mistake, or other trouble? If God is in control, why does He allow those things?

Look at what happened to Job. Did he bring his misfortune upon himself? Was it his fault? Had he sinned? No. It happened because the Devil asked God if he could test and tempt Job to see if he could break him and make him deny God's goodness. God let the Devil take away all Job's wealth, then his family, and finally his health. It was all a test—perpetrated by the Devil but allowed by God—in order to show that Job really loved God in spite of it all.

God will not allow us to be tempted beyond what we are able to bear (1 Corinthians 10:13). He doesn't let the Devil give us more than we can take, but He does let him test our faith to see if we will flee to the Lord and quote His Word and take a stand of faith. It's one way God has of trying to keep us close to Him, constantly dependent upon Him and His protection. And when we pass the test, God delivers us, like He did Job.

God works, and that's all you need to know!

WE ALL USE ELECTRICITY IN OUR EVERYDAY LIVES, even though none of us has ever seen it, only its effect. In the same way, we must accept the existence of God, even though we can't see Him. We simply know He does exist and He is here, ever-present, all-knowing, and all-powerful.

All that most of us know about electricity is that it works. We flip the switch and make contact with this invisible power, and it does the work for us. Likewise, we must learn to make personal contact with the power of God through prayer, a spiritual seeking of contact with His Spirit through obedience to the laws of His Word. We must avail ourselves of God just as we do electricity, and let His light and power into the rooms of our lives to give us light and power and joy in living by doing many things for us that we cannot do for ourselves.

Just reach out your hand of faith and turn the switch of decision, which makes the contact and starts the flow of that power into your life. You don't have to personally know all the answers. Just flip the switch and God will go to work!

Have you been filled with the Spirit of God's love?

BEFORE THE TIME OF CHRIST, God only anointed certain leaders, kings, and prophets with His Spirit, but now His Holy Spirit is available to *all* who receive Jesus.

Ever since the Day of Pentecost, when the first disciples were filled with the Holy Spirit, Jesus has made it possible for every Christian to have a direct connection with Him by means of the Holy Spirit. Now everybody can have the Holy Spirit and be led individually by the Lord. Now we can all enjoy Him together anywhere, everywhere, any time, all the time, in all His power and fullness, and we can all be reached equally, fairly, and simultaneously through the communication of the Holy Spirit.

Everyone who receives Jesus as their Savior is given a certain amount of the Spirit, but receiving a complete infilling or "baptism" of the Holy Spirit is usually a subsequent experience to that of salvation. This is why the apostle Paul inquired of certain Christians that he met, "Have you received the Holy Spirit *since* you believed?" (Acts 19:2 KJV).

If you are saved, this power from God is yours for the asking. "If you then, being evil, know how to give good gifts to your children, how much more will your heavenly Father give the Holy Spirit to those who ask Him" (Luke 11:13).

"We walk by faith, not by sight"
(2 Corinthians 5:7).

So many people today say, "I'll believe it when I see it. Seeing is believing." But that's not the way faith works. To the Christian, believing is seeing. God wants us to trust Him and believe first of all, and then we'll see the answer. He puts us through that period of believing and trusting by faith to see if we really love Him and are willing to trust Him. He wants to see if we really have faith. He appreciates our faith to believe what we cannot see.

We can't expect to receive faith from God for a situation when we're looking at ourselves or conditions instead of looking to Him. Man says, "Tie up in port. Don't attempt the impossible; you'll sink!" God says, "Launch out into the deep! Cast forth your nets and I'll give you such a catch of fish there will not be room enough to hold it" (Luke 5:4–9). Man says, "Look at the waves! Look at the condition of your vessel! You can't do it!" God says, "Look at Me. With man it is impossible, but with God *nothing* is impossible, and all things are possible to those who believe" (Matthew 14:29–31; Luke 1:37; 18:27).

> Keep your eyes on Jesus.
> His promises avail!
> Keep your eyes on Jesus.
> His Word can never fail![1]

[1] Author unknown.

God is still on the throne and prayer changes things.

MOST PEOPLE TODAY SEEM TO PUT THE STORIES OF JESUS and His disciples way back in the past. They're looked on as fairy tales; they have no reality to them. God is far away, Heaven is far away, Jesus has long been dead—everything's so far away. But the day of miracles is *not* past!

God is still alive, well, and working just as powerfully as ever amongst those that trust in Him. He says, "I am the Lord, I do not change" (Malachi 3:6). Jesus is just as real as ever (Hebrews 13:8). God's Word hasn't changed; His promises still have no restrictions, no limitations, and no qualifications except our faith.

All God asks of us is that we honor Him with faith by believing His promises in His Word. When you pray, bring those promises with you to remind Him. When you remind God of His Word, it shows you have faith in it. This positive declaration of your faith pleases God and moves Him to work on your behalf, so quote Scriptures and hold God to His Word. "There has not failed one word of all His good promise" (1 Kings 8:56).

Keep on believing, God answers prayer.
Keep on believing, He's still up there.[1]

[1] Lucy Milward Booth-Hellberg (1868–1953),
"Keep On Believing," paraphrased.

He is no fool who gives a life he cannot keep for a love he will never lose.

WHATEVER THIS LIFE AND THIS WORLD HAVE TO OFFER, it's only for a little while. But salvation, souls, and service for the Lord are forever; they are eternal. "And the world is passing away, and the lust of it; but he who does the will of God abides forever" (1 John 2:17). "For the things which are seen are temporary, but the things which are not seen are eternal" (2 Corinthians 4:18).

Moses esteemed the reproach of Christ greater riches than the treasures in Egypt, which could have been his, because he looked to the reward (Hebrews 11:26). He looked beyond his day and all of its problems and temptations and saw Jesus. He had an eye on eternity and its great rewards, and counted the riches of Christ greater than all the riches of Egypt, the richest, most powerful nation on earth in that day, of which he could have been pharaoh (Hebrews 11:24–27).

If we pay the same price and make the same sacrifices, we too can look forward to eternal rewards and everlasting glory. By giving our all to the Lord, we are going to receive so much more. What a small price to pay for all we're getting in return!

Winter's over, spring is here!

It's a pity to live in unhappiness, when just around the corner your life can be thrilling and fulfilling and wonderful beyond all expectation.

> Beyond the blue horizon waits a beautiful day.
> Goodbye to things that bore me, joy is waiting for me.
> I've found a new horizon, my life has only begun.
> Beyond the blue horizon, waits a rising sun![1]

For all of us who have found Jesus, that certainly is true. Our lives are constantly full of new horizons from which the rising Son, Jesus, brightens each new day.

He came so we may have life, and so we may have it more abundantly (John 10:10). He wants us to enjoy life to the fullest, here and now—not just pie in the sky and Heaven hereafter, but "a hundredfold now in this time ... and in the world to come eternal life" (Mark 10:30 KJV). All this and Heaven too! Heaven on earth and Heaven hereafter! When we found Jesus, it was like the end of a cold, hard winter and the beginning of a beautiful new spring-like awakening of the spirit of life. Hallelujah! We have heaven on earth in our hearts!

> Truth and spring our God can bring,
> And happy you can be.
> Take Jesus' joy right here and now,
> And live a life that's free!

[1] Leo Robin (1895–1984).

The secret of victory is the Word.

WHAT IS THE LIFE-GIVING FLOW THAT GIVES US LIFE FROM GOD?—It's God's Word. It's His Word that gives us life and food and nourishment and strength and spiritual health. Jesus Himself said, "The words that I speak to you are spirit, and they are life" (John 6:63).

Some people become "alienated from the life of God" (Ephesians 4:18). How is this possible?—It happens when they become separated from the Word, because Jesus is the Word (John 1:14). The minute you start crowding the Word out of your life, you are getting too busy. If you're not faithfully living in the Word—reading the Word, absorbing the Word, and practicing the Word—beware! Eventually you will lose confidence in the Word because of your own double-mindedness and double-heartedness, and you will drift further from the Lord. When you neglect the Word, you neglect the Lord, and when you do that, you are programmed to self-destruct spiritually.

There's nothing more powerful than the Word! The Word is the secret of power and victory and overcoming and fruitfulness and fire and life and warmth and light. The secret of everything good is the Word!

"God is a Spirit"
(John 4:24 KJV).

GOD IS THE SPIRIT OF LOVE. He's the Great Spirit, the Creator. He's not some old bearded gentleman way off somewhere, or some kind of ferocious monster that you can't understand, but He is the guiding light of the universe, the all-powerful, omnipresent, omniscient, omnipotent spirit that pervades all things. He is in everything, and everything is part of God, in a sense (Acts 17:28; Colossians 1:16–17).

God dwells in life. He dwells more in one little sparrow than He does in all of the buildings and monuments supposedly dedicated to Him. "The most High does not dwell in temples made with hands" (Acts 7:48). He said even the Heaven of heavens cannot contain Him! Nevertheless, the High and Holy One dwells in the heart of the meek and the lowly (Isaiah 57:15). He will live in your heart if you'll ask Him to come in.

He's everywhere. He is the very spirit of love in your heart. He's inside of you—so close. His love is there wherever you are, whenever you ask for it. As King David so beautifully expressed in the Psalms, "If I'm up in Heaven, You are there. If I descend into the depths of Hell, You are there. Wherever I am, You are with me. I can never depart from Your Spirit" (Psalm 139:7–12).

Ask for prayer.

GOD ENCOURAGES US TO CALL FOR HELP AND ASK OTHERS TO PRAY WITH US, and He promises us greater results if we do. "If two of you agree on earth concerning anything that they ask, it will be done for them by My Father in Heaven. For where two or three are gathered together in My name, I am there in the midst of them" (Matthew 18:19–20). "Pray for one another. … The effective, fervent prayer of a righteous man avails much" (James 5:16). One can chase a thousand, but two can put ten thousand to flight (Deuteronomy 32:30). That's why it's important that you make your request known, not only to the Lord but also to your brothers and sisters in Christ.

If God knows your needs before you call (Matthew 6:8), why doesn't He just go ahead and supply them without your having to ask?—Because He wants you to confess your dependence on Him and manifest your faith in Him. Similarly, you can pray for yourself and God will answer, but the answer won't be as great a testimony. When you ask others for prayer it's not only a manifestation of your faith in God, but also a confession of your need for and dependence on Him and therefore a greater testimony to all when He answers—and that, of course, greatly pleases Him.

No matter how good you are, Jesus can make you better!

It's not possible for you to truly change yourself, but it's possible for Jesus to change you by His miracle working power. He'll do things you can't do!

His coming into your life not only renews and purifies and regenerates your spirit, but it also renews your mind, breaking old connections and reflexes and gradually giving you a whole new outlook on life and new reactions to nearly everything around you (Ephesians 4:23; Romans 12:2). This is what it means to be "born again" in spirit so that you become a "new creation" in Christ Jesus, with old things being passed away and all things becoming new (John 3:3; 2 Corinthians 5:17).

It's impossible for you to make such a change as this yourself. "With men this is impossible, but with God all things are possible" (Matthew 19:26). If you want this change, it's necessary for you to ask Jesus to come into your heart. He's the One who makes "new creations." All you do is ask Him to come in, and then *He* works the miracle.

Some changes are instantaneous; others take a while. But if you're saved and truly want Jesus to change you, you'll be changed—because Jesus changes people!

"He who rules his spirit is better than he who takes a city"
(Proverbs 16:32).

WE CAN'T BLAME ALL OUR PROBLEMS ON THE DEVIL. Our number one problem is often with us. The evil spirits are subject to us (Luke 10:19–20); it's our own spirits that are often not as submitted to the Lord as they should be.

If we're saved, then Jesus will never leave us nor forsake us (Hebrews 13:5), but we can lose His power by our disobedience and wrong attitudes. Our spirits have free will and must be brought voluntarily under the Lord's control, otherwise they can certainly lead us astray just as bad as an evil spirit. In fact, our own spirits *become* evil when we disobey and are out of fellowship with God and out of His Spirit (Romans 6:16). When we don't control our spirits, we leave ourselves wide open to spiritual attack. "Whoever has no rule over his own spirit is like a city broken down, without walls" (Proverbs 25:28).

God leaves the choice up to us which way we want to go, but if we will make the right choice to go God's way, then He can step in to help us overcome our weaknesses. We need to yield to the Holy Spirit, then the Lord will help us rule our spirits.

Trust in the darkness brings triumph at dawn.

GOD'S WORD SAYS, "Count it all joy when you fall into various trials, knowing that the testing of your faith produces patience. But let patience have its perfect work, that you may be perfect and complete, lacking nothing" (James 1:2–4). Through every difficulty you face, God is molding and making you, so trust Him!

Trust Him through it like every man of God and every woman of God has had to do. That's what made them the women and men of God that they became—they trusted through the dark spots, they trusted through the storms, they trusted through the trials, they trusted through the afflictions. And because they trusted, He bought them through those dark spots and into the light of a brighter day. In the end those trials of their faith didn't seem so bad, because they worked for them "a far more exceeding and eternal weight of glory" (2 Corinthians 4:17).

So when the times get rough and storms rage, when the nights get darker and the discouragement deeper, don't give up! Just look to Jesus, the author and finisher of your faith (Hebrews 12:2). Jesus is there with you. He is with you in the darkness. He is with you in the trial. He is with you in the depths. He is with you there because He loves you. He is there to pull you through.

Ask God to give you direct revelations, straight from Him, to show you exactly what to do.

GOD STILL SPEAKS TODAY. He's still speaking and revealing, and He can speak and reveal to you directly. You can get your orders directly from the Lord Himself.

How do you test your inspiration?—Scripture is the yardstick, the final authority by which you can measure anything that's said. True revelations won't teach anything contrary to the Word, but they can fill in a lot of gaps and instruct you in your present circumstances. Just be sure that your revelations are in line with and don't contradict the Word of God. Ask Him for Scriptures to confirm what you receive directly from Him.

It's wonderful to be able to go straight to the Lord for the answers, instructions, and guidance you need. When you get His statement on the matter in question, you know you're on the right track and you can go ahead and act with conviction and faith, without hesitation. You've heard from Heaven, and that settles it!

Praise brings down the blessings of God.

PRAISE IS VERY IMPORTANT IN HEAVEN, because in Heaven everyone praises the Lord all the time. It's part of being there. And when you praise the Lord, it takes you there in the spirit and you partake of that praiseful atmosphere. "Enter into His gates with thanksgiving, and into His courts with praise" (Psalm 100:4).

Praise is one of the greatest powers of Heaven. When you praise the Lord, you open yourself to the healing balm of Heaven and it clears your mind, relieves stress, and refreshes your spirit. Strength and power lie in praise—not only power that lifts your spirit, but power to draw more power from the heavenly realm. Praise opens a channel to the heavenlies that allows the heavenly blessings to pour down. You don't just praise your way to victory, you also praise down the blessings of God.

Praise is a form of love. It's you telling the Lord how much you love Him and how thankful you are for all He does for you. As you praise and love Him, He loves you in return and pours His blessings on you. So sing those praises, pray those praises, pour forth those praises to the Lord. The blessings come down as the praises go up!

Help us to stay close to You, Jesus, and to others in the faith.

GOD ALWAYS SEEMS TO BLESS HARMONY, people living at peace with each other, helping each other, and showing a large measure of love. His dynamics of the spirit operate amazingly: He says that one can chase a thousand, but two can put ten thousand to flight (Deuteronomy 32:30). In other words, it doesn't just double your power, but it increases it tenfold! There is tremendous strength in unity.

One of Jesus' last earthly prayers was that His followers would be one, just as He and His Father were one (John 17:21–23). If we truly love Jesus, we should try to work in unity with other Christians for the sake of His kingdom, not in competition with each other but yoked together in love, pulling the load together.

Blest be the tie that binds our hearts in Christian love;
The fellowship of kindred minds is like to that above.[1]

"Now I plead with you, brethren, by the name of our Lord Jesus Christ, that you all speak the same thing, and that there be no divisions among you, but that you be perfectly joined together in the same mind and in the same judgment" (1 Corinthians 1:10).

[1] John Fawcett (1740–1817).

There are some things that God cannot do.

THERE ARE SOME THINGS THAT GOD CANNOT DO, because He has bound Himself within certain limitations so as not to interfere with your power of choice. Just like Adam and Eve in the Garden, everyone is given a chance to choose. In fact, when all is said and done, that's the main reason we're here in the first place: to learn how to make decisions under God's guidance. *You* have to make the decision; He's not going to force you to do His will. "Whoever *will* may come" (Revelation 22:17).

God never forces Himself on anyone. He just gives people the opportunity to receive His blessings. If they refuse them, it's their loss. "Each of us shall give account of himself to God" (Romans 14:12). We cannot hide behind others when it comes to our majesty of choice. God wants you to make your *own* choice according to *your* faith, not somebody else's. He wants you to learn to trust Him personally, and to not always lean on others. No one else can make your choices for you, not even God. "According to *your* faith let it be to you" (Matthew 9:29).

Jesus has left the cross!

LET'S NOT ONLY REMEMBER JESUS' DEATH ON THE CROSS. Let's not always be seeing a Christ on the cross and the sense of suffering and death and fear that image sometimes generates. We don't have a Jesus on the cross; He's left the cross! We have an empty cross. "O death, where is thy sting? O grave, where is thy victory?" (1 Corinthians 15:55 KJV). We don't have a Christ in the grave. We have a live Jesus living in our hearts.

> Up from the grave He arose;
> With a mighty triumph o'er His foes;
> He arose a victor from the dark domain,
> And He lives forever, with His saints to reign.
> He arose! He arose! Hallelujah! Christ arose![1]

He rose in victory, joy, liberty, and freedom, never to die again, so that He could redeem us as well and prevent our having to go through the agony of death of spirit. What a day of rejoicing that must have been when He rose and realized it was all over. He had won the victory; the world was saved; He had accomplished His mission! He had gone through the horrors of death and Hell for us, and it was over!

[1] Robert Lowry (1826–1899).

Prayer is not just speaking your piece, but most of all letting God speak His.

If we're truly trying to follow and PLEASE GOD, we have to play it by ear—and it better be *our* ear and God's music! To some Christians, playing it by ear means getting God's ear and trying to put their program across on God. Prayer for them is a one-way street; they do all the talking. They are more concerned with having God hear what they have to say than they are with hearing what God has to say. They're trying to get Him to sign His name to their program. They'd get a lot farther by signing their name to God's program—or better yet, signing a blank sheet of paper and letting God add His program to it.

We need to learn to listen to the Lord most of all. Instead of praying, "Hear, Lord, Your servant speaks," we should be like dear little Samuel, the child prophet, who said, "Speak, for Your servant hears" (1 Samuel 3:10).

God always knows what's best and chooses only what's best for you—the unbeatable choice. So don't make the mistake of telling Him what to do or how to do it. Learn to get His answers, and you will find that His program is best.

If there's anything good about us, it's only You, Jesus.

JESUS IS OUR ONLY HOPE! Every one of us is a mess, and if we don't keep our eyes on Jesus and our mind on His Word, we're doomed to defeat, doubt, disillusionment, and final failure. When Peter walked on the water, as soon as he took his eyes off of Jesus, he started to sink (Matthew 14:28–31). Jesus is the only One who can keep you from falling. Hold onto His hand and don't look at the waves.

God knows you're anything but perfect, can't be perfect, and never will be perfect. In fact, you're probably pretty much of a mess, like the rest of us. So the only standard is this: Do you depend on Jesus and His grace, love, and His mercy, and give Him all the credit? Whenever you do a good job or get something right, do you say, "Thank You, Jesus! Don't thank me; thank the Lord. It's all the Lord"?

(Prayer:) Help us to keep our eyes on You, Jesus. Help us to always remember that if we accomplish any real good or appear to be good, it's only because You're working in us and through us (Philippians 2:13). You're the One who does it all. We're nothing. We just have to depend on You, Jesus, and we do!

Let the voice of God's Word speak directly to you.

YOU CAN READ A SCRIPTURE ALL YOUR LIFE AND NOT REALIZE ITS MEANING until the Holy Spirit opens it to you and brings it to life. When the Lord applies a verse or passage to you or some situation you've been praying about, that's called the voice of His Word. Suddenly that verse or passage becomes alive. It's no longer just mere words, but you really get the point.

Have you ever been reading the Word when all of a sudden what you're reading really hits you? *That's for me! That's the answer!* God couldn't have spoken any more emphatically if He'd screamed it in your ear! It may have been written for somebody else thousands of years ago, yet all of a sudden it hits you personally. The Holy Spirit grabbed ahold of that arrow, pulled back the bow, and hit the mark, your heart.

The Lord only has to speak the Word and it can unlock a whole situation. It's the key that unlocks the door that reveals the whole truth. If there's a Scripture that fits the situation, He will likely use it to give you the answer. Thank God for His Word!

"By His stripes we are healed"
(Isaiah 53:5).

WHAT DOES THAT MEAN, "By His stripes we are healed"? The original Hebrew word translated here as "stripes" literally means "bruises, hurts, wounds." Similar to how Jesus' blood was shed for the salvation of our spirits, His body was broken for the healing of our bodies.

Jesus didn't have to suffer in His body for our sins. He only had to shed His blood and die for our sins. But to save *our* bodies it took *His* body. His body suffered and was broken for us in a number of ways—the crown of thorns, the scourging, the nail and spear wounds—so that through this He could also atone for our infirmities.

What does "atone" mean? It means to make amends or pay for something. Jesus bought our souls with His blood so that we could be saved, but He also bought our bodies with His sufferings. So if you've been sick and you need healing, claim it by faith. It's there for you!

Do you believe that Jesus suffered for you, not only for your salvation but also for the healing of your body? If so, you can claim the miraculous power of God's healing.

Isn't it wonderful to know Jesus? Isn't it wonderful to be saved?

"OUR GOD IS THE GOD OF SALVATION" (Psalm 68:20)—total salvation of body, mind, and spirit. God has rescued us from the very gates of death and Hell. If you have received Jesus, the battle for your soul is won, and it's a *permanent* victory. You'll never have to worry about whether you're going to go to Heaven or not. You *have* eternal life through Jesus, which is the gift of God, and you cannot lose it (John 3:36; Ephesians 2:8). He will keep you. You are His.

God says that He's blotted out your sins as a cloud and put them behind His back, to be remembered no more (Isaiah 44:22). You're all clean now and no longer under the power of sin (Romans 6:14). You can start life all over with the Lord, for you're a new creature in Christ Jesus. "Old things have passed away ... all things have become new" (2 Corinthians 5:17).

You're born again, a new person, God's new child, with a new plan and purpose in living. He'll give you peace of mind, purity of heart, rest of soul, and happiness of spirit now and forever.

> Happy now, happy now,
> Since I found the favor of my loving Savior.
> All the past is gone at last,
> And I don't care where or how, praise God![1]

[1] Author unknown.

When God can get you out of the way, then He has a chance.

At THE AGE OF 40, when Moses was cocky and overconfident and tried to free his people himself, he was a big flop and had to run for his life in a personal exodus of his own. It took God 40 years in the wilderness to teach Moses humility and utter dependence on God, until he no longer even wanted the job! It wasn't until he thought he wasn't ready or able that he was. Man's extremity is God's opportunity. When you come to the end of your rope, then God has a chance to work.

Sometimes God has to break us—and it's not fun being broken. It almost makes you feel like you want to die, but then you're willing to live for Jesus. Only from such death to self can life be born anew (John 12:24–25). Then it is no longer you that live, but Christ that lives in you (Galatians 2:20). You are now dead and your life is hid with Christ in God (Colossians 3:3).

So if you feel incapable or insufficient, cheer up! That's when God has a chance to take over and do things to suit Himself. Only He can do it anyway, so give Him a chance. Let go and let God! Surrender to Him today.

We all need the encouragement and prayers of others.

WHEN YOU'RE HAVING A TRIAL OR A PROBLEM, you should never complain or dump your doubts and fears on others, but that doesn't mean you can't ask for counsel or prayer about your problem.

Some people keep things in and suffer through their trials without asking for help or prayer. Well, you can admire them for being able to take it, but wouldn't it be better if they would just honestly confess that they need help and prayer? Spilling it all out prevents a lot of misunderstandings and it gets you some prayer and sympathy, at least—the very things you like to have when you're going through a trial.

Many times it really helps to talk about your problem, but of course you should try to find someone who is spiritually strong, because you don't want to stumble others or bring them down or discourage them in any way.

"Confess your trespasses to one another, and pray for one another, that you may be healed. The effective, fervent prayer of a righteous man avails much" (James 5:16). "Bear one another's burdens, and so fulfill the law of Christ" (Galatians 6:2).

"Bear fruits worthy of repentance" (Matthew 3:8).

TRUE REPENTANCE IS NOT JUST BEING SORRY, it is *metanoia*, Greek for a complete change of direction. Many people are always being sorry but never really changing, like King Saul. Poor Saul never learned. He apologized and was sorry many times, but he never really repented, he never really changed, he never turned and went the other way. Saul would break down and weep before the prophet Samuel, but he didn't weep because he was repentant; he wept because he was sorry he was about to lose the kingdom (1 Samuel 15:24–30). He didn't really confess and forsake his sin, the evil root beneath the outer show (Proverbs 28:13).

Though King David also committed great sins, he had great repentance and a genuine change. Therefore God had great forgiveness for him. David sought God's heart (1 Samuel 13:14; Psalm 51). David deeply loved God, and he really wanted to glorify God and please Him. God loved David in spite of all his sins and mistakes because David was willing to confess and change—and he went on to become one of God's greats, in spite of himself.

It's not forever that loved ones will be gone.

DEATH IS A SAD PARTING, even for Christians. It's a sad parting for those of us who are left behind, and in a way it's even sad for those who go on, to have to leave us behind for a little while. But thank God, our sorrow is not as those who have no hope, for we know we're going to be reunited again soon. We may have to be apart for a little while, but we'll appreciate each other more than ever when we're reunited in Heaven. What a day of rejoicing that will be!

Does Jesus care when I've said goodbye
To the dearest on earth to me?
When my sad heart aches, till it nearly breaks,
Is it aught to Him? Does He see?

Oh, yes, He cares, I know He cares,
His heart is touched with my grief;
Though the days be weary, the long nights dreary,
I know my Savior cares![1]

Our dear ones are with Jesus, so if we stay close to Him, we cannot be far from them.

Death hides but it does not divide.
Thou art but on Christ's other side.
Thou art with Christ, and Christ with me.
In Him I am still close to thee.[2]

[1] Frank E. Graeff (1860–1919).
[2] Author unknown.

One of the Devil's jobs is to help keep us in line.

In a way, the Devil is our friendly adversary. He has his own agenda, of course, but even that can serve God's purpose when it helps keep us in line. The Devil can be pretty lenient with his own—or at least he gives that impression to keep them firmly in his grip—but he doesn't let active Christians get away with anything! He's the Accuser of the saints (Revelation 12:10).

The Lord is like a shepherd, we are His sheep, and the Devil and his demons are like sheepdogs. Sheepdogs help the shepherd by keeping the sheep in the flock. They don't bother the sheep as long as the sheep stay together, but if one sheep gets out of line or strays from the shepherd, the sheepdogs bark and yap and nip at the stray sheep's heels to get it to rejoin the flock—and the little sheep runs back to the shepherd real quick!

Stay close to the Lord like a little lamb at the shepherd's side, because if you get out of touch with the Lord, the Devil gets in touch with you! He'll start nipping at your heels, so stay close to the Lord.

"Sing to the Lord a new song!"
(Psalm 98:1).

GOD'S CHILDREN HAVE USED MUSIC AND SONG FOR MANY PURPOSES THROUGHOUT HISTORY. In fact, they not only played music and sang songs, but they recorded them as well—not with the advanced methods we use today, but in whatever ways they could. You can read in the Bible the lyrics of some of the earliest songs of God's children.

Moses was a singer and songwriter. David wrote lots of songs, and many of them are recorded in the book of Psalms, a whole book of songs. Jeremiah wrote a song now known as Lamentations. Hannah, the mother of Samuel, wrote at least one song (1 Samuel chapter 2), and Deborah and Barak sang a duet before the children of Israel (Judges chapter 5). God even used musical instruments to save His children from their enemies, like the trumpets made of rams' horns that caused the walls of Jericho to fall (Joshua chapter 6) and the Midianites to flee from Gideon's meager army of 300 men (Judges chapter 7).

You can read all through the Bible how God's children sang and made a "joyful noise unto the Lord" (Psalm 100:1 KJV). Even Jesus and His disciples sang songs (Matthew 26:30), and Paul exhorts that we should all sing psalms and spiritual songs (Colossians 3:16). The apostle John even heard singing in Heaven—the song of Moses (Revelation 15:2–3).

"Come, let us sing to the Lord!" (Psalm 95:1).

The hand that rocks the cradle rules the world.

WHAT AN IMPORTANT JOB A MOTHER HAS! The mothers of the next generation are the ones who are molding the future. Motherhood is just about the greatest calling in the world. Of course, taking care of a baby may not always *seem* very important, but don't ever minimize it. Who knows what an impact that child may have on the lives of many others one day.

Motherhood takes the strength of Samson, the wisdom of Solomon, the patience of Job, the faith of Abraham, the insight of Daniel, and the courage and administrative ability of David. It also takes the love of God, that's for sure! What a job!

The thing that makes a mother so wonderful is her selfsacrificial spirit that is willing to sacrifice her time and strength and even her own health, if necessary, for the sake of that child. Any woman can have a baby, but it takes a real mother to learn how to "train up a child in the way he should go" (Proverbs 22:6).

> The bravest battle that ever was fought!
> Shall I tell you where and when?
> On the maps of the world you will find it not;
> 'Twas fought by the mothers of men![1]

[1] Joaquin Miller (1837–1913), "Motherhood."

God can open doors that no man can close (Revelation 3:8).

CIRCUMSTANCES AND CONDITIONS ARE NOT ALWAYS THE BEST WAY OR FINAL CRITERIA in finding the will of God, but they can be a helpful indication. This is referred to as "open and closed doors" because this is how God sometimes operates—by opening some doors of opportunity and closing others.

If you're trying to please God, He will put golden opportunities in your path. God works in mysterious ways, His wonders to perform, and sometimes we're just swept along by His current. Where God guides, He provides, and where He is providing open doors, He's obviously guiding. So don't hesitate—just walk right in! Take advantage of those golden opportunities He sends your way.

But if He is *not* opening doors for you, don't get impatient and try to batter them down. Trying to force the situation and push your way through just won't work. We sometimes have to accept God's no in order to find His yes. Be patient and wait, and He will make an opening for you.

(Prayer:) Lead and guide us, Lord, according to what You know is best. If we follow Your leading and want to do Your will, then we know You'll open the doors and work everything out.

If your heart's desire is to please the Lord, the Lord will usually let you do as you please.

Our personal desires in a matter are often a fairly good indicator of the Lord's will for us, because as long as our motives are right, He gives us what we want and have faith for. "Delight yourself also in the Lord, and He shall give you the desires of your heart" (Psalm 37:4). "According to your faith let it be to you" (Matthew 9:29).

The Lord is able to help you *want* to do what *He* wants you to do. If a certain thing is God's will for you and you're open and yielded to what He wants, He will give you an inner conviction about it—what is sometimes called "the witness of the Spirit." This is how God often works: He gives different people desires for different ministries and mission fields, and then He gives them faith to see through what they and He want done.

If you love the Lord, your personal desires are usually the right ones because you only want to please Him. So delight yourself in the Lord most of all, and seek to do His will. When you do, it is His delight to also give you the desires of your own heart, because He's the One who puts them there when you're pleasing Him.

"I have given you the authority over all the power of the Enemy [the Devil]" (Luke 10:19 TLB).

Don't underestimate the power that GOD HAS GIVEN EACH OF HIS CHILDREN. "He who is in you is greater than he who is in the world" (1 John 4:4). In other words, "My power in you is much greater than the Devil's power in his children—much greater!" In fact, the power of Satan's children is so puny by comparison that they're like little kids playing with matches, while we've got lightning bolts! The power of God's Holy Spirit of love is the greatest power on earth!

If you humbly yield to God, then He will empower and fill you with His Spirit. You then become a powerhouse, a generator of the Spirit of God. It's like you have a big electric power cable in your hand, but you're so in tune with it yourself that you can hold the cable and use its power to create, to mend, to heal, and to love. "For with God nothing will be impossible" (Luke 1:37), and "all things are possible to him who believes" (Mark 9:23). Are you "strong in the Lord and in the power of His might"? (Ephesians 6:10). If not, receive power now by asking Him to fill and renew you with His Holy Spirit, and He will! (Acts 1:8; Titus 3:5).

"Though Jesus was a Son, yet learned He obedience by the things which He suffered" (Hebrews 5:8).

WHY DID JESUS HAVE TO LEARN? Wasn't He the Son of God? (John 5:18; Philippians 2:6). Didn't He already know everything?

The main thing His heavenly Father was trying to show Jesus was how to love sinners enough to be willing to die for them—to understand their suffering, to have compassion on them, to want to heal their sick and save their souls. That's what Jesus learned while He was here.

Why did He learn those things? Just so they would be forgotten and left behind when He left this world?—No! It was so He could take all that knowledge and experience with Him and thereby have even greater sympathy and love for us and be a greater help to us, both now and hereafter. "For we do not have a High Priest who cannot sympathize with our weaknesses, but was in all points tempted as we are, yet without sin. Let us therefore come boldly to the throne of grace, that we may obtain mercy and find grace to help in time of need" (Hebrews 4:15–16). "He is also able to save to the uttermost those who come to God through Him, since He always lives to make intercession for them" (Hebrews 7:25).

Spend your life losing your life for others; that's the secret of saving it.

JESUS SAID, "Whoever desires to save his life will lose it, but whoever loses his life for My sake and the Gospel's will save it" (Mark 8:35). "Seek first the kingdom of God" (Matthew 6:33). And what is His kingdom? His kingdom is souls. His kingdom is reaching the lost with the Gospel. Jesus didn't call us to save ourselves; He called and commissioned us to save others.

Do you want to save your life? Then lose it for Jesus, spreading the Good News to others. Live for Jesus, and He will take care of you. Obey Him and do His will, tell others about Him and win others to the kingdom of God, and then help them do the same.

The fastest way to lose your life is to live selfishly, like the man who set out to build bigger barns for all his goods. "But God said to him, 'Fool! This night your soul will be required of you; then whose will those things be which you have provided?'" (Luke 12:20). What a warning!

How much better to heed His call, take up the challenge, and do your best to share His love with others. Then you will hear Him say to you, "Well done, good and faithful servant. Enter into the joy of your Lord" (Matthew 25:21).

Give *no* place to the Devil
(Ephesians 4:27).

W HEN WE LOVE THE LORD AND GIVE HIM OUR ALL, our entire lives are in His hands, under His loving care, and the Devil has nothing that he can lay claim to—nothing he can use to make us feel condemned and distant from God.

It's like the story of Huddersfield: There was once a rich landowner who decided to buy the entire village of Huddersfield, and over time he bought every piece of land in the area—every piece, that is, except one little plot. One stubborn old farmer refused to sell his tiny piece of land, and nothing would change his mind. The landowner even offered the farmer much more money than his property was actually worth, but the farmer was so fond of his land that he absolutely refused to sell. When the landowner finally gave up, he tried to encourage himself by saying, "What difference does just one little plot of land make? I've bought everything else, so Huddersfield is *mine*. It belongs to me!" But the stubborn old farmer overheard him and said, "Oh, no it doesn't! *We* own Huddersfield. It belongs to you and *me*!"

Don't let the Devil be able to say that of you to God! "Aha! Look, God! Even though he belongs mostly to You, a little bit still belongs to me!"

"We are fools for Christ's sake" (1 Corinthians 4:10). Whose fool are you?

SOME PEOPLE JUST DON'T SEEM TO UNDERSTAND THE MIRACLE OF CONVERSION or the idealistic desire to devote one's time to God's service. "The natural man does not receive the things of the Spirit of God, for they are foolishness unto him" (1 Corinthians 2:14). Because there was such a sudden change in their lives, many new Christians have been thought to have suddenly gone mad, like the apostle Paul, or been "driven crazy by religion" (Acts 26:24; Mark 3:21; John 10:20).

In fact, nearly all the prophets and men of God throughout the Bible and past ages were thought to have been nuts by the rest of the world—misfits and dreamers who heard voices and had hallucinations and were pretty well flipped-out over religion.

It all depends on who is calling whom mad. If people think *we're* a little eccentric or off center, it's not because we're off the center; it's because they're wobbling around themselves, way off the one and only true center, Jesus Christ. Man without God is off center. They're the ones who are not in their right minds, because they can't possibly know what's right without Jesus!

What's every Christian's duty?— To love others into the kingdom of God.

If THE WHOLE PURPOSE OF OUR EXISTENCE IS TO FIND AND RECEIVE GOD'S LOVE IN JESUS, then why doesn't the Lord just take us home to Heaven the minute we do?—Because once we're saved, we have a job to do; we have a responsibility. There are lots of other people who need to know Jesus, and we are the means by which He has chosen to make Himself known.

Jesus alone saves, but He doesn't want to save us alone. He wants to save the whole world, but in order to do that He needs us to tell others about His love, to give His love and message of salvation to the whole world.

Jesus told His closest followers, "As the Father has sent Me, I also send you" (John 20:21). He says this still to His followers of today, calling them to give their lives daily in loving concern and care for others, to share His heart and love with those who are seeking for "the Way, the Truth, and the Life" (John 14:6). He came to love the world, and He calls us to do likewise.

Will you answer His call? Will you do what you can to win others to Him? Will you spread the Word, spread the message, spread His love?

Only the Lord can keep you faithful.

Too many people think about faithful-ness as being something that they must work up. But faithfulness is a result of faith, and faith is a gift of God. You just have to depend on the Lord to keep you faithful.

If you feel you don't have enough faith, read the Word; that's the source of faith. You have to give Him a little cooperation, you have to listen, you have to read, you have to obey, but that's the easy part. It's His job to keep you faithful, full of faith, which comes from Him!

So quit trying so hard! Quit worrying about it! Quit trying to work it up or even pray it down! Trust the Lord and don't worry. He'll give you all the faith you need!

"Now to Him who is able to keep you from stumbling, and to present you faultless before the presence of His glory with ex-ceeding joy, to God our Savior" (Jude 24–25), commit your way, your life, your mind, your thoughts, your time! "I know whom I have believed and am persuaded that He is able to keep what I have committed to Him" (2 Timothy 1:12). Praise the Lord! Only He can do it!

One way to find the will of God is to ask for a sign, a "fleece," some visible indication.

GIDEON LAID THE WOOLLY COAT OF A SHEEP ON THE GROUND AND SAID, "Lord, if the fleece is wet in the morning and all the ground around it is dry, then I'll know that such-and-such is Your will." But when God gave Gideon the sign he had asked for, Gideon still wasn't sure. So the next evening Gideon said, "Lord, if the fleece is dry and the ground is wet, I'll believe it." So God did that, too, and Gideon then knew that God was with him. If God hadn't given him those signs with the fleece, Gideon might have lost heart and quit. But when God answered, that convinced Gideon he was doing the right thing (Judges 6:36–40).

A fleece is like a contract between you and God. You specify the sign you want, like Gideon did. When God answers a fleece, then you've got to have the faith that the outcome was really God's answer. When you make a deal with God, you'd better stick to it no matter what. It's just as important for you to keep your part of the bargain as it is for God to keep His. It's a test of faith. So make a wise fleece and stick to it.

You are Jesus' proof!

THE APOSTLE PAUL WAS A TREMENDOUS WITNESS FOR JESUS, and almost every time he was brought before governors or magistrates or kings to answer the accusations of those who opposed him and his message, he took the opportunity to try to win them to Jesus—and he started with his own personal testimony: "This is what happened to me!" (Acts chapter 26).

People are interested in people. Life stories are more effective than getting into theological arguments and preaching sermons. When you start telling people your life story, instantly you have their attention and they quickly become fascinated. When you tell them your own personal experience, if you say it with sincerity in the power of the Spirit, they will believe that you're telling the truth. Your testimony is one thing they cannot deny. And the moment they admit that it has happened to you, then they have to admit that it's possible for it to happen to them. Win them to yourself and your own happiness first, then they will want whatever it is that makes you that way.

You're the proof of the pudding. You are the product of the Gospel and the love of Jesus. So tell others how His miracle-working power has worked in your own life, as a genuine living example and proof of what He can do.

"Whatever you spend," God says, "I will repay."

Do you remember who else said that? The Good Samaritan. It's from the parable that Jesus told about the poor traveler who was beaten and robbed by thieves, and the Good Samaritan who picked him up and took him to an inn and cared for him, then told the innkeeper, "Whatever you spend, I will repay you" (Luke 10:30–37).

The Good Samaritan is like the Lord, and the innkeeper His steward, like you or me. Whatever you spend in His work of rescuing lives and saving souls, He will more than repay. In fact, He has promised that if you obey Him and give, "your gift will return to you in full and overflowing measure, pressed down, shaken together to make room for more, and running over. Whatever measure you use to give—large or small—will be used to measure what is given back to you" (Luke 6:38 TLB).

That's the way God is: As you pour out, He'll pour in, and He'll never let you outgive Him. He gives you back much, much more than you could ever give. As long as you continue to overflow on others, God will continue to overflow His blessings upon you. The more you give, the more He'll give you back in every way.

Why did the Devil and man cook up the ridiculous, idiotic scheme of evolution?—To try to get rid of God!

THE DEVIL KNEW THAT TO PREVENT PEOPLE FROM BELIEVING IN JESUS, he had to destroy their faith in the Bible, beginning with the book of Genesis, the story of Creation. Charles Darwin was the Devil's dupe to finally give the world the excuse it needed to not believe in God.

People often think of evolution when they hear a mention of God, because that's the whole purpose of evolution: to eliminate faith in God and to foster the false doctrine of devils that the creation created itself. If it could have happened without God, there doesn't need to *be* a God.

Evolution is really a religion of unbelief in God—a religion that has to be believed by faith because there is no proof. Margaret Mead (1901–1978), the famous anthropologist, admitted, "We as honest scientists must confess that science has yet to discover one single iota [tiny speck] of concrete evidence to prove evolution."

Evolution is one of the Devil's greatest lies and most clever pieces of teaching, because if he can get people to doubt one word in the Bible, they'll soon doubt the whole Bible. Don't let it happen to you!

God can make a living saint out of little old you!

A LOT OF CHRISTIANS EXALT THE GREAT MEN AND WOMEN OF GOD OF THE PAST to such heights that they forget those people were just as human as everyone else. "It's impossible to be like that today," they say. "Ordinary Christians aren't supposed to even try to be like that. It's impossible!"

That's a lie! The apostle Paul writes in Romans chapter 3, "There is none righteous, no, not one" (verse 10), and "All have sinned and fall short of the glory of God" (verse 23). And that includes whom?—Not only you and me, but the saints and the apostles and everyone else except the Lord Himself.

Now that changes the picture! That means it *is* possible to become more like them. So if you think that you'll never amount to anything for the Lord because you're too bad, that isn't so! Regardless of your faults or failings or supposed limitations or whatever, you too can be greatly used by the Lord if you want to help further His kingdom and are willing to do things His way.

God can use even you—weak and bad as you are. And when He does, you'll give Him all the glory because you will know that whatever good you accomplish is only due to His working through you.

God is our Sun.

GOD CREATED THE SUN, THE MOON, THE STARS, AND THE PLANETS in part to illustrate His spiritual truths, so we could better understand our relationship with Him and how necessary He is to our spiritual solar system.

Life itself wouldn't be possible without the Sun. Without the light of the Sun we'd be in total darkness except for starlight, just as without the Lord we would be in almost total spiritual darkness. Without the warmth and heat of the Sun's rays, we'd also freeze to death, just like without the Lord we'd be dead cold spiritually. Without the Sun's rays, the plants that provide our food wouldn't grow; likewise, we would die spiritually of hunger without the Lord and His Word. Without the Sun's gravitational pull on Earth, instead of staying in its well-planned orbit, Earth would go wandering off through space. Just so, without God's guidance—His gravitational pull on us in the spirit—we too would certainly get out of the well-planned orbit of His will and go wandering off into the darkness of spiritual space.

If the Sun has that much power, think how much power our spiritual Sun, God, has and how much we need Him!

For God's sake, know what you believe and stand up for it!

For life to have real meaning and purpose, we have to believe in something. Then we have to be ready to stand up for what we believe; we have to have conviction.

God likes wholehearted, stouthearted men. If He is what you believe in, have you got the guts to be one of these? If you're going to serve God, know what you believe and serve Him no matter what anyone else says. Be prepared to take a stand of faith, like Martin Luther (1483–1546) did on the issue of salvation by grace before the religious council of his day: "Unless I am convinced by the testimony of Scripture, I can and will not retract. Here I stand. I can do no other. So help me God!"

You cannot stop the man of faith. You cannot dissuade him. You cannot divert him. He'll go on with or without you or right over you, if necessary. He is determined to go on by faith because he has found the truth. He is of one mind, one heart, one soul, one spirit, one purpose, and will not quit!

"No good thing will God withhold from those who walk uprightly" (Psalm 84:11).

WHAT ARE YOUR HEART'S DESIRES? If you delight yourself in God and His service, He's promised to give you the desires of your heart (Psalm 37:4).

God apparently feels that nothing is too good for His obedient children. If we please Him, we not only get what we need, but usually even what we *want*, above our needs, "exceedingly abundantly above all that we ask or think" (Ephesians 3:20).

He's willing to give us anything that's good for us, but He doesn't always let us have those things that He knows *aren't* good for us. He tried that on the children of Israel. He let them have the desires of their hearts a few times when it wasn't good for them, but then He had to send leanness to their souls to try to teach them a lesson (Psalm 106:15).

(Prayer:) Lord, help us to put You first, to delight ourselves in You and Yours most of all so You can trust us with other things—everything we need and even things we want—because they will not come between You and us. If it's good for us, let us have it, but if it's *not* good for us, please keep it from us. Amen.

Your talents are nothing if you don't have love.

You CAN READ THE BIBLE ALL YOU WANT, but if it doesn't come to life in you by the Spirit, what's it all for? You can quote the Bible word for word, but if you don't live it in love, it doesn't do any good. You can have all the gifts of the Spirit, but without love it is meaningless. You can be tops in your field, but if you don't manifest God's love to others, then it's all in vain, because love is the most important thing (1 Corinthians chapter 13).

Faithfulness is important, to endure as a good soldier and to work hard (2 Timothy 2:3), but if you don't have love, you don't have anything. If you don't have love and show love for others, then in God's eyes your good works don't really count.

What's the thing that proves we are Jesus' disciples?—Love! Jesus said, "By this all will know that you are My disciples, if you have love for one another" (John 13:35). "This is My commandment, that you love one another as I have loved you" (John 15:12). That's an order! He ordered us, His followers, to love one another, so love!

Jesus is the ultimate manifestation of God's love.

THE BIBLE TELLS US, "God is love" (1 John 4:8). He is the great Spirit of Love who created you and me, this beautiful world, and the entire universe. Then, to show us His love and to help us understand Himself, He sent us His own Son, Jesus Christ, in the form of a man.

God is pictured in Jesus, a man who loved everybody, even the poorest and the worst of all. He came for love and lived in love and died for love that we might live and love forever. His death brings life, forgiveness, and eternal happiness to those who love Him in return.

God shared His love with the whole world, but He also loves everyone individually. God loves *you* so much that He gave His most priceless possession, the most cherished thing He had— "His only begotten Son"—so that you could have everlasting life (John 3:16). He loved *you* enough to send Jesus to take the punishment for your sins, if you'll just receive Him and thank Him for it.

He loves you dearly, more dearly than the spoken word can tell. You can never understand the love of God. It's too great; it passes all understanding (Ephesians 3:19). You just have to receive it and feel it with your heart.

Jesus is coming soon!

DESPITE ALL THE WARNINGS OF GOD'S PROPHETS and all of the world events that point to the Second Coming of Christ, most people today still won't believe. They think, *Oh, they've been saying for centuries that Jesus is coming back, and He hasn't come yet.* Unwittingly, they themselves are a fulfillment of an Endtime prophecy: "Scoffers will come in the last days, saying, 'Where is the promise of His coming? For since the fathers fell asleep, all things continue as they were from the beginning of creation'" (2 Peter 3:3–4).

Jesus said that it would be "as in the days before the flood [when] they were eating and drinking, marrying and giving in marriage, until the day that Noah entered the ark, and did not know until the flood came and took them all away." What did He mean, they "did not know"? Noah had been telling them for 120 years! What He really meant is that they wouldn't *believe* until it happened. "So also will the coming of the Son of Man be" (Matthew 24:38–39).

Will *you* be ready when Jesus comes? If so, you won't be taken by surprise and can actually look forward to that great day with hope and faith.

The day is coming when even the fields and trees are going to be glad and rejoice!

Many OF THE SOUNDS OF NATURE ARE IN A MINOR KEY and have a melancholy note to them, like the sighing of the wind as it blows through the trees. "The whole creation," Paul says, "groans and labors with birth pangs together until now. ... Even we ourselves groan within ourselves, eagerly waiting for the adoption, the redemption of our body" (Romans 8:22–23).

But the coming thousand-year reign of Christ will be heaven on earth, like the Garden of Eden, only better. There will be worldwide peace, Satan and his forces will be bound, the Curse will be removed, and we'll have Paradise regained. There will be no more of man's cruelty toward man, no more of man's inhumanity to man allowed. At last God will redeem the earth (Revelation 20:1–4).

The earth will blossom like a rose, and all of God's creation will be in perfect peace and beautiful harmony. "You shall go out with joy, and be led out with peace; the mountains and the hills shall break forth into singing before you, and all the trees of the field shall clap their hands" (Isaiah 55:12). Can you imagine such a thing? So beautiful!

Our greatest need is love, and love is God's great answer.

PEOPLE'S HEARTS ARE THE SAME THE WORLD OVER: Everybody needs love. Most people are searching for real love, but can't find it. They know it must exist, they hunger for it, they need it, but so many of them can't find it because they don't find God. It's so sad!

But wherever people have problems, God has answers. And in this case it's such a simple answer—love! Love is the key, love is the answer, and Jesus is the Way, the Truth, and the Life (John 14:6). He's the only way they'll ever find love, joy, peace, and heavenly happiness, both here and now and in the life to come.

(Prayer:) Help us, Jesus, to be faithful to show Your love to others, to encourage and help them, to heal them and lift them by giving them the message of Your love that has the power to solve all their problems and heal their bodies, minds, and spirits. Thank You for giving us the opportunity to help others by giving them Your answer, and it's such a simple answer, Jesus—just You and Your love!

The first place we look for the will of God is in the Word of God.

G OD'S WRITTEN WORD IS THE KNOWN, SURE, ABSOLUTE, REVEALED WILL OF GOD. So when you aren't sure what to do or how to go about it, look in His Word at all He's said before. If God never tells you another thing, if you never get a revelation, if you never see a vision, if you never receive a message from Heaven in prophecy, if you never have the gift of knowledge, if you never have wisdom, if you never have discernment, if you never have the gift of healing, if you never have the gift of miracles, if you'll just operate according to the written Word of God, you'll accomplish a whole lot.

Jesus said, "Heaven and earth will pass away, but My words will by no means pass away" (Matthew 24:35). The Bible also tells us: "Forever, O Lord, Your Word is settled in Heaven" (Psalm 119:89). When God speaks to you right from His Book, you know it's right. There's no question or any doubt about it! It never fails!

> How firm a foundation, ye saints of the Lord,
> Is laid for your faith in His excellent Word!
> What more can He say than to you He hath said,
> To you who for refuge to Jesus have fled![1]

---

[1] John Rippon, *A Selection of Hymns from the Best Authors*, 1787.

"Sown in weakness ...
raised in power"
(1 Corinthians 15:43).

IN HEAVEN, your new body is going to resemble your present body, only it will be much more beautiful and wonderful. It will be eternal, thrilling, and glorious (Philippians 3:21).

When God created the life cycle of butterflies, it was almost as though He was illustrating resurrection. They hatch from eggs into little wormlike caterpillars. Then, after a short life as an earthbound bug, they wrap themselves up in a cocoon called a chrysalis, almost like a coffin, and it seems they die. But then spring comes and suddenly the coffin splits open and out comes a beautiful butterfly. Once it was just a little crawling insect, the lowliest of all creatures, but all of a sudden it breaks out of its cocoon in the form of a beautiful butterfly that flies in the heavens—one of the prettiest of all creatures!

Like the difference between a grain of wheat and the full-grown, full-blown stalk and head that comes from that grain, or the flower that comes from one tiny seed, that's how much better your new heavenly body is going to be (1 Corinthians 15:35–38, 42–58). You're going to be like the angels of God (Luke 20:36).

It pays to serve Jesus;
it pays every day.
It pays every step of the way.[1]

IF YOU LOVE JESUS, delight yourself in Him, and do your best to love others and help them, He will do anything for you. He'll supply all your need according to His riches in glory (Philippians 4:19). He'll even give you the desires of your heart—not only whatever you need, but your wants as well (Psalm 37:4). Those are His promises to you, so believe them, claim them, step out by faith and do your part, and expect the Lord to fulfill them.

Most of the Lord's blessings and rewards are dependent upon obedience and worthiness, on doing a good job faithfully. The Lord doesn't reward loafing; He rewards faithful hard work. But the minute you start obeying and working, He will start doing His part. He will bless!

Believe His promises, His guarantees, and put your faith into action. Be a good and faithful servant, and He will reward you here and now and in Heaven when that time comes.

> Go work in My vineyard; oh, work while it's day!
> Your strength I'll supply, and your wages I'll pay;
> And bless with My best the diligent few
> Who finish the labor I've given them to do.[2]

[1] Frank C. Huston (1871–1959).
[2] Tullius Clinton O'Kane (1830–1912), paraphrased.

Praise your way through!
That's how you get the victory!

Even the greatest men of God, such as King David, sometimes got discouraged. David was a great psalmist and he usually sang beautiful praises to the Lord. But once before he was king, he was sure that King Saul was going to kill him, and he said, "I shall perish some day by the hand of Saul" (1 Samuel 27:1). Thank God David never wrote a psalm saying that! How could you sing that? Did David ever die at the hand of Saul? No, he never did. So that was just the Devil trying to discourage him.

If you let the Devil get you down and use your mouth to speak doubt and discouragement and lies to others, you are preaching the Devil's own doctrines. Don't do it, or you're just letting the Enemy in. Take a positive stand against the attacks of the Devil. Fight him and fight his doubts. The minute you feel discouraged, start praising the Lord. Go on the attack! As long as you have praise on your lips, you can't complain or speak doubt.

The Devil hates praise. He hates songs that praise the Lord, and he hates God's Word most of all, so keep full of it.

God gives us the majesty of personal choice, to go His way or our own.

IF GOD HAD WANTED ROBOTS, He could have programmed everybody to love Him. Instead, He made us with a free will and gave us the majesty of choice, so we could *choose* to love Him. This is the age of grace in which we have to make our own decisions to love and serve Him. We have to voluntarily choose God and His way, as revealed to us through His Word.

One of the main reasons we're here in the first place, from the Garden of Eden to the present, is to learn how to make decisions under God's guidance. All of life is that way. We must constantly make decisions and choices. If we know and love and want to please Him and do what's right, this causes us to seek Him in prayer and ask Him for the answers. It makes us dependent on Him as we try to make the right decisions so we'll go the right direction.

He put us here to make decisions. He tells us what's right and wrong, but then He doesn't make us do either; He lets *us* make the decisions. Are you choosing God's way?

Eternal salvation by grace means once saved always saved.

"H<small>E WHO BELIEVES IN THE</small> S<small>ON</small> *HAS* <small>EVERLASTING LIFE</small>" (John 3:36). Right now! No ifs, ands, or buts about it! If you've received Jesus, you already have it. You don't have to worry if you are going to have it, if you are going to fall from grace, if you are going to manage to stay saved, or if you are going to manage to keep true and then finally be given the reward of salvation for your faithfulness. Salvation is *not* a reward. It's not pay; it's not wages. It is a *gift* that you don't earn by faithfulness or by any righteousness or works of your own (Titus 3:5). None of these can keep you saved any more than they can save you in the first place. Only *Jesus* can do it. "The gift of God is eternal life in Jesus Christ our Lord" (Romans 6:23).

A works salvation is no salvation at all. You cannot be good enough. No matter how many good deeds you do, they won't save you. "For by grace you have been saved through faith, and that not of yourselves; it is the gift of God" (Ephesians 2:8). It's impossible to save yourself. You have eternal life, which is the gift of God, and you cannot lose it, for He will keep you. You're the Lord's forever!

It's wise to "wait on the Lord."

You're never going to accomplish much for God if you try to do things yourself in the energy of the flesh. This is a problem that most of us seem to have. We jump to conclusions, make hasty decisions, or simply push ahead in our own strength, doing what seems natural or logical, without really praying and making sure that's what the Lord wants us to do and how He wants us to go about it.

You need to learn to stop and pray, "Now, God, what do *You* want me to do?" Seek the Lord. Don't just lean to your own understanding, even when a course of action seems obvious. Ask the Lord and make *sure* (Proverbs 3:5–7).

Remember, God is hardly ever in a hurry. The greatest works of God take time. It takes God time to make a baby or grow a flower or even to paint a sunset. So when you haven't yet made certain that a thing is God's will, the best thing to do is to wait on the Lord until He reveals it to you one way or the other.

"Wait on the Lord; be of good courage, and He shall strengthen your heart" (Psalm 27:14). "Those that wait upon the Lord shall renew their strength; they shall mount up with wings like eagles" (Isaiah 40:31).

Always remember, everyone is hungry for praise and appreciation.

EVERYBODY NEEDS ENCOURAGEMENT. Most people have a certain amount of inferiority complex and tend to get discouraged, so encouragement is a very important thing. We all need the encouragement of others, and yet most of us fail all too often to express appreciation to those around us. As we will account for every idle word, so we will for every idle silence (Matthew 12:36–37).

The Lord knows that encouragement is very important. He appreciates us and commends us, and He promises to reward us for our good work. It has nothing to do with our salvation—we get salvation as a free gift by His mercy and grace and love—but He especially commends our service for Him. He really appreciates our service and our sacrifice and the things we do for Him beyond the call of duty, and He wants us to likewise show appreciation to those who give of themselves for Him and others.

"Whatever things are of good report, if there be any virtue and if there is anything praiseworthy—meditate on these things" (Philippians 4:8). We need to apply that to those around us, and try to remind ourselves constantly to think positively about others and to thank and praise them for their good qualities, just as the Lord does with us.

"He has filled the hungry soul with good things, but the rich He has sent away empty" (Luke 1:53).

JESUS FOUND AND LOVED THE LOST SHEEP, the hungry ones, the sinners who knew they needed help and were thankful for it, not the self-righteous ones who "had no need of a physician" (Matthew 9:12). There is not much hope for those who are satisfied with their lives the way they are.

The hardest person in the world to win to the Lord is the moral man who thinks he is good enough and thinks he doesn't need God. Sometimes the guiltiest people are the most utterly deceived and actually think they are innocent and righteous. They're "glad they're not like the sinner," when actually they're worse because of their self-righteous pride that goes against God's spirit of love (Luke 18:11).

But there are others who have hungry hearts and really want to hear the truth, and when you give it to them they receive it, believe it, accept it, and follow Jesus. Because they are willing to confess that they need answers, the Lord has an opportunity to give them answers. For those who are seeking, hungry, unhappy, and yearning for the spiritual, He has this promise: "Blessed are those who hunger and thirst after righteousness, for they shall be filled" (Matthew 5:6).

The Word of God is like a beautiful string of pearls!

GOD'S WORD IS AN ABSOLUTELY INEX-HAUSTIBLE SOURCE OF WISDOM AND KNOWLEDGE in which you can constantly find treasures new and old. It will stand a thousand readings, and he who has gone over it most frequently is the surest of finding new wonders there. Each time we delve into the Word, we bring forth priceless truths by the handful!

But these pearls of knowledge are nothing without the Holy Spirit. No matter how much you study, it takes the Spirit of God and the hand of God to string the pearls of His Word together in proper order, sorted out and made into a wonderful, beautiful string of truths to adorn your mind and heart in proper order, sequence, size, importance, and beauty. That's the difference between knowledge and wisdom. Wisdom is knowing how to apply what you already know—in this case, knowing how to rightly use your knowledge of God's Word.

So don't neglect the beauties, riches, and treasures of the Word of God. Ask God for wisdom. "Wisdom is the principal thing; therefore get wisdom. And in all your getting, get understanding" (Proverbs 4:7). It is better than gold (Proverbs 16:16).

Heaven is here!

EVEN NOW, GOD'S INVISIBLE HEAVENLY KINGDOM IS ALREADY IN EXISTENCE and operation. It not only surrounds us, but is *within* us. Jesus said, "The kingdom of God is within you" (Luke 17:21). If you have Jesus and are filled with the Holy Spirit, it's already entered you. If you live in the continual heaven of His love, peace, and joy, you're already in Heaven in spirit. So if you are looking for the kingdom of God on earth, at this time you will only find it within your own heart and in the fellowship of God's children.

We who have found Jesus and faith in God have found heaven on earth, the promised land of His kingdom within. He's made a heaven of our hearts. But those who don't know God and have no faith have nothing but fear, and some have hell on earth.

Have you got a little bit of Heaven in your heart? If not, take Jesus into your heart and you'll have Heaven here and now!

> Heaven is here, is here right now.
> Heaven is here and I'll tell you how!
> Jesus to know is Heaven below,
> Heaven is here, is here and how![1]

[1] Author unknown.

Pray! Jesus has the answer!

ALL THE ANSWERS TO OUR QUESTIONS AND PROBLEMS ARE SIMPLE FOR JESUS. In fact, sometimes this is why He lets us have a problem, so that He can give us the answer. He likes for us to find out that we can't always solve our problems on our own, so we'll turn to Him for help. After all, if we could figure it all out and solve all our own problems, we wouldn't need Him. He likes to give us answers to remind us that we're dependent on Him. He likes for us to appreciate His help, and to love Him for it.

He even knows what things we have need of before we ask (Matthew 6:8), but He usually waits for us to ask. Jesus can solve our problems so easily when we ask Him, but He likes us to ask Him. Sometimes our own pride and independence get in the way. We don't want to ask for help because we don't want to admit that we don't have the solution. So we try to do it ourselves to the point of frustration, when all we need to do is ask and receive His answer.

If you're smart, you'll be like the man who said, "I may not know all the answers, but I know the Answer Man!" God's got all the answers. He *is* the answer!

MAY 18

"Follow Me," Jesus says, "and I will make you fishers of men."

WHEN JESUS CALLED TO SOME FISHERMEN
who had just caught the biggest haul of their lives, "Come follow
Me, and I will make you fishers of men," immediately they
forsook everything else—the fish, their nets, their boat, their
livelihood, and their old life—and followed Him (Matthew
4:18–20; Luke 5:1–11).

How could they do such a thing? How could they forsake their
very living and their own family and friends without notice
to follow this stranger and become part of His motley crew?
Because He offered them a better life, a better job in a better
place with a better boss, and greater rewards—and those simple
fishermen wandered off with a perfect stranger and made history
that has helped save countless millions of souls for eternity.

Doesn't it seem ridiculous now to compare those few fish, a boat,
and a business—all of which soon perished—with the millions
of immortal souls who have been saved for eternity through the
decision of those simple fishermen to put God first that day, drop
everything, and follow Jesus? Now that we can see the results,
it's easy to know they made the right choice!

God will not take second place, even to His service.

We can sometimes get so busy serving the Lord that we forget to love Him. This is one of the greatest temptations of workers for the Lord, and one of the greatest dangers. If we neglect our fellowship with the King of kings because we're so busy with the affairs of the kingdom, it can be disastrous to our spiritual life and communion with the Lord.

No matter how sincere our motives or how faithful we are to His work, we must put *Him* first—not the work or even others. God doesn't fit second place, and He won't take it. "You shall have no other gods before Me. ... For I, the Lord your God, am a jealous God" (Deuteronomy 5:7,9). That is probably the greatest mistake of sincere Christians: to make a god of God's service.

Your service is nothing if you don't give the King your attention, your love, your time, your communion. He desires your love and intends for you to love Him first of all and above all. You cannot do the Master's work without the Master's power and guidance, and to get it you must spend time with the Master.

It's impossible to make a sacrifice for God.

THE GREATEST MANIFESTATION OF OUR LOVE FOR GOD AND OTHERS is not the mere giving of our material things, but the sharing of ourselves and our personal services for others.

When you first begin to give of yourself, it may look like you're losing or sacrificing, but in the long run you're going to find out you're really not going to be sacrificing at all. You're just going to be investing, and the returns are going to be far beyond anything you have invested and will far surpass any sacrifice you could possibly have made. Dr. David Livingstone (1813–1873), the Scottish missionary and explorer who pioneered the jungles of Africa and died there, said, "I never made a sacrifice." He gave everything, but he knew that what he was getting in return was worth much more than everything he could possibly give. Although he gave his life, he reaped eternal life and dividends in immortal souls— thousands saved forever.

So invest your life and your all in the Rock, Christ Jesus, and invest it in God's work, and you'll have eternal dividends that you will never lose, but reap forever. God will bless you for it!

Jesus took upon Himself the sins of the whole world on the cross (1 Peter 2:24).

ONLY JESUS WAS PERFECT, and that's why He could pay the price of our sins and take our punishment so that God could forgive us. Jesus fulfilled the Law and its requirement of death to the sinners. He died in our place so that we wouldn't have to die. He voluntarily gave Himself to be crucified—He loves us that much!

What caused Jesus the greatest agony on the cross was not our sins, because He knew that we were going to be forgiven and saved. What broke His heart was thinking that His Father had turned His back on Him. He went through an experience that, thank God, *we* will never have to go through—not just crucifixion, not just the agony of the body, but the agony of mind and spirit, feeling that God had actually deserted Him. "My God, My God," He cried out, "why have You forsaken Me?" (Matthew 27:46). Had God forsaken Him? Yes, momentarily, that He might die the death of a sinner, without God.

Jesus loved us enough to give His own life for us and take the punishment of our sins upon Himself on that cross, so that we could be forgiven and be saved (Romans 5:8; 1 John 4:10). Such love!

The best thing you can do for others is pray for them.

GOD HAS HIS REASONS FOR ALLOWING PROBLEMS IN LIFE, and one of the main reasons is to teach us to pray. He lets us come to the end of our rope, the end of our strength and what we think we can do to solve the problem at hand, so we will realize that He's the One who has got to do it and pray for Him to work, by His power.

If there's something we can do to help the situation and we ask Him what that is and how to go about it, He will show us and help us do it. But in the end, the thing that will help more than anything and without which all our labors are incomplete, is prayer—to pray for *Him* to do the work in the *spirit*.

He's the only One who can change hearts and minds. He's the only One who can bring people to the point where they're willing to change or do whatever's necessary to make progress or fix the problem. So the best thing we can do to help people who are having problems is to pray for them. We can't do the miracle that's needed, but the Lord can. Our prayers move His hand and make things happen in the spiritual realm that change things in our physical realm.

You have the Holy Spirit if you ask for it.

HOW DO YOU KNOW IF YOU HAVE BEEN FILLED WITH THE HOLY SPIRIT? That's simple. Jesus said, "Everyone who asks receives, and he who seeks finds, and to him who knocks it will be opened. If you ... know how to give good gifts to your children, how much more will your heavenly Father give the Holy Spirit to those who ask Him!" (Luke 11:10,13). Like salvation, you can't earn it or deserve it or be worthy of it; it's a gift, received by faith.

Sometimes people receive the Holy Spirit but they don't get any particular evidence and they're disappointed because it wasn't manifested by some supernatural or physical experience right then and there. But it doesn't matter how you feel; when you've asked God for the Holy Spirit, you *have* it.

You know you have it because He promised it. It's just like salvation. How do you know you got saved when you received Jesus as your Savior?—Not because of whatever you may have felt or experienced at the time, but because of what He said about it in His Word. Your faith is built on fact—God's Word—not on feelings.

Pray and ask Jesus to fill you with His Holy Spirit and He will. He's promised to.

Start your day off right. Hear from Jesus!

You OUGHT TO TRY A LITTLE PRAYER TIME EVERY DAY, early in the morning before beginning your day's work, asking Jesus to help you. When you first wake up, before you do anything, talk to Jesus. Get your orders from Him for the day, and you'll be amazed at how He'll solve or prevent a lot of your problems before the day even starts, simply by listening to what He has to say.

But if you go plunging into all your problems and troubles and your day's work without stopping to talk to Jesus and get your directions from Him, you'll be like a musician who decided to have his concert first, and then tune his instrument. Begin the day with the Word of God and prayer, and first of all get in harmony with Him.

Don't ever think that it's too hard to pray or that you don't have time to pray. The busier your day, the more reason you have to pray and the longer you ought to pray. If you'll spend a little more time praying, you will find that you'll spend a lot less time working to get things done later. If your day is hemmed with prayer, it is less likely to unravel. It's that simple!

Jesus has all the help you need to overcome your natural weaknesses.

EVERYONE HAS WEAKNESSES, and everyone makes mistakes. That's just part of life. We shouldn't resign ourselves to failure, though, and we shouldn't keep making the same mistakes; we should try to do better. The best thing to do with faults and failures and mistakes and weak areas is to recognize them, be honest about them, and then try to overcome them if we can.

The first step is to face the facts. If we can honestly admit our problems to ourselves, then we can fight them. The second step—and here is where the Christian is at a distinct advantage—is to be honest with the Lord about ourselves and ask for His help. We don't have to fight to overcome these things on our own. If we're willing to bare our souls to Jesus, He will step in and help us as only He can.

Another wonderful thing about this arrangement is that Jesus always offers us hope. He doesn't throw us out when we make mistakes. If He did, we'd all have been thrown out a long time ago because we all make so many mistakes. Instead, He tries to help us learn from our mistakes, tells us how to do better next time, and encourages us to try again.

Only one life, 'twill soon be past. Only what's done for Christ will last!

Every Christian was intended to lay down his life and take up his cross and follow Jesus in order to bear fruit, more Christians like himself (Luke 9:23– 24; John 15:8). Jesus said, "Unless a grain of wheat falls into the ground and dies, it remains alone; but if it dies, it produces much grain" (John 12:24). If we will bury our lives in the soil of God's service, if we will "die daily" for the Lord by giving our lives to help others (1 Corinthians 15:31), we will bring forth much fruit—more Christians to preach the Gospel to more of the lost and win them to Jesus—that He may have much fruit.

What a small price to pay for all the blessings, happiness, and eternal rewards in Heaven that He has promised you in return! If you give your all, God will reward you a hundred times over (Matthew 19:29). You can't beat that kind of investment. There's no other investment in this world that guarantees that kind of return.

What are *you* doing and for whom? Will it last forever for Jesus and others? Don't waste another day! Spend its precious time for Him and His, for eternity!

If you can't be a missionary, support one.

JESUS SAID THAT WE ARE TO "SEEK FIRST THE KINGDOM OF GOD" (Matthew 6:33). What is God's kingdom? It's the people who love Him and those He loves. If people are God's kingdom, we are supposed to witness and win more people for His kingdom, or help others win them.

To help His kingdom is to help His people, and the way He helps people is often through other people. He likes to use us as His means in order that we too might be blessed and have a share in His work and its fruits and receive part of the rewards. That's part of His plan.

The multimillionaire R.G. LeTourneau (1888–1969) went bankrupt early in his career. He asked God what God wanted him to do, and God told him that He wanted him to make money for His work. So LeTourneau started off promising God 10% of his income if He'd pull him out of debt, and God did. God made him a success, and he made millions. Toward the end of his life LeTourneau gave 90% of his income to foreign missions and lived very well on the other 10%—all because He put God's kingdom first!

Are you called to raise funds for missions? Will you share forever in the eternal rewards of souls won as a result of your giving?

"Take, eat; this is My body, which is broken for you"
(1 Corinthians 11:24).

THE BREAD USED FOR COMMUNION REPRESENTS JESUS' BODY, which was broken for us in a number of ways—the crown of thorns, the beatings, the stripes, the injuries and pain He suffered. He didn't have to suffer all that for our sins, He only had to shed His blood and die for our sins. But His body suffered so that through this, He could also atone for our sicknesses: "By His stripes we are healed" (Isaiah 53:5). To save *our* bodies, it took *His* body.

The best medicine in the world is the body of Jesus Christ, which was broken for our healing. When we partake of the bread, it shows we have faith that His body was broken for our health, so we can claim His healing by faith when we partake. If we eat of it by faith, we are healed by faith. It's part of His atonement for salvation for the whole man—body, soul, and spirit.

(Prayer:) Thank You, Jesus, for the communion bread that represents Your body, which was broken for us and our physical health. As Your body was broken for our healing, so let us have faith to partake of it accordingly, in Your name we ask. Amen.

"Dying grace" means perfect peace, perfect rest, no worry, no fear.

SOMEONE ONCE ASKED DWIGHT L. MOODY (1837–1899), "Do you have dying grace?"

"No, I don't," he answered. "I'm not dying yet!"

But when the time came, he did. Moody's last words were: "I see earth receding; Heaven is approaching. God is calling me. This is my triumph. This is my coronation day. It is glorious. God is calling and I must go."

If you know Jesus and have His love in your heart, He will also give you dying grace when your time to go comes. "As your days, so shall your strength be" (Deuteronomy 33:25). He'll give you peace and faith.

Even the martyrs of the early church didn't die sadly or sorrowfully, but singing and shouting and praising God. God will never let anything happen to you that is more than you are able to bear—not even death (1 Corinthians 10:13).

When the moment of death comes, God will give you such grace and peace and love and confidence and perfect faith that you will have no fear, only joy and thankfulness for Heaven and all that lies ahead. One life is past, and a new one begins. Heaven forever! Happiness for all eternity!

Do all you do to the glory of love.

W_{HATEVER WE DO IN WORD OR IN DEED,} we're to do all to the glory of God (1 Corinthians 10:31). God is love (1 John 4:8), so we're to do it all to the glory of *love*. There is no law but love in God's kingdom of love (Galatians 5:14). God now only judges according to whether we have love or no love, whether what we do is done in love or selfishness and lack of love. Whatever is done in God's love is right.

The Law of Moses spelled out in detail what people should or shouldn't do if they loved God, loved others, and acted in love. But once we're saved, once we've received and are ruled by the Spirit of love itself, we don't need that old law because we just won't do those things we shouldn't, and we will voluntarily do those things we should. "If you are led by the Spirit, you are not under the law" (Galatians 5:18). If your actions, thoughts, words, and deeds are motivated by love and guided by love, you can't go wrong.

Love is what counts. God is love, His law is love, and our faith and practice are love. Isn't that a wonderful religion?

Here's the secret to successful witnessing:
Fill your heart with God's love and Word.

WE'RE THE VESSELS OF GOD'S LOVE TO POUR OUT HIS LOVE TO OTHERS. It's His love, but He works through us. We're His channels, tools in His hand.

God says, "Open your mouth and I will fill it" (Psalm 81:10). But where does He fill it from? He fills it from your heart. "Out of the abundance of the heart the mouth speaks" (Matthew 12:34). If you have filled your heart beforehand, if you're full of His love and the knowledge of His Word, the message you want to get across to others, when you open your mouth He will fill it, right out of your heart. It will just roll out by inspiration.

God doesn't expect you to do it. All He expects you to do is yield to Him and then He will do it through you. When you turn on a water faucet, the faucet doesn't do the work. It's the power from outside that causes the water to flow effortlessly through the faucet. The faucet is just the channel, just the hole, to let the water flow out. If you're full of the Spirit, full of Jesus and His love, full of the Word, then you can ask God to turn you on and let it roll.

Jesus wants us to grow into the stature of full-grown mature Christians.

WHEN WE ARE SAVED OR "BORN AGAIN" (John 3:3–8), at first we're like babies, spiritually speaking. Like babies need nourishment and exercise every day to be healthy and grow, we need spiritual nourishment and exercise every day. But a lot of Christians stop growing when they are only a few months or years old. They never grow up; they never mature. They think they've learned all they need to and so never grow into the kind of Christians that Jesus wants them to be—mature Christians who are able to carry a lot of responsibility and make sacrifices when necessary.

God's Word says that even Jesus "learned obedience by the things which He suffered" (Hebrews 5:8), and "Jesus grew in wisdom and stature, and in favor with God and men" (Luke 2:52 NIV). Every day we learn some new obedience, and although some things get harder, others get easier—like growing up. That's what it's all about!

Spiritual maturity is not entirely a matter of time; it's mostly a matter of your connection with Jesus and His Word and your obedience and humility. A child becomes a true adult when he learns to act responsibly and think of others, and it's the same with Christians. That's spiritual maturity.

Only we can sing salvation's story.

IN SOME WAYS WE'RE MORE IMPORTANT THAN THE ANGELS. God didn't send His Son to die for the angels; He sent Him to die for *us*.

"Holy, holy," is what the angels sing,
And I expect to help them make the courts of Heaven ring;
But when I sing redemption's story, they will fold their wings,
For angels never felt the joys that our salvation brings.[1]

The angels wish they could sing the same message, but they can't because they were never lost. They can't know the joy of salvation; they can only witness it.

This is the message that I bring,
A message angels fain would sing:
"Oh, be ye reconciled,"
Thus saith my Lord and King,
"Oh, be ye reconciled to God."[2]

What is the message we bring?—"Get saved. Be reconciled." It means make peace with God. There's only one way you can make peace with God, and that's through Jesus (Acts 4:12; 1 Peter 3:18; Revelation 5:9). Salvation is one story that hasn't got any end, because it's eternal. You can't say, "And that's the happy ending," because that's just the happy beginning! But you can say, "And they all lived happily ever after!"

[1] Johnson Oatman, Jr. (1856–1922).
[2] E. Taylor Cassel (1849–1930).

God leaves a lot up to us and our concern and prayer.

You'd be surprised how much God depends on our prayers. When we're faced with a needy situation, He wants us to show concern and pray specifically about it. If we really believe, every prayer is heard and answered, but if we don't pray, it is *not* done. God can do anything, but He puts the responsibility of prayer on us.

The very intensity with which we pray and really mean it or desire it is reflected in the answer. The objects of our prayers are not going to receive any more than we send. We have to visualize the people or situations we're praying for and pray for them with that thought on our heart, asking God specifically for what we want Him to do.

Prayers are answered in proportion to the intensity with which they originate. Like a beam of light focused on a mirror, it will bounce back with as much power as it began with. If we only pray with half a heart, we only get half an answer. But if we pray with our whole heart, we get a wholehearted, strong answer.

Are you exercising your prayer power? Heaven will reveal what good we have done—or could have done—through prayer!

For goodness sake, people don't need to see perfection!

DON'T WORRY IF YOU FEEL YOU'RE A MESS, because we *all* are. But Jesus is everything! Just talk about Jesus. Forget about your problems and just talk about Jesus. Praise Jesus and love Jesus, and you can't go wrong. When others see that you're just like them, when they see that you also stumble and fall but let Jesus pick you up again, when they see you give all your trials and problems to Him and let Him carry you through, this will encourage their faith.

The fact that you feel like a mess but keep on keeping on for Jesus is what matters. The fact that you keep giving all your problems to Jesus and keep trusting Him is a far greater testimony than if you were perfect, because that points others to Jesus and glorifies Him, not yourself.

So keep loving Jesus. Keep running to His Word. Keep depending on Him every minute of every day, for everything, at every turn. Keep tuning in to His voice and following Him. This is what others need to see, and this is what will inspire them to do the same. They'll know that if Jesus can do it for you, He'll do it for them.

What God has done for others, He can do for you!

ALL THROUGH THE BIBLE GOD MIRACU-LOUSLY EMPOWERED AND PROTECTED HIS CHILDREN, and the same miracles of power and protection that occurred back in Bible times can happen now. "Jesus Christ is the same yesterday, today, and forever" (Hebrews 13:8). If Jesus could do those miracles in His day and through the apostles in theirs, then He can still do them today! God is still the God of miracles, and what He's done before He can do again! In fact, Jesus said, "He who believes in Me, the works that I do he will do also; and greater works than these he will do, because I go to My Father" (John 14:12).

Jesus also said, "All power is given unto Me in Heaven and in earth" (Matthew 28:18 KJV). So if you have Jesus, you've got all that power! God has not only promised all this power, but He's promised it for right *now* if you need it and have faith to claim and exercise it. Think how much good you can do in His name!

It is no secret what God can do!
What He's done for others, He'll do for you!
With arms wide open, He'll carry you through!
It is no secret what God can do![1]

[1] Stuart Hamblin (1908–1989).

Our spirits are contagious.

SOMETIMES JUST A WORD OR A SMILE CAN MAKE A BIG DIFFERENCE—how we look or sound or seem. If it's not cheerful and victorious and uplifting, it's bound to drag somebody else down with us. Others will partake of our spirits and be influenced by our attitudes. This is why it's so important that we dwell on the positive, not the negative. Think about the *good* things (Philippians 4:8). Be encouraging, loving, and cheerful. Love begets love. If we are peaceful, trusting, patient, restful, and full of faith, this is the way others will also react. A little real love goes a long, long way!

No man is an island. Everybody has influence. One person walking in love will encourage others to do likewise. If you show love, others will catch the same spirit. It's such a contagious thing—the love of Christ in action. It spreads from heart to heart.

If we live enough with God, like Moses did, a little of God will rub off on us too and we'll be happy and our faces will shine with joy and the Spirit of God (Exodus 34:29–34; Numbers 6:25–26). That's the secret! If we shine forth with enough love, others will reflect it.

"It is God who works in you both to will and to do for His good pleasure" (Philippians 2:13).

Too MANY CHRISTIANS HAVE BEEN TAUGHT TWO CONFLICTING DOCTRINES: first, that they can't be saintly and perfect, and second, that they can't be saved unless they are. Both are the Devil's own doctrines! It's no wonder that a lot of Christians give up trying to be or do anything for the Lord!

Of course you can't do it! Of course you can't save yourself! Of course you can't live a perfect Christian life! Of course you can't be good or do anything good of yourself! Jesus Himself said, "Without Me you can do nothing" (John 15:5). But the wonderful truth of the matter is that you can do *anything* with Jesus' help. "I can do all things through Christ who strengthens me" (Philippians 4:13). With His help you can do anything, go anywhere, and be anybody God wants you to be.

God doesn't want you to try or pretend to be something you're not and couldn't possibly be. However, He teaches in His Word that almost anybody can be almost anything if they have faith and it's according to His will. Anybody can be somebody or somebody can be anybody, because with God nothing is impossible and all things are possible to those who believe (Luke 1:37; Mark 9:23).

"Let us not be weary in well doing, for in due season we shall reap, if we faint not" (Galatians 6:9 KJV).

SOMETIMES WE DON'T MIND BEGINNING A GOOD WORK, but when we see what the final cost is going to be, we don't want to complete it. Well begun is half done, but if we don't finish the thing, nothing is done. Jesus said we should count the cost first before we start any big project—from building a tower to waging war—to make sure we'll be able to finish it (Luke 14:28–32). If we begin a job for the Lord, we need to see it through. Otherwise it would have been better if we had never started.

We need to remind ourselves that the men and women who have accomplished the most for God were mostly ordinary people who stuck to their jobs through thick and thin. There's really no limit to what God can do through us, too, if we'll just be faithful and stick to it.

(Prayer:) Help us, Lord, to remember that You're the One who has begun a good work in us, and what You have started You have promised to complete (Philippians 1:6). Give us faith and patience and perseverance to stick to the tasks You have given us until they're finished or You have something else for us. Amen.

It is impossible to have faith unless you have the Word.

THE BIBLE SAYS THAT FAITH COMES FROM THE WORD OF GOD (Romans 10:17). That's a basic spiritual law, as sure as what goes up comes down. So if you're weak in faith it's because you're weak in the Word.

The cure for doubts is the Word. Faith comes, it grows, by hearing the Word of God. It's not a sudden boom. It is something that is built by faithful study of God's Word.

Faith isn't something you work up, muster up, or polish up by your own efforts and strength. Accepting faith through His Word is a work of God's grace. All *you* have to do is desire and receive it. Jesus even gives you faith to believe His Word. Jesus is the "author and finisher of our faith" (Hebrews 12:2).

Don't neglect His Word. It is food for your soul and gives you strength for the daily battles of life. It is His Word by His Spirit in His love that makes you strong. So read it prayerfully and ask God to increase your faith, and He will. He never fails! He'll always answer the hungry heart.

Everything God has created is for our pleasure and our good.

GOD MADE ALL THE BASIC NECESSITIES OF LIFE PLEASURABLE—breathing, eating, sleeping, exercising, and loving. The Bible says that He created all things for His pleasure (Revelation 4:11 KJV), but He also created them for ours. God made life to be enjoyable, and he equipped us to enjoy it. He created our senses and the nerves that register pleasure. He gave us the gift of sight so we could look upon things that are pleasing to the eye, taste to be able to enjoy delicious food, hearing so we could listen to the beautiful sounds of nature and beautiful music, touch so we could feel pleasurable sensations, and smell so we could enjoy the lovely fragrance of a flower.

God created pleasure for our good, but some people have been taught that pleasure is sinful, that it's wrong to enjoy certain things that bring pleasure. According to the Bible, that's simply not so! Pleasure only becomes ungodly when it's not as God created it or intended for it to be used—when it's perverted, overindulged in, or put before Him and what He wants for us.

The rule of thumb is simple: Put God first in everything you do, and then you can enjoy all His goodness in full faith. All this and Heaven too!

Let Jesus lead.

To be successful for the Lord, we have to stay close to Him and make sure we're in His will. There's a sure and simple formula for that: "Trust in the Lord with all your heart, and lean not on your own understanding; in all your ways acknowledge Him, and He shall direct your paths" (Proverbs 3:5–6).

We can't even do things that seem good and reasonable unless we're sure they're what the Lord wants. If we're leaning to our own understanding and forgetting to acknowledge Him, if we're not listening to the voice of His Spirit and letting Him lead and guide us every moment, then we're apt to get sidetracked or step into one of the Devil's traps. We can't guard ourselves from everything, but we can stay so close to Jesus that we are always in the charmed circle of His blessing and protection. "Your ears shall hear a word behind you, saying, 'This is the way, walk in it,' whenever you turn to the right hand or whenever you turn to the left" (Isaiah 30:21).

(Prayer:) Thank You, Jesus, for being our ever-present companion and coworker—the best help that we could ever ask for! Help us to do our part, to be sensitive to Your voice and to follow it. Then we can act in full faith and You'll be able to bless and use us to the full. Amen.

There's power in Jesus' name!

SOME PEOPLE ASK, "Why can't you just leave 'Jesus' out of it? Why do you have to use *that* name? Why can't you just speak of God's love and do what you're doing in God's name?"—Because these are *God's* conditions.

Jesus is the One you have to approach God through. He's our Mediator and High Priest (1 Timothy 2:5; Hebrews 4:14). Jesus is the only One who ever rose from the dead and can give you power to do the same. The Bible says, "Nor is there salvation in any other, for there is no other name under heaven given among men by which we must be saved" (Acts 4:12). We're to pray in His name, heal in His name, cast out devils in His name, baptize in His name, and preach in His name. Without that name, there is no power. Everything we have is in Jesus' name. "Whatever you ask the Father in My name," Jesus said, "He will give it you" (John 16:23). Expect miracles, and in Jesus' name you'll get them!

Look how much emphasis the early disciples in the book of Acts put on the name of Jesus. That's all they preached and talked about—Jesus! That's the name they did all those miracles in, and that's the name they won the world in. That's the only name we'll win it in too—Jesus!

Take God at His Word!

WE'RE SUPPOSED TO BELIEVE THE WORD SIMPLY BECAUSE GOD SAID SO! He wants us to have faith in His Word and not always have to have a sign.

Why does God insist we have to believe in something we cannot see or feel, purely by faith in His Word, trusting Him just like a little child has to trust a parent? It's because the Lord loves faith! He loves us because we believe Him, just because He said so. It's a way of showing our love and our confidence in Him. "But without faith it is impossible to please Him, for he who comes to God must believe that He is, and that He is a rewarder of those who diligently seek Him" (Hebrews 11:6).

It's like a child who has to trust his parents even though he doesn't always understand why he must do or not do this or that. He just has to "do it because Daddy says so." Because the child trusts his parents and feels secure in their love, he takes their word for it. That's the way we should be with God. We should say to Him, "Yes sir!" and believe it and do it simply because He says we should.

Let's get back to the Garden of Eden.

THERE IS ONLY ONE WAY THAT WE CAN REGAIN THE FREEDOM THAT ADAM AND EVE HAD in the Garden, and that is to find God and His truth. Those of us who have received Jesus Christ as our Savior and King already have Paradise in our hearts. He has forgiven us of our sins and brought us peace and love and happiness that we never knew before.

Would you like to live in this Garden of Eden—to enjoy Paradise, true freedom, and all the wonderful things and pleasures that God has given us to enjoy, His whole creation? Well, you can, just by inviting Jesus into your heart. Take Him as your Savior and you'll be there! He'll make your heart a Garden of God's love! There it will always be sunshine and gladness, because you'll be forgiven for every wrong you ever committed and made sinless and pure and perfect in God's sight.

And once you've found the Paradise of God, you'll want to lead others there also, that they too might experience its joys—and you can. You can bring Eden to every heart by telling others about Jesus and helping them to ask Him in.

You can pray all the time.

GOD'S WORD TELLS US THAT WE ARE TO "PRAY WITHOUT CEASING" (1 Thessalonians 5:17). You don't have to be down on your hands and knees praying frantically to be heard. Prayer is something you can and should be doing all the time, no matter what else you're doing—like thinking on your feet. You can be anointed and led by Him in anything you do. If you're thinking and praying about what you're doing and asking God for wisdom, He will give it to you (James 1:5).

Ask the Lord about *everything* before you do it. Make sure that's what He wants you to do. "In all your ways acknowledge Him, and He shall direct thy paths" (Proverbs 3:6). Stopping your activity and asking the Lord for His help shows your reliance on Him and brings a hush to your spirit. The Lord wants to be recognized, and He wants you to remember that you need Him.

(Prayer:) Keep us close to You, Lord, and help us to stay in the center of Your will, obedient and following You moment by moment. Every moment, keep our hearts right, our minds right, our motives right, and everything right with You. Amen.

You can't take your money with you when you die—but you can send it on ahead.

WHEN IT COMES TO GOD AND HIS WORK, it's good business to give. It's a good investment because it will earn the highest interest rate possible and dividends that outstrip anything else you could possibly invest in—a hundred times over in this life, and in the world to come, life eternal (Mark 10:30). That's His promise!

The richest people in God's kingdom are going to be those who shared the most with Him and His children. But there is also the other side of the coin, as illustrated by the tale about the selfish rich woman who was led to her heavenly home by an angel. They walked past many beautiful mansions where other Christians were living, until they came to a section of Heaven where the homes were small and humble.

As the angel led her to a tiny cottage, the woman asked, "What's the big idea? I'm used to very fine living!"

"Well," the angel answered, "our abodes up here are built from what each person sends on before, and this is all we could do with what you sent. Others sacrificed and lived their lives for the Lord and others, so great is their reward."

Are you investing in God's service and in His kingdom by giving to Him?

"The blood of Jesus Christ His Son cleanses us from all sin" (1 John 1:7).

GOD SAID THROUGH MOSES THAT WITHOUT THE SHEDDING OF BLOOD THERE IS NO REMISSION OF SIN (Leviticus 17:11). That was the Law, and that is why Jesus died for us.

Jesus died on God's altar, the cross, believed upon by every Christian, trusted by every son and daughter of God who believes in Jesus Christ for their salvation. Jesus was the ultimate sacrifice for sin. He was the ultimate Lamb of God, slain for the remission of our sins. He took the punishment of our sins in His own body on the cross, and that was the last sacrifice of blood for sin as far as God was concerned.

Our salvation is a gift from God (Ephesians 2:8), but it cost Jesus dearly. That was the highest price anybody could have paid for our salvation, and only Jesus could do it. No matter how much you sacrifice and try to pay for salvation by your own works, it's impossible; the price is too high! God did not spare His own Son, Jesus Christ, but let Him die on the cross so that He could then freely give us all things (Romans 8:32).

The truly loving are truly humble, and the truly humble are truly loving.

You've got to admit, a big part of love is humility. It takes humility to be affectionate and to receive affection. If you want to fall in love and accept real love, you have to be humble enough to forsake your pride and receive it.

This is true even of our relationship with the Lord. When we first hear that God loves us so much that He sent His only Son, Jesus, to die in our place, we have to humble ourselves to receive God's love. Receiving salvation is a humbling experience. Those who humble themselves receive not only forgiveness, but also an infilling of love they could never have imagined. But those who are too proud miss out on both, for "God resists the proud, but gives grace to the humble" (James 4:6).

Humility and love are inseparable. You cannot have real love and not be humble, and you cannot have genuine humility without a lot of love. Pride's fear of failure or refusal also prevents us from reaching out to and loving others as much as we should. Not so with humility. Humility has love and faith without fear (1 John 4:18). Love doesn't care what other people think; it just loves in spite of what they think. So be humble—and love!

Jesus is the door.

HAVE YOU PASSED THROUGH THE DOOR OF SALVATION, Jesus, into the heavenly world of new life in Him? You can! It's wonderful—like passing from darkness into light, from death into life, through God's love, mercy, and salvation in Jesus!

Jesus called Himself the door (John 10:7,9). "Behold! I am the Door you have to get through to get into My Father's house. There isn't any other entrance but by Me!"

Jesus is an *open* door, not a locked door or even a shut door. You don't even have to be able to reach the doorknob. The door is standing wide open. All you have to do is see the door, believe it is open for you, walk through it by faith, and you're saved! You've entered the heavenly sphere of salvation, heaven on earth and Heaven hereafter, the kingdom of God, just by walking through that open door!

Once you believe Jesus Christ is the Son of God and receive Him as your Savior, then He knows you and you know Him, and every time you come to His door it will be standing wide open and He will say, "Welcome! Come in! I love you!"

What's the good news?—"God is love" (1 John 4:8).

ALL YOU NEED IN ORDER TO SHARE GOD'S LOVE WITH OTHERS is a simple faith in a simple salvation and a simple Gospel for people to simply believe and receive and be saved—the Good News summed up so simply in one beautiful verse: "For God so loved the world that He gave His only begotten Son, that whoever believes in Him should not perish but have everlasting life" (John 3:16).

That's the best single verse in the Bible to explain the concept of salvation to people from almost any background. If you can help them understand each part of that verse, that's all you really need. "For God so loved the world"—who is God?—He's the Spirit of love. Are they part of the world? "For God so loved you"—put their name in there—"that He gave His only begotten Son"—who's that?—Jesus—"that whoever believes in Him"— do they believe in Jesus?—then they "will not perish"—they won't go to Hell—"but have everlasting life."

John 3:16 is all the education you need to go out and win the lost. That's all the preparation you need to be a missionary. Simply go out where the lost are to be found and give them His love and the Good News of salvation in Jesus!

The name of the game is faith and trust.

SOMETIMES GOD LETS OUR FAITH BE TESTED RIGHT TO THE BRINK in order to prove that it's real faith. He can even make it appear as if He is being a little too hard on us, so we're tempted to think, "How could God let that sort of thing happen?" The Devil is always around to try to make us doubt and even criticize God, like he did with Job.

We've got to be willing to trust God, live or die, sink or swim, like Job. Despite the loss of everything dear to him, Job kept trusting God. He finally overcame, and in the end God gave him back more than he had lost. Job's is one of the most glorious testimonies in the whole Bible. In the face of suffering and defeat and discouragement, his faith carried him through.

That's the greatest victory of all—when we seem to be defeated and still trust God. He must really be pleased with that kind of faith. "This is the victory that has overcome the world—our faith" (1 John 5:4). God loves to watch us make it in spite of all the tests and trials. He loves to watch us run and win the race, endure the affliction, and fight through to victory!

Miracles come naturally to God.

WE USUALLY THINK OF THINGS THAT ARE BEYOND OUR COMPREHENSION as supernatural or miraculous, but those things aren't supernatural to God because He operates in the spiritual realm where everything is "natural" to Him. It's like saying there is nothing impossible with God (Luke 1:37). A lot of things God does are beyond our power and grasp of things and what we consider natural, so when they happen we say they are supernatural. But with God nothing is impossible, so nothing is supernatural to Him!

God can do things that are contrary to what we consider His natural laws. When someone gets healed of an incurable disease, for example, we call it a miracle because we're seeing the evidence or manifestation of some of God's laws that link the spiritual and the physical realms—laws that we know little about. To God, on the other hand, it's simple! He knows how to undo whatever damage the disease may have done and thereby creates what to us is a miracle—a supernatural act that is beyond our capabilities.

God is always ready, willing, and able to work miracles on our behalf—miracles of healing, supply, protection, or whatever else we may need when we ask Him to in faith and claim the promises from His Word. We can't work miracles; we can only pray for Him to do it and marvel at His power when He does.

Faith is the title deed.

"FAITH IS THE SUBSTANCE OF THINGS HOPED FOR, the evidence of things not seen" (Hebrews 11:1 KJV). The word translated as "substance" here is the Greek word *huposta-sis*. When the New Testament was first translated into English from Greek, the translators were puzzled by this word *huposta-sis*. It seemed to be some kind of business terminology not found in classical Greek literature, and all they could determine was that it meant something fairly substantial, so they translated it as "substance."

Hundreds of years later, archaeologists uncovered the charred ruins of an old inn in Palestine. There they found a small iron chest apparently containing the legal papers of some Roman noblewoman who had owned real estate in the area. Most of the papers in the chest had written in large Greek letters across the top: *hupostasis*. They were all title deeds to her properties! Before her apparent visit, this Roman woman had perhaps never seen her properties, but she knew they were hers and could prove her ownership because she had the title deeds.

So what is faith?—It's the title deed! Had those translators known what we know now, that verse might instead read, "Now faith is the title deed to things hoped for."

God can do anything but fail.

THE DIFFICULT GOD DOES IMMEDIATELY; the impossible might take a little longer. So if you need a miracle, never give up and never take no for an answer. Nothing is too hard for God (Jeremiah 32:27). He can do anything if you'll just give Him a chance.

> God can do anything, anything, anything,
> God can do anything but fail!
> He can save, He can heal,
> Just believe and He will,
> God can do anything but fail![1]

> Got any rivers you think are uncrossable?
> Got any mountains you can't tunnel through?
> God specializes in things thought impossible
> And He can do what no other friend can do![2]

(Prayer:) We know, Lord, that You can do whatever we need done, and we know You *will* do it if we'll believe and trust You. You always make a way if we obey and do it Your way. If we do all we can do, You'll do the rest. Even when it comes to the impossible, You're an expert at that (Luke 1:37). So help us to do all we can and then trust You for the impossible. You can do anything but fail, and *we'll* never fail as long as we trust You!

[1] Ira Stanphill (1914–1994).
[2] Oscar C. Eliason.

Every time you're tempted to think negatively about yourself, thank God for the good instead.

You're a very special creation of God's love, so don't worry about a few blemishes. Imagine how self-righteous and proud we would be if God had made us all perfect! Instead, He gave us a few blemishes—and we *all* have them. But God doesn't want you to look at the blemishes; He wants you to look at the *good*.

Every time you're tempted to think something negative about yourself, thank God for something He blessed you with—your good health, your sound mind, or some quality or talent that others admire in you. There are so many things you could thank God for!

Think how much worse off you could be—and think of others who *are*. Pray for someone who is battling a long-term illness or coping daily with a debilitating handicap. Job was delivered from his problems when he prayed for his friends (Job 42:10).

Take a positive approach and pretty soon the instigator of your negative thoughts, the old Devil himself or one of his henchmen, will give up. When your spiritual enemy sees that your praises and prayers are defeating him every time, he'll think twice before tempting you with negative thinking—and you can be thankful for that!

Love is more than righteousness, and mercy is greater than justice!

LOVE IS THE LAW OF CHRIST TODAY. "For all the law is fulfilled in one word, even in this: 'You shall love your neighbor as yourself'" (Galatians 5:14).

Love is really stricter than the Mosaic Law because it goes further than the Law. In the Law there was virtually no forgiving and it was "an eye for an eye and a tooth for a tooth." But Jesus said that even if our brother offends us seventy times seven times and is sorry, we should forgive him (Matthew 5:38–39; 18:21–22). Now everything must be done in His love. We must have more mercy and more love than the Law!

People only obeyed the Law because they *had* to, and most people only did as much as they were made to do. But love goes all the way. Love will do the right thing and go the distance for someone else. The Spirit of God in us will give us the power and the strength to love others more than ourselves.

This is what God has been working on all the time: to persuade us to do things through the right, loving motivation, because we love Him and others and therefore want to do what's right.

Fill your heart and mind with God's truth.

GOD HAS GIVEN YOU THE BEST COMPUTER EVER CONSTRUCTED—your own mind—but it's up to you how you fill it. It has to be filled with something, good or bad, and your reflexes are mentally conditioned to react in a certain way according to what you have learned or experienced. That's why you could hardly accomplish anything more important than to memorize the Word of God.

God Himself is like the Great Central Computer. You can plug into Him and by His power, His Spirit, He can give you all the information, all the wisdom, and all the answers you need. If you'll be faithful to read, study, and memorize His Word, then He can spiel it off by the Spirit when you need it. He will just pop it up in your little computer whenever you make the right connection in your programming (John 14:26).

Once you've downloaded God's Word into your heart and mind, you just need to be a yielded instrument. Then God can sit down at the keyboard and get out of your computer the information that He wants, because your little memory chips will have the right data, as much as you've programmed them to contain.

Faith for God to heal is found in the promises of His Word.

OFTEN A LACK OF FAITH IS DUE TO IGNORANCE. If you feel like you don't have much faith for God to heal you, it may be because you don't have a sufficient background of faith and knowledge of God's Word. But the provision is there for you. God has made lots of promises for our healing throughout the entire Bible, God's personal Word to each of us.

You can't say, "I'm trusting the doctor, but I don't like to follow his prescriptions." You have to follow through and obey whatever you're putting your faith in. If it's God, you're going to take the scriptural pills and follow the treatment He prescribes. You will claim His promises by faith.

"I am the Lord who heals you" (Exodus 15:26).

"Many are the afflictions of the righteous, but the Lord delivers him out of them all" (Psalm 34:19).

"He sent His word and healed them" (Psalm 107:20).

"Behold, I am the Lord, the God of all flesh. Is there anything too hard for Me?" (Jeremiah 32:27).

"To you who fear My name the Sun of Righteousness shall arise with healing in His wings" (Malachi 4:2).

"Jesus the Christ heals you" (Acts 9:34).

Turn on and tune in.

GOD IS LIKE A BROADCASTING STATION, broadcasting all the time. Just like the radio waves that are unseen in the air all around you this very minute, God's Spirit is ever present, waiting for you to make contact. And much the same as a radio, you have been designed by your Creator to receive those signals. God's power is always on. The message is always there. But in order to receive it, you must turn on and tune in to His frequency.

Compared to the tremendous power and complex operations of the broadcasting station, you, the receiver, need not have much power, and only the basic components. Prayer is the hand of faith that flips the switch and turns on what little power you have. Then the hand of hope tunes with expectancy, searching for the frequency upon which God is broadcasting, and suddenly His great broadcasting station booms in with tremendous volume and power, and the messages come through loud and clear.

If you concentrate and wait with faith and patience, without distraction, you'll receive some of the most powerful, thrilling, and amazing messages that will stir you to action. The messages you receive from Him minister faith, joy, hope, love, and praise. You'll dance to His tunes, move according to His signals, and you'll know you're fulfilling the purpose for which you were created.

The divine, supernatural, miraculous, infinite, marvelous love of God is love enough to forgive!

GOD'S MERCY IS ENDLESS, from everlasting to everlasting. His love and mercy and forgiveness and salvation never end. He never stops loving us, no matter what we do. He never rejects us or withdraws His love. He always has hope for us no matter how far we've strayed (Psalm 103:3–14).

Even in spite of our sins and shortcomings and misdeeds and crimes, whatever they may be, the blood of Jesus covers all our sins, past, present, and future. If we will forsake our sin and turn to the Lord, our God will abundantly pardon (Isaiah 55:7). The Bible says, "If we confess our sins, He is faithful and just to forgive us," no matter what we have done (1 John 1:9). The only unpardonable sin is refusing to believe in Jesus, rejecting Him as your Savior. Most people suffer for pardonable sins for which they fail to ask forgiveness.

We have a God big enough to forgive not only our mistakes but also our sins. He always has and always does and always will, forever and ever. Like a river, God's love and mercy just keep flowing, no matter what.

Don't be self-conscious; be Christ-conscious.

SHYNESS IS A COMBINATION OF TWO THINGS: fear and pride. We are afraid of what people think about us. A certain amount of this is all right; we should like to be well thought of. But on the other hand, the Bible says we're not to be worried about the opinions of men, nor to fear what men think or say about us if we're doing what we know is right (Proverbs 29:25; John 12:42–43).

Timidity, shyness, and bashfulness are manifestations of a form of fear, which is the opposite of faith. So to overcome fear you must have more faith. The cure is faith—strong faith in God—and this comes through reading His Word and being filled with His Spirit. If you think about how much He loves you, you become less self-conscious and more God-conscious, and this is the cure.

Keep your mind on Jesus. He will keep you in perfect peace, when your mind is stayed on Him (Isaiah 26:3). Immerse yourself in the Lord, and He will help you forget yourself. Throw your whole heart into pleasing Jesus and sharing Him with others, and He will help you to lose that selfconsciousness.

Heaven on earth will one day be a literal reality!

T HE PLACE WE'RE GOING TO DWELL WITH
GOD AND JESUS FOREVER HEREAFTER is not some fanciful
dreamland way off in outer space, but an even more amazing
dream city that is going to come down from God, out of space, to
earth. God is going to come down and live *with* us and we with
Him. Think of that! The dwelling place of God is going to be
with men (Revelation 21:2–3).

But first God is going to purge, purify, and renew the whole
earth so that it will be perfect and beautiful, like the Garden
of Eden. Then the heavenly city is going to come down. Jesus
will be restored forever as the King of kings and His kingdom
will finally be established "on earth as it is in Heaven"
(Matthew 6:10). It will be indescribably beautiful—the most
gorgeous sight you'll ever see, full of precious stones and
jewels and, best of all, full of precious souls!

Are you going to be able to walk in that city? The Bible says that
only the saved shall walk therein (Revelation 21:24). You don't
want to miss that, do you?—Then receive Jesus as your Savior, if
you haven't already!

"There is one who scatters, yet increases more; and there is one who withholds more than is right, but it leads to poverty" (Proverbs 11:24).

GOD LOVES TO OUTGIVE US. The more we give, the more He gives us back. But if we're not willing to give, God's apt to take. If you won't give Him an offering when you can, He might take a collection that will far outweigh what you could have given.

It's like the story of a certain rich man in the Bible who had a big harvest and many riches, but instead of sharing with others, he decided to build bigger barns to hold more for himself (Luke 12:16–21). It wasn't the big crop that was his sin; God gave him that. His problem was his selfishness—the barniness of his own soul, his unwillingness to share his blessings with others. God told him that he would die that very night and he couldn't take anything with him, so he lost it all. That's selfishness and its reward. But if you are willing to give, God will reward and repay and bless you with much more than you gave. He's promised that!

Which are *you* doing?—Withholding or scattering? "Whatever measure you use to give—large or small—will be used to measure what is given back to you" (Luke 6:38 TLB).

If we can trust God with our lives, why can't we trust Him with our deaths?

For the Christian, thinking ahead about death is not a burden anymore. It's no longer something to worry about. It's a victory, a release, a graduation. "O death, where is thy sting? O grave, where is thy victory?" (1 Corinthians 15:55–57). Death has no sting and the grave is no defeat for the Christian who has salvation and is promised resurrection. Our death will be a victory over the grave and sin and the Devil—a glorious victory and a glorious entry into the heavenlies.

God knows when and how we're supposed to die, and we'd better let God make that decision and leave it in His hands. "For this is God, our God forever and ever; He will be our guide even to death" (Psalm 48:14). When it comes time to die, if we are Christians and love the Lord, He'll give us dying grace. We trust God for everything else, so why not trust Him to determine the time, place, and way we die?

God bless and keep you trusting even through death—and don't worry, He will. You'll die like you lived, still trusting!

Nothing is ever going to stop us but Jesus!

THE FORCES OF EVIL WILL NEVER BE ABLE TO COMPLETELY DESTROY GOD'S CHILDREN. In spite of innumerable major persecutions, they have never been stopped. In spite of all the wrath and atrocities bestial man will bring against God's children during the Great Tribulation—the coming three-and-a-half-year worldwide reign of terror against people of all faiths by the devilish dictatorship of the Antichrist and his regime—multitudes of us Christians will still be here to joyously welcome Christ's triumphant re-entry into the earth's atmosphere (Matthew 24:21, 29–31). He's the only One who can stop us, and He *will* stop us then for a little while to take us home for a party, the marriage supper of the Lamb in Heaven! Then we'll come back here and put a stop to the reign of the wicked! (Revelation chapter 19).

So praise the Lord, beloved. Don't feel defeated, don't get discouraged, and don't worry. No matter what the enemies of Christ do, they can never stop us completely. As Martin Luther (1483–1546) said, "We will not fear, for God hath willed His truth to triumph through us!" We can't fail, because Jesus is on our side. There will always be some of His children somewhere in the world as a witness right up to the very end!

Waiting and learning patience is part of your training.

Look at all the examples in the Bible of patience, like Job, Moses, and David.

Job lost everything—his family, his fortune, and finally his health—but he kept on believing and obeying. "Though He slay me," he said, "yet will I trust Him" (Job 13:15). He hung on and would not give up. The patience of Job has given Christians down through the ages a wonderful example to follow.

When Moses was in a hurry to deliver the children of Israel, he killed an Egyptian and had to flee alone for his own life. But after 40 years of humbly and patiently tending sheep in the wilderness, with plenty of time to listen to the voice of God instead of his own impulses, he was finally ready for the slow, laborious, patient work of the Exodus—slow, but sure!

David spent 17 years working under King Saul, and learned from Saul's mistakes. Saul got all upset and tried to do things in his own strength, and he found he wasn't strong enough. David learned he had to let God do everything, and wait for Him to work.

Learning patience is one of the most frequent lessons God has for us all, so "let patience have its perfect work, that you may be perfect and complete, lacking nothing" (James 1:4).

God alone can satisfy your deepest yearning for total love and complete understanding!

Do you sometimes feel lonely, empty, dissatisfied? Are you longing for love you have never known before, true love, sincere love, genuine love, the truly great love of your life, love that will never leave? The answer is waiting for you if you are willing to receive it!

There is something more than the flesh, there is the spirit—the real you that lives inside your body—and it will never be satisfied with the things of this earth. It must have the things of the spirit; it must have God. Within each heart, God has created a vacuum that can only be met spiritually. Only God and His true love can ever fill that aching spiritual void of your heart, which He created for Himself alone!

If you haven't already, you can receive God's love by receiving the Spirit of His Son, Jesus Christ, into your heart in a definite, individual decision. He can give you everything you've always longed for, including forgiveness of sins, faith in God, peace of mind, health of body, and joy and happiness and love and laughter now and forever after. He'll meet all your needs and solve all your problems. He's that wonderful, and it's that simple!

Do your best, and God will do the rest.

GOD EXPECTS US TO DO ALL WE CAN, and then He will do what we can't. When Jesus went to raise Lazarus from the dead, He told the people, "Take away the stone" (John 11:39). He could have made the stone roll away by itself, or He could have made Lazarus walk right through the stone, so why did they have to roll it away? Rolling the stone away from the door of the tomb was something *they* could do. They couldn't raise him from the dead, but they could roll the stone away.

Jesus said we are to ask, seek, and knock. "For everyone who asks receives, and he who seeks finds, and to him who knocks it will be opened" (Matthew 7:7–8). But if you don't look, you're not going to find. Maybe nine out of ten doors you try are locked and you're only going to find one open, but you've got to do what you can. You can't just sit there and say, "God, reveal it to me!" God expects you to put feet to your prayers, to get out and do a little hoofing and look.

If you're doing your best to please and obey Him, God will do almost anything for you—some of the most amazing things you could possibly imagine!

Let's not be so self-righteous.

If you're going to be so self-righteous and holier-than-thou and hypocritical as to think you're better than somebody because they have sinned against you, but oh, no, you've never sinned, therefore you're not going to forgive them, then you are the biggest sinner of all! If you have self-righteous feelings of being better than others and look down on them, like the Pharisee who said, "God, I thank You that I am not like other men" (Luke 18:9–14), then that attitude in itself is the worse sin. In fact, self-righteousness is one of the greatest sins of all.

We should take a kind, loving, sympathetic, and forgiving attitude toward others and *have* mercy as we *want* mercy. We should treat others in their errors as we want God to treat us in ours. We must forgive those who've wronged us, seek forgiveness of those we've wronged, and then take them back into our circle of love and fellowship.

May we all be kinder, more humble, more patient, more loving, more forgiving, and more long-suffering with each other—and may we sincerely pray, "Forgive us our sins, for we also forgive everyone who sins against us" (Luke 11:4 NIV).

Beware of compromise.

THE DEVIL WILL DO EVERYTHING HE CAN TO TEMPT YOU TO FORSAKE GOD'S WAY. If he can't get you to stop, he will try to get you to compromise. He tempts you with half-truths that make you doubt your convictions or not live up to them fully.

Most people don't realize that if they hold one little thing back from God, if they make one little compromise, they are distancing themselves from God. One little disobedience leads to another, one little refusal and denial leads to another, and one bit of selfishness leads to more. You may think, "Oh, just this one little sin, just this one little thing, it's not important," but that crack in your armor is all the Devil needs. His gas of deceit begins to seep in and poison your mind because you disobeyed what you knew God wanted you to do, and pretty soon you're totally off the track.

Don't let that happen to you. Be faithful to the Lord. Be faithful to the voice of His Spirit when He tells you to do this or that, or to not do this or that. Be loyal. "Resist the Devil and he will *flee* from you" (James 4:7). Don't give him an inch, or he'll take a mile—everything you've got. Give *no* place to the Devil (Ephesians 4:27).

You believe in love as much as you love.

IF YOU HAVE REAL LOVE, you can't face a needy situation without doing something about it. You can't just pass by the poor man on the road to Jericho. You must take action, like the Good Samaritan did (Luke 10:30– 37). It's not enough to say, "Oh, I'm so sorry, how sad!"

There was a time when Jesus was very tired and He tried to escape the multitude for a little rest, but when He looked on the multitude, the Bible says He was moved with compassion, and taught and healed them (Mark 6:31–34; Matthew 14:13–14). Compassion must be put into action.

You can't say that you believe in something if you don't practice it. We should apply love as God intended for it to be applied— with all our heart, with all our soul, and with all our mind (Matthew 22:37–39). That means to be truly concerned. It's not saying, "I love you," and then walking off and forgetting people in need. It's not saying, "Be warmed and filled," but not giving them the things they need when it's in your power to help (James 2:16; Proverbs 3:28). Love without physical application is like faith without works, which is dead (James 2:26). Show love and compassion by putting kind deeds to your kind words (1 John 3:18).

Lord, help us to be humble and not hardened or bitter.

SOMETIMES THE VERY THING WE DON'T WANT IS WHAT GOD PUTS US THROUGH, because our unwillingness is due to our pride. He does some things to humble us, and sometimes later lets us go through similar things to see if we're still humble. It's a real test when this happens, and it often ends in complaining and holding it against God. "God doesn't love me, because He didn't do what I wanted Him to do."

That seed of resentment or bitterness can grow and grow, and soon it can become a pretty big weed. That's why His Word warns us to watch out "lest any root of bitterness springing up trouble us, and thereby many be defiled" (Hebrews 12:15). That is a serious warning against bitterness! If we let bitterness take root, it can poison our whole spirits.

Sometimes we feel the only way we can bear the hurt is to harden our hearts, but that's not the Lord's solution. His Word says, "Cast your burden on the Lord, and He shall sustain you" (Psalm 55:22).

(Prayer:) Lord, help us to learn our lesson—whatever You're trying to teach us—and to be better for it, not bitter. Help us to thank You in spite of our tests and trials, hurts and disappointments. Help us to come through them more humble and closer to You. Amen.

Every calling is great when greatly pursued for God's glory!

God CAN INSPIRE YOU IN ANYTHING YOU DO. No matter what it is, you can do it in the Spirit; He can make every task glorious. Even if you don't have the most talent or experience, God can use you. In fact, that's the way God usually works. He chooses people who aren't strong or wise or anything great in themselves in order to show what *He* can do (1 Corinthians 1:26–29). Although you may not be the greatest in the eyes of the world, if God has called you to serve Him in some capacity and you said yes, you're the greatest in *His* eyes; that's what counts. He can make you strong when you're weak, to show it's His strength and His miraculous power (2 Corinthians 4:7; 12:9).

But before God is able to do great miracles in your life and ministry, you need to realize that it is nothing of you, that it is only a gift from Him. What makes you really great is the greatness God gives you, the Spirit, the inspiration. It's God behind it all—behind and above and underneath and on all sides. He does all of it through you. When you acknowledge this to yourself and others, then He'll be able to show what great things He can do!

First impressions are usually the right ones, if you're truly following the Lord.

IF YOU LOVE JESUS, are filled with the Holy Spirit, and are sincerely seeking God's will, usually your first reaction is the right one. God speaks first. It can just be in that "still small voice" (1 Kings 19:12) that you feel inside of you. Sometimes it's not even words, but just an impression. God doesn't have to communicate in words. He can just give you a feeling or a picture or an idea.

When you are in tune with the Holy Spirit and doing your best to stay in His will and obey Him, you have a strong clear channel with Him and pick up His signals—His answers and leadings—loud and clear. You've got to get not only in prayer, but you've got to get in the Spirit. Point your antenna in His direction, tune in, and the Lord will tell you exactly what you're supposed to do.

When you're asking the Lord to speak to you about a question or problem, you have to have faith. When you ask the Lord for an answer, expect an answer and take the first thing that comes. If you really believe and ask the Lord, you won't be disappointed. That thing you see or hear with the eyes or ears of your spirit, that's the Lord speaking to you. Expect God to answer!

Breathe deeply!

LIKE THE FLAME OF A CANDLE, your body needs a continual supply of oxygen in order to stay alive. That is a fact of this natural life that also illustrates an important spiritual truth: If you want to keep burning brightly for the Lord (Matthew 5:16), you need to have a constant supply of the Holy Spirit. The Holy Spirit is like your spiritual oxygen supply, the very air that you breathe that keeps you alive spiritually.

The Hebrew word used throughout the Old Testament for "spirit" is *ruwack*, which also means "air" or "breath," and the Greek word *pneuma*, translated as "spirit" in the New Testament, means the same thing. You need to be breathing that breath of the Spirit constantly or you'll suffocate and die spiritually. Like the flame of a candle, your spiritual fire will go out.

Just eating is not enough to keep you alive; you also have to have air to burn that food, to give you energy. Just so, the spiritual food of God's Word is not enough by itself; you have to have the oxygen of the Spirit to make it burn to give you power and energy spiritually. One or the other is not enough. You have to have both—God's Word, combined with the breath of His Spirit!

"Behold, a king [Jesus] will reign in righteousness, and princes will rule with justice" (Isaiah 32:1).

CHRIST'S COMING IS LITERALLY GOING TO BE AN INVASION FROM OUTER SPACE. When He finally returns to set things right, He is going to take over "with power and great glory" (Matthew 24:30). Out of Heaven will come the great hosts of Heaven with Jesus in the lead on a white horse to destroy the Antichrist and his kingdom in the great Battle of Armageddon (Revelation 19). Jesus and His saints—all of His children from down through the ages—will take over the world by God's power and make this world live the way it should have lived (Revelation 20:4).

His Word says we shall then rule and reign with Him over the nations with a rod of iron (Revelation 2:26–27). The nations will then be compelled to submit to the laws of God and to recognize His authority. It's going to be an iron rule over those left on earth; otherwise many of them would never obey. Only then shall all wicked and vengeful men of war be stopped at last, and only then shall the men of peace and the God of peace and the Prince of Peace rule and reign and bring peace on earth.

> Hail the heavenly Prince of Peace!
> Hail the Sun of Righteousness!
> Light and life to all He brings,
> Risen with healing in His wings.[1]

[1] Charles Wesley (1707–1788).

The best ability is availability.

GOD DOESN'T CREATE SAINTS OUT OF THIN AIR; He creates them out of flesh and blood, normal people who love Him and let Him use them. Most of the greatest saints the world has ever known were people who just did what they thought needed to be done, whether or not others heard about it or even knew they were around. They were always there when someone needed them, always willing to see the need and respond.

If you have real love for God and others, you will be aware of the needs around you and do whatever needs to be done. And when God sees that you will do the lowly little tasks lovingly and faithfully and well, He will know He can trust you with bigger, more important jobs (Luke 16:10). But He won't force you. It all depends on you and your yieldedness, your willingness to be made willing. Yieldedness requires humility, which is a manifestation of love—the kind of love that is willing to go anywhere, anytime, and do anything, for anybody, and be nobody, to please God and help others.

Are you ready for anything God wants you to do? "I beseech you therefore, brethren, that ye present your bodies a living sacrifice, holy and acceptable unto God, which is your reasonable service" (Romans 12:1 KJV).

Love is the most important thing in our religion.

T HE BIBLE PREACHES LOVE—the love of God through Jesus Christ, His Son. He also blesses us with other kinds of love and they are all important, but His is all-important. This is the cornerstone of the religion we Christians are supposed to practice: love for God and love for others. Love is what Jesus Himself taught—the Good News that God is love (1 John 4:8). True love, real love, unselfish love, sacrificial love, God's love, is all the religion we need.

"Love the Lord your God, and love your neighbor as yourself. On these two commandments hang all the Law and the Prophets" (Matthew 22:37–40). That's all the laws of the whole Bible put together—love! If you have love, you have everything. If you do everything out of genuine love for God and others, you are fulfilling all the laws of God.

Herein is our salvation and message: love, true love, the love of God and fellow man, for it is God's divine love working in us that helps us fulfill His great commandment to love one another. Thank God for such sweet love in the Lord!

Isn't it wonderful to have love? When you have God you have love, because God *is* love (1 John 4:8).

"See me, feel me, touch me, heal me!"—This is the heartcry of the world!

So MANY PEOPLE ARE ALWAYS SEARCHING FOR LOVE BUT SELDOM, IF EVER, FINDING IT. People everywhere are looking around for some little ray of hope, some bright spot somewhere, a little love, a little sympathy, a little mercy, some salvation, someplace where they can find relief from their loneliness and heartache. We who have found God and His love have what others have been searching for all their lives and need desperately.

The greatest thing we can give others is love—to show them love. If we can prove to them that *love* exists, then they can believe that *God* exists. Even the little things you do can mean a lot. A little bit of love goes such a long way! The light of your smile or the kindness of your face can have an amazing effect on people, including some you think might be the least likely to be impressed. When people feel your love and you tell them it's God's love, they can't help but think, *Maybe Somebody up there does love me!* It can change their whole outlook on life!

Thank God for Heaven and for the hope of such wonderful things to come!

WOULDN'T YOU JUST LOVE TO ENJOY ALL THE BLESSINGS YOU HAVE RIGHT NOW without any pain, sickness, death, weariness, or any of the other difficulties of this present life? We will never get to truly enjoy life to the full as long as sin and its results are in the world, but in Heaven there will be none of these (Revelation 21:4). There all of our heart's desires will be fulfilled.

It's going to be a sinless new world where everything will be a joy and a pleasure and perfect, with peace and harmony and cooperation and love for all. Everything there will be true—the truth, the whole truth and nothing but the truth! Everybody there will be like Jesus—good and honest and loving and caring and kind. It will be the perfect society, where everyone will be in perfect fellowship with each other and the Lord. Isn't that beautiful?

God's plan is not going to be defeated. He's going to bring us through to final perfection the way He originally intended. We will have eternal, wonderful happiness, joy, and paradise, similar to what we who love the Lord have now, only it will be far better and it will be forever!

We're always on trial with God, passing tests all our lives.

GOD NEVER ALLOWS US TO BE TEMPTED BEYOND WHAT WE ARE ABLE TO BEAR (1 Corinthians 10:13), but He does allow the Devil to test our faith to see if we will flee to Him and His Word and take a stand of faith.

With every grade, the tests get harder and the choices more difficult. The more God can trust you to stand the test, the tougher it's going to be. But no matter how great your trial may be, if you have faith to trust in God to bring you out of that difficulty, you won't murmur or complain. You'll rejoice and praise God and thank Him for the trial because you know He is able to save you, like He did Job. Job endured his suffering to prove his faith and love for God, but when Job gave the right answer: "Though He slay me, yet will I trust Him," he passed the test and earned his diploma (Job 13:15).

God allows tests and sufferings not only so He can see if we've got faith, which He already knows, but also for *us* and others to see if we've got it. It's a test and a testimony. And when you finally pull through, it makes you stronger in the Lord and brings out the best in you.

The only difference between us and other sinners is that we're *saved* sinners because we have received Christ.

L<small>ET'S FACE IT</small>: All of us are sinners. "*All* have sinned and fall short of the glory of God" (Romans 3:23). God is not so angry with the sinner for breaking the rules, because He knows the sinner is a sinner and *can't* be perfect. So the great condemnation is not that we're sinful, which God can forgive and does forgive if we receive His pardon through Jesus, but "this is the condemnation, that the light has come into the world, and men loved darkness rather than light, because their deeds were evil" (John 3:19).

The only unpardonable sin is rejecting Jesus as your Savior—to have been shown the love of God and resisted it. This is blasphemy against the Holy Ghost (Mark 3:28–29). He'll forgive every sin in the Book except that.

So you either belong to Jesus or you don't. That's the only difference God sees. God sees nothing but the blood of Jesus Christ and the blood-washed soul.

> All glory and praise
> To the Lamb Jesus that was slain,
> Who hath borne all our sins,
> And hath cleansed every stain.[1]

[1] William Paton Mackay (1839–1885).

"She has done what she could!"

REMEMBER WHAT JESUS SAID about the dear woman who anointed His head with costly, fragrant oil before His death? He said, "She has done what she could" (Mark 14:3–9).

Maybe you feel you can't do very much, but at least you can do what you can! If you will be faithful to do your best at the job God has given you to do for Him, however great or small it may be, He will greatly reward you one of these days soon when you stand before Jesus at the "judgment seat of Christ" (Romans 14:10). You will reap eternal rewards and everlasting glory, and have a feeling of genuine permanent accomplishment from your investment in His work. "Well done, good and faithful servant," you will hear Him say. "Because you were faithful over a few things, I will make you ruler over many things. Enter into the joy of your Lord" (Matthew 25:21).

Have you done what you could, or are you going to be sorry for your sins of omission? Don't lose your reward or let another take the crown that God has for you (Revelation 3:11).

I am satisfied with Jesus, but the question comes to me,
As I think of Calvary, "Is my Savior satisfied with me?"[1]

[1] B.B. McKinney (1886–1952).

Obedience comes before the anointing.

YOU DON'T GET THE ANOINTING *TO* OBEY; you get the anointing *because* you obey. Look how much the Lord hinges on your doing what He asks, just because He says so. Even if you don't know all the whys or wherefores, you've just got to do it. But once you do, it will usually become clear why He asked it of you, or He will explain.

Jesus commanded His disciples to wait together in Jerusalem until they were "endued with power from on high" to carry the message of God's love to the world (Luke 24:49; Acts 1:4–5,8). After ten days of obedience, there came that final tremendous explosion on the Day of Pentecost when they were all filled with the Holy Ghost. It was such an explosion that thousands gathered to see what in the world was going on, and three thousand people got saved that day (Acts chapter 2).

If you'll believe God's Word, He will give you the faith to take that first step of obedience. The moment you obey by faith, you get the anointing to carry on. The test is to see whether you're going to obey or not, but as soon as you do, God steps in and does His part without fail.

Every day can be a holiday for Jesus!

Every day can be a holiday, because every day can be a holy day if we live them all for Jesus. Every day can be holy, sacred, cleansed, and set apart to serve Jesus.

Some esteem one day above another, but we should esteem all days the same (Romans 14:5). They are all the Lord's days, so they are all holy days—not mere holidays, but holy days. We shouldn't love God and Jesus any more on one day than we do every other day of the week. We should love and worship the Lord just as much every day.

We can have Thanksgiving Day every day. We should be thankful and treasure every moment of every day and constantly be praising and thanking the Lord for it. We can have Christmas every day. If Christmas lives in our hearts and minds, we can live each day like Christmas day. We should love Him better every day, grow sweeter every day, and try to be a greater blessing to others every day. Then every day will be Christmas and Thanksgiving and Happy Birthday and New Year all in one!

> Jesus saves and keeps me,
> And He's the One I'm living for.
> Every day with Jesus,
> Is sweeter than the day before![1]

---

[1] Robert C. Loveless.

"I fear, lest ... your minds may be corrupted from the simplicity that is in Christ"
(2 Corinthians 11:3).

THE FIRST TIME THE DEVIL TEMPTED MAN, he tempted him with something that supposedly would make man wise—knowledge (Genesis 3:1–6). Likewise today, many books are written with the demonic wisdom of the Devil himself, cunningly devised to deceive and lead people astray, to pervert, to warp, and twist them spiritually to where they don't know what is true.

"God is not the author of confusion" (1 Corinthians 14:33). God likes to keep things very simple. That's why it's wonderful to have the Bible as a guide. Then you know what's perverted and what's normal, what's right and what's wrong. "The wisdom of this world is foolishness to God" (1 Corinthians 3:19). You cannot fill your mind and heart with worldly wisdom, the foolishness of man, without it affecting your spirit, just like you can't wade through the garbage and the gutter without getting besmirched (Colossians 2:8).

Why waste time on complicated and confusing theories and thoughts of man when the Word is right there, so simple and direct to the point? Stick to the refreshing water of the Word that feeds your soul, renews your mind, lifts your spirit, encourages your heart, and purifies your whole being!

God sometimes has to correct us, but He always does so in love.

GOD IS JUST AND MERCIFUL AND LOVING. He deals with us, His children, with much love and long-suffering and patience, but He also deals with us firmly when He sees that we're getting off the track. Like a shepherd with an errant sheep, He sometimes has to let us feel His shepherd's rod in order to turn us off the wrong path. He is a loving God, but He's also a very good Father who knows how to correct us when we need it.

Although God's corrections are sometimes hard to take, they're a token of His love—His "intolerable compliments"—and are good for us if we learn our lessons and are thereby brought into harmony with Him and doing what He knows is best for us and others.Therefore, don't forget "the exhortation which speaks to you as to sons: 'My son, do not despise the chastening of the Lord, nor be discouraged when you are rebuked by Him; for whom the Lord loves He chastens'" (Hebrews 12:5–6). God's chastenings are proof that He loves you.

Let the light in, and the darkness will flee.

THE DEVIL IS THE ACCUSER OF THE SAINTS (Revelation 12:9–10). He accuses us for what we *haven't* done or *could* have done or *should* have done but didn't. He picks at all the lacks and shortcomings and weaknesses and little failures. If you start listening to him, you're beaten, because there will always be something more you could have done or something you wish you hadn't done. There will always be something— some neglect, some oversight, some mistake or fault, some bad habit—that the Devil can pick on if he wants to, and he sure wants to!

But thank God for Jesus! He's the antidote! Jesus always points out the *good* things. He never loses faith in us and He never stops loving us, even when we do make mistakes. So when the Devil descends on you with his dark thoughts about yourself or others, don't listen to him. Listen to Jesus instead. Let the light in! Think positive thoughts. Remind yourself constantly of the good. When you think positively about yourself and others, it chases away the doubts and the fears and nagging little accusations from the Devil. Fill your mind and heart and mouth with positive things. Chase away the Devil and all his shades of night by letting the light in. Count your blessings and put the Devil on the run!

What everybody needs is love!

P~EOPLE ARE HUNGRY FOR LOVE~—love they
have never known before, true love, sincere love, genuine love,
the truly great love of their life, the love of all loves from the
Lover of all lovers, who alone can satisfy that deepest yearning
of every human soul for total love and complete understanding.

People's hearts are the same the world over. Their longings,
loves, hunger for God and His truth, for joy and happiness and
peace of mind are God-created and universal. People can never
be happy with a heavy heart, a troubled mind, a discouraged
spirit, and an unsaved soul. The human soul can never be completely satisfied with anything but utter union with the great
and loving Spirit that created it. Flesh can satisfy flesh, but only
Spirit can satisfy spirit.

Do you want the key to every heart?—Try love! It never fails,
because God is love and it's impossible for Him to fail!

> Ah, sweet mystery of life, at last I've found thee!
> Ah, at last I've found the reason for it all!
> Ah, 'tis love and love alone the whole world yearns for,
> And 'tis love that bids us heed Thy call![1]

---

[1] Rida Johnson Young (1869–1926), "Ah, Sweet
Mystery of Life," paraphrased.

Every day, Jesus has to cleanse us.

BELIEVE IT OR NOT, everybody who believes in Jesus is a saint. Most people think that to be a saint they must be made perfectly and permanently holy, but actually the ancient Greek words *hagios* and *hagiazo*, which are translated as "saint" and "sanctify" in the New Testament, both mean to be cleansed and separated and set aside for further use. We may not be perfect or sinless saints, but we're cleansed and made holy by His blood. Jesus takes us, dirty as we are with sin, and He washes away our sins with His blood and our evil thoughts with His Word (1 John 1:7; Revelation 7:14; Ephesians 5:26).

Sanctification is not just a one-time thing that takes place when you receive salvation. It is a constant process. When Jesus washed His disciples' feet at the Last Supper (John 13:4–12), He was illustrating that even after we get saved and He cleanses us of our sins, if we wade through the filth of this world as we serve Him, we have to have a little bit of washing every day. Is there ever a day that passes that we don't sin?—Not really. We're human, so daily He has to cleanse us—our minds, our thoughts, our bodies, our actions, our words. If we want Him to continue to use us, we have to be washed and set aside again and again.

If we're going to grow and mature spiritually, then we need to grow in love.

LOVE IS THE MOST IMPORTANT THING (1 Corinthians chapter 13). That's really the whole purpose for living, to love God and others. That means not only winning the lost wherever they are, but winning our brothers and sisters in Christ who are right beside us. The whole purpose for everything is love.

Some of our relationships are directly between the Lord and us, like praise and prayer and obedience to His Word, but most of our relationships are on a personal level with others. And the main lesson we're supposed to learn from these is to love one another. If we haven't learned to work well with others or how to treat them in love, then we're missing one of the major lessons of life.

We're not going to grow very much or learn very much unless we learn to interact lovingly with other people, and that's not always easy. It takes patience, love, and humility. Jesus gave the simple key when He instructed us to do unto others as we would have them do unto us (Matthew 7:12). It takes a lot to learn how to carry that out, but that's what we're here to learn. Do you want to grow?—Then love!

Life itself is proof of God, because life is a miracle.

ONE HUMBLE LITTLE CHICKEN out in some poor man's yard is proof of God because it produces a marvel of His creation every day—an egg, new life from the hand of God.

God's marvelous creation is alive, life giving, creative, and regenerative. It is constantly multiplying and being reborn and repairing itself. This is true of all forms of plant and animal life. When God created the world, He ordained it that each variety and species "whose seed is in itself" would bring forth more life of the same kind (Genesis 1:12, 21–22).

God's production system is the most effective there is in the world. God has a plan for everything, and His plan is perfect. Nothing is wasted and there is no pollution. Everything that God produces is pure and good. If it weren't for sin, there wouldn't even be any dying (Romans 5:12). There would be absolutely no waste and no destruction, only God's original all-life, no-death, can't-lose system. That's the way it will all be again one day soon for all those who receive God's love in Jesus and love Him in return. Isn't that wonderful?

May you always be known by your love!

WHAT WAS JESUS' MESSAGE TO HIS DISCIPLES AT THE LAST SUPPER, before He was arrested, beaten, and killed? "By this all will know that you are My disciples, if you have love for one another" (John 13:35). He talked about love, that love was the most important thing.

The early Christians turned the world upside down with the love of God that they found in Jesus Christ. Even their Roman rulers marveled at the love of the Christians and said, "Behold, how these Christians love one another!" The way the Christians lived convinced the Romans that their faith was real, and the Romans wondered, "Who is this Christ and how does He make you so happy? Even though you have nothing, you've got everything! How can I find this kind of happiness that I don't have?"—And within 200 years, when Christianity was still outlawed, one out of every five people in the Roman Empire was a professing Christian and the known world had been saturated with the Gospel of Jesus Christ!

Just a little love can go a long way—much further than you could ever dream—so love the Lord and others, and be faithful in your witnessing to others of the love of Jesus Christ!

"Blessed are the meek, for they shall inherit the earth" (Matthew 5:5).

THE WHOLE WORLD IS GOD'S. In a sense, the Devil has stolen it away for a little bit, but it will soon be back fully in the hands of its rightful owner. Then at last the meek shall inherit the earth. Right now the ungodly powers of this world reign by their cruel, selfish, dog-eat-dog philosophy that gives the world to the strongest, but during the coming kingdom of Christ on earth it will be given to those who really have the right to govern because of their love and meekness and forgiveness and faith in God and His Word. Then, under the supreme reign of Jesus Himself, the pitiful little bands of persecuted Christians and believers are going to inherit the earth and run it by love and the power of God (Daniel 7:27).

These weakest and meekest will become the most powerful influences on the earth, and will rule the world with both love and a "rod of iron"—love and loving force, when necessary, to compel the nations to submit to the laws of God and to obey His rules of life, love, health, and happiness. Then at last will there be peace on earth toward men of good will (Revelation 2:26–27; Luke 2:14).

Our labors are not in vain; they're going to last a lot longer than some of us think.

WHAT WE'RE DOING NOW IS IMPORTANT, and it's not going to be wasted. The preparation we, God's saved children, are doing now is all a part of His plan to prepare us for bigger and better things to come.

There's going to be a lot that's the same in the coming world, especially during the coming thousand-year kingdom of Christ on earth, known as the Millennium. This may come as a disappointment, but we won't be absolutely perfect in the next world. We'll be partly human and partly divine, and we'll still be using a lot of the knowledge, experience, talents, languages, and skill that we have gained in this world. God's not going to waste all these years of training.

What we're doing is of eternal value. "Lay up for yourselves treasures in Heaven" (Matthew 6:20). What treasures? The Bible tells us that we brought nothing into this world with us, and we can't take anything out of it—no material things, that is (1 Timothy 6:7). We're going to take our children and all the souls we win to Jesus, and that's not all. We'll also take the knowledge and experience we gain in this life.

Are you getting ready here and now for there and then? It won't be lost, but used forever.

Never underestimate the advantage of a handicap.

GOD KNOWS WHAT HE'S DOING. He has a reason and a purpose for everything. We don't always understand, and we don't have to. All we have to do is let each thing that He sends our way accomplish His purpose.

"All things work together for good to those who love God" (Romans 8:28), no matter what they are or how "good" they seem to us. It may not always seem like it at the time, but in the long run God often gets His greatest victories out of seeming defeat. Perhaps that handicap is meant to strengthen you in other areas, such as faith and love, and to equip you to impart those strengths to others.

When William Moon (1818–1894) of Brighton, England, was stricken with blindness, he said, "God gave me the talent of blindness to use for His glory. Without blindness I should never have been able to see the needs of the blind." Then God enabled him to invent the Moon alphabet for the blind, by which thousands of blind people were able to read the Word of God, and many of them were gloriously saved.

So don't give up! Don't drown in your sorrows. Make an advantage out of your handicap. Build a bridge out of your broken dreams, and set those ships a sail again. That handicap need not be the end. In fact, it may only be the beginning!

Little things can make us or break us—they're that important!

ALTHOUGH SOME THINGS MAY SEEM UNIMPORTANT TO US, they may be very important to God and very important to our happiness and success. Look at what resulted from one wrong decision in the Garden of Eden (Genesis 3:1–11), one tiny boat in a worldwide flood (Genesis chapter 7), and one little deal that brought death to the Savior (Matthew 26:14–16).

Little mistakes and little lacks can be costly. It's like the maxim: For want of a nail, the shoe was lost; for want of a shoe, the horse was lost; and for want of a horse, the rider was lost.[1] —All because of one tiny nail! "A little leaven leavens the whole lump" (Galatians 5:9), and it's the little foxes that spoil the vines (Song of Solomon 2:15).

Conversely, little things can also lead to great things. One little stone brought down a giant (1 Samuel chapter 17), one little manger changed the destiny of mankind (Luke 2:7), and a little mustard seed of faith can move mountains (Matthew 17:20).

"He who is faithful in what is least is faithful also in much; and he who is unjust in what is least is unjust also in much" (Luke 16:10). Be diligent and faithful in the little things, and God will use you for greater things.

[1] Benjamin Franklin (1706–1790), maxims prefixed to *Poor Richard's Almanac*, 1757.

Enjoy yourself and enjoy life— but enjoy the Lord most of all!

GOD INTENDS FOR YOU TO ENJOY LIFE. He made all things for you to enjoy, and He created the very senses with which to enjoy them. Every good and perfect gift that God has sent down from above, He created for you, His child, to enjoy (James 1:17).

Enjoy the pleasures that God has given you as much as you please and as much as you need. Just don't enjoy them more than Him. If you have an inordinate desire for too much of certain things, then it becomes a form of worship, and that's a sin. "Do not love the world or the things in the world," the Bible cautions us. "If anyone loves the world, the love of the Father is not in him" (1 John 2:15). Don't let the blessings of God take first place in your life, because God will not take second place. He wants your love above all else. He says, "You shall have no other gods before Me" (Exodus 20:3).

Be sure that you put God first. Love and worship Him above all, and thank Him for all of these other things that He has given you to enjoy. Then you can have all this and Heaven too!

When you first decide to serve God, all hell breaks loose!

IF THE DEVIL CAN SCARE YOU OUT BEFORE YOU EVEN BEGIN, you'll never accomplish what God wants you to do. So the Devil pulls out all of his big guns and everything in his bag of dirty tricks to try to keep you from starting to serve God, because he figures that if he can keep you from starting, you'll *never* serve God.

It's your witness the Devil fears. He knows he's going to lose others from his clutches because of you and your influence and testimony. Every person you win to Jesus is a threat to hundreds of others that the Devil has claimed as his, so he's out to stop each one as best he can.

In the testing time before the beginning of His ministry, Jesus was led by the Holy Spirit into the desert where He fasted for 40 days and afterward was tempted by the Devil. Imagine, the Devil was allowed to test even Jesus! But Jesus never yielded under the attack. Instead, He resisted the Devil with the Word of God. When the Devil saw that Jesus wasn't going to give up, that He claimed the Scriptures, then the Devil quit.

So for God's sake, the sake of others, and your own sake, don't let the Devil bluff you out of what God wants you to do. "Resist the Devil and he will flee from you" (James 4:7).

AUGUST 9

The best way is the love way.

THIS IS WHAT GOD'S BEEN WORKING ON ALL THE TIME: to persuade us to do things with the right motivation, because we love Him and others and therefore want to do what is right. Following God's example, we also should try to persuade others to do the right thing out of love.

A horse can either love and obey its master, or it can be stubborn and willful. A horse that is gentled through love takes a lot more time and patience to train, but it will be a far better horse and much more obedient than if its will is broken and it's forced to obey for fear of punishment.

If you teach that horse to *want* to obey you and follow your every instruction because it loves and trusts you, it will be the best mount you could ever ride. But a horse that's had to be broken because it was stubborn will continue to want to break the rules whenever it gets a chance. The best way is the gentle way, not the breaking way.

Certainly God has to have a lot of patience and love with us, so we, in turn, should have patience and love with others. "Be kind to one another, tenderhearted, forgiving one another, just as God in Christ forgave you" (Ephesians 4:32).

God's sinning saints give hope to you and me.

GOD LETS US HAVE A FEW GREAT SAINTS AS EXAMPLES, but nearly every great man or woman of God in the Bible was a hero with clay feet and just as human as we are.

Many consider this proof that the Bible was written by God and not man, because when man writes history he covers up all of the mistakes and sins of his heroes, whereas God's book, the Bible, tells the whole story, not just the good parts. God's Word tells the truth, the whole truth, and nothing but the truth. God paints the picture just as black as it really is sometimes to show how bad man can be without knowing Him or being in His will. We're to learn from the things that He taught others in the past. These things didn't happen for their sakes only, He says, but were written for *our* sakes, that we might learn God's ways (1 Corinthians 10:11).

God's Word always portrays its heroes as they really were— ordinary men and women like you and me. They made big mistakes just like you and I have, and some committed horrible sins. Yet when they repented, God forgave. That gives all of us sinners hope!

"Do you not know that you are the temple of God and that the Spirit of God dwells in you?" (1 Corinthians 3:16).

WE OURSELVES ARE THE VERY TEMPLE OF GOD—you and me, His children who live with Him day by day and worship Him in our own hearts.

God's true Church has always been the body of believers, the fellowship of the saints, the assembly of the saints. The word "church" comes from the ancient Greek word *ekklesia*, meaning the called-out ones, or the separated ones. The church is not the building; it's the people. Christian worship in the early days needed no buildings, no great temples built with hands of men, which could not contain God anyway (Acts 7:48). They worshiped Him in homes, in upper rooms, in basements, in the marketplace, beside the river, and in the forest under the trees—wherever they happened to be. And Christianity soon covered the earth because the apostles obeyed and went out. Instead of building buildings, they went out and built the true Church of Jesus Christ in the hearts of men, a temple built of "living stones," as Peter calls us (1 Peter 2:5).

God dwells within the human heart. Buildings cannot contain Him, but your heart contains the Lord Jesus Christ if you have received Him (Galatians 4:6).

Conscience is God's presence in man.

It's an amazing and wonderful thing that the world over, in nearly every culture and even in the most remote places, everyone seems to know the difference between right and wrong. People understand that certain things are sins, and they have laws against them. God's basic moral standards are pretty universal.

The Holy Spirit is faithful and speaks to the hearts of all, telling them when they're doing wrong. They know the difference between good and evil. They may not know their Master or the whole truth, the Good News of salvation, but they know the difference between right and wrong. "God's laws are written within them; their own conscience accuses them, or sometimes excuses them" (Romans 2:12 TLB). God gives everybody *some* light, and God is going to judge each one according to how they follow the light he or she is given.

God created man as a free moral agent. He gives each of us the majesty of personal choice to choose between good and evil, between obeying the guiding voice of God and obeying the voice of Satan. Which will you do?

You don't have to be a millionaire to give what you've got.

THERE IS NOT ONE OF GOD'S CHILDREN who cannot afford to give something to His work. You may think you can't afford to give, or you may not be able to give a lot at first, but God blesses everybody that gives. If you're *not* rich, that's all the more reason to give, so God can bless you and help you have more.

God's finances work the opposite from the world's. The world says, "When I've got my million, *then* I'll start giving." But the Lord says, "Start giving what you've *got* now, and then I'll give you more." Man says, "Me first. Self-preservation is the first law of nature." But God says, "Put Me and Mine first, and I'll take care of you afterwards" (Matthew 6:33).

God's way to plenty is to give sacrificially of what you now have. "There is one who scatters, yet increases more; and there is one who withholds more than is right, but it leads to poverty" (Proverbs 11:24). The faster you give it away and share it, the more He'll heap it on and the richer you'll become so you can share more. Covetousness hoards itself poor, but charity gives itself rich.

It's better to stay healthy than to have to be healed.

Remember, an ounce of prevention is worth a pound of cure. A fence at the top of the cliff is better than a hospital at the bottom. The best way to prevent illness is to obey God's natural laws: Live right, eat right, work right, play right, rest right, love right, and maintain a right relationship with Him.

You cannot violate God's health rules or abuse your body and expect to be healthy, because God made you with built-in self-destruct mechanisms to punish you if you do. It's not that God enjoys punishing you or seeing you suffer. To the contrary, He made His health rules because He loves you and wants to protect you from harm. The rules are to help you be happier and get more out of life by making sure you do what you can to keep yourself healthy and whole. It's a case of, "If you know these things, blessed are you if you do them" (John 13:17 KJV).

God created you, and He knows what is best for you. So work on the ounce of prevention now, rather than worrying about the pound of cure later. Take care of God's creation by following His commonsense rules, and God will bless you with good health.

What a wonderful place to meet, at Jesus' feet.

JESUS SAID THAT WE SHOULD SIT AT HIS FEET AND LEARN FROM HIM, like Mary in the Scripture (Luke 10:39–42). Mary hungered for His words of love and wisdom, gave Jesus her full attention, and received this commendation and promise: "Mary has chosen that good part, which will not be taken away from her."

"Where two or three are gathered together in My name," Jesus promises, "I am there in the midst of them" (Matthew 18:20). Jesus is in our midst every time we're together in His name, so we always meet at His feet.

Jesus always rewards those who unite in His love, when we give our time and attention to Him and His Word. He loves to give the answers we need when He sees we're united in love and prayer and purpose and mind and heart and spirit, of one mind (1 Corinthians 1:10). This is the marvel of the Day of Pentecost. Jesus was in the midst of them, and the Holy Spirit was poured out upon them (Acts chapter 2).

As we read His Word, study it, share it, pray over it, and follow the light of its truth, we are melted together in His love, blended together in His truth, joined together as one body, fitly joined together according to His Word.

God loves a mystery!

GOD HAS FILLED LIFE FULL OF PUZZLES AND PROBLEMS and mysteries and suspense to challenge our intellect, our faith, and our trust in Him as we set out to try to find the answers.

In trying to show us His will, God sometimes sets a mystifying puzzle before us. He sometimes speaks in riddles and mysteries that are hard to understand in order to get us to think and pray, but He almost always gives us a starting clue. Then He leads us on step by step. We never know what's going to happen until we take the next step.

He likes to make us seek His answers, because this causes us to exercise our faith in Him and His Word and His divine guidance and magnanimity, His parental love. It shows we trust in Him when we obey Him, even if we don't know what's at the end of the road. We may not see the answer, we may not know the solution or the place He's leading to or what we're going to find, but we're trusting God to fulfill His promises, like Abraham did when he obeyed God and went out, not even knowing where he was going (Hebrews 11:8).

"There is joy in the presence of the angels of God over one sinner who repents" (Luke 15:10).

Each time another soul is born into the kingdom of God when someone accepts Jesus as their Savior, it's similar to the birth of a child. Although a baby is delivered in pain, afterwards the pain is forgotten in the delight of a new soul born into this world. The same joy, only greater, is experienced at the birth of a new spiritual baby into the kingdom of God. One saved soul makes all Heaven rejoice, and is certainly sufficient payment for whatever work or sacrifice or difficulties we may go through to help bring that about.

All Heaven rejoices and all the angels rejoice more over one lost "sheep" that's found, over one soul that's saved, than over the ninety-nine—all the rest who are already found and saved and rescued (Luke 15:7).

If the angels of Heaven rejoice over every soul that's saved, they certainly must also rejoice over our service for the Lord because of what that ultimately leads to—more souls for the kingdom of God. When your time of reward and recognition comes, are the angels of Heaven going to jump for joy over your sacrificial giving of yourself so others could also find God's love in Jesus and be won to His eternal kingdom?

Keep on believing.

MANY OF US HAVE GONE THROUGH DRY, DESERT-LIKE EXPERIENCES, wandering about in the spiritual wastelands of this world, feeling lost and seemingly separated from God. If you find yourself in such a state, instead of lamenting that you have somehow missed His will, keep on believing and praising the Lord. Encourage your faith with His Word. Repent of any wrongdoing and ask God to forgive you, so you can have another chance at His highest will for you. Then, like a bird whose pinion once was broken but now is healed, you may fly even higher than before.

Don't ever quit! Don't ever give up! Don't be discouraged! Maybe you missed the first opportunity, but maybe you haven't missed the last one.

> Keep on believing, Jesus is near,
> Keep on believing there is nothing to fear,
> Keep on believing, this is the way
> Faith in the night as well as the day.[1]

Ask God for another chance, and He will send along another golden opportunity to encourage you and carry you along in the power of His Spirit to the glorious victory of your heavenly destination. Keep on holding on to His promises, and whatever you do, keep on going for Jesus!

[1] Milward Booth-Hellberg (1868–1953).

A tree is a vision of perfection.

Do you know why a tree is perfect?— Because it does nothing but obey God. It grows just for His glory and according to His will, and produces exactly what God has ordained it to produce. It's fruitful and flowering, strong and beautiful, fulfilling its mission in life. It never resists, it just yields and bends and nods its head to the will of God. It smiles all day, and lifts its leafy arms in praise to the Lord.

"Blessed is the man ... whose delight is in the law of the Lord. ... He shall be like a tree planted by the rivers of water, that brings forth its fruit in its season, whose leaf also shall not wither; and whatever he does shall prosper" (Psalm 1:1–3).

(Prayer:) Lord, help us to be like sturdy, healthy trees, planted strong in Your earth, watered by Your Word, and fertilized with the food of Your very body. You are like the earth in which we grow and on which we stand. Without You, we couldn't exist. Help us to be strong and true, like the trees, growing only for Your glory, fruitful and performing the mission for which You've ordained us: to bear fruit and be a blessing to others. Amen.

"Abide in Me, and I in you"
(John 15:4).

In the beautiful 15th Chapter of John, Jesus says, "I am the Vine, you are the branches. He who abides in Me, and I in him, bears much fruit; for without Me you can do nothing. If anyone does not abide in Me, he is cast out as a branch and is withered; and they gather them and throw them into the fire, and they are burned" (John 15:5–6). If ever you, as a branch, don't abide in the Vine, Christ—if you don't abide in His love, His Word, and His service—then you will become unfruitful and withered, and you will be pruned from the tree as a dead branch. You won't lose your salvation, but you will be cast aside as being no longer useful to God and His kingdom.

Without the flow of God's Spirit there is no life. You must be firmly implanted in the Vine where you're receiving the spiritual sap and life and nourishment that you need directly from the Lord Himself. A lot of how you grow is up to you and how much nourishment you receive, so don't cut yourself off from the Vine.

Jesus said, "Without Me you can do nothing" (John 15:5). But if you are dwelling in the Vine, as one of the branches, then you can produce beautiful leaves and beautiful fruit so that He and the Father may be glorified and have much fruit (John 15:8).

"Wait on the Lord"
(Psalm 27:14).

W<small>HAT DOES THAT MEAN</small>, "Wait on the Lord"? A lot of people take it to mean that they're supposed to sit around doing nothing while they wait for God to do something. They're waiting for God to do something *for* them rather than *with* them. That's one form of waiting on God and there's a time for that, but it just might be that God is waiting for *them* to get *busy*.

Very often the best way to find God's will is to get busy doing what we can and what we know we should do. So think about it like that. "Wait on the Lord," like a servant who waits on his master, or like a waiter or waitress waiting on a customer, where the customer is king. Don't just stand around or sit there; put yourself at His service. Get busy *serving* the Lord and He'll tell you what He'd like for you to do next.

That's what we're supposed to be: servants in the house of God, tending to His business, caring for His children, and doing His bidding. He is very grateful for our help, and admires us for our loyalty and faithful, cheerful service. He always has plenty for us to do, and is happy to tell us how He would like it done. How is that for a picture of waiting on the Lord?

Jesus is better to us than He was to Himself.

"FOXES HAVE HOLES AND BIRDS OF THE AIR HAVE NESTS, but the Son of Man has nowhere to lay His head" (Matthew 8:20). Jesus never owned a home, He never had a wife or children, and it seems the only material thing He owned on earth was His clothes.

Jesus said that it was enough that a disciple be like his master (Matthew 10:25), and Paul said, "Having food and clothing, with these we shall be content" (1 Timothy 6:8). Yet look at all that Jesus has given us besides that! All the rest are extras.

Jesus loves us and wants us to be happy and comfortable. He also knows what we need and what's good for us. He's pretty smart about that because He knows that when He's extra good to us we'll want to show our appreciation by working harder and doing a better job for Him.

Jesus believes in happy employees. To Him, our happiness is worth more than money. He's willing to let you have almost anything you want as long as you put Him first (Matthew 6:33). Look how Jesus tries to make it easy for us to be good and serve Him. As long as we delight ourselves in Him, He gives us the desires of our hearts (Psalm 37:4).

He that would win some must be winsome.

In order for people to communicate well, they must have some things in common. So in your witnessing, approach others in a positive way with a positive attitude. Establish points of contact. Develop a rapport. Be friendly, loving, understanding, compassionate, and sympathetic. Find as much common ground as you can. The apostle Paul said that he became all things to all men in order to win some (1 Corinthians 9:22).

Fighting false systems and false doctrines can be a temptation when you know you're so right and others are so wrong, but that's a negative type of witnessing—the kind that doesn't show love or win people. The best way to handle points of disagreement is not by refuting what the other person says, but by hearing them out and then presenting the truth in a loving and positive way. "Sanctify the Lord God in your hearts: and be ready always to give an answer to every man that asks you a reason of the hope that is in you with meekness and fear" (1 Peter 3:15 KJV).

Dwell on the positive, not the negative. Instead of preaching *against* things, preach Jesus. Then He will draw all men unto Himself (John 12:32).

Healing is a sample of resurrection.

Pain is a touch of Hell; healing is a touch of Heaven. Healing is a sample of everlasting life, renewal of the body, and cure of disease. It's a touch of resurrection.

When we experience salvation, we get a little sample of what eternal life and Heaven are going to be like. We have tasted of the heavenly gift and the powers of the world to come (Hebrews 6:4–5). Likewise, when we get healed we get a little sample of what God is going to do for us one of these days. We don't have the full resurrection yet, but we can have a little touch of it once in a while (Romans 8:11). We already have His healing power manifest in our bodies but it won't be complete until we receive our eternal, supernatural, indestructible bodies on which death no longer has any power or claim whatsoever.

When Jesus returns for us and we're transformed as we receive our new bodies, that will be the best healing of all. That will be the final healing. Then we won't have any more diseases, or sickness, or pain. That's permanent healing, final resurrection (1 Corinthians 15:51–57).

Life is like a garden.

IN THE BEGINNING, Adam was the first gardener. Even the Garden of Eden, as perfect as it was, had to have somebody taking care of it, and God gave that job to Adam. God expected man to tend and, in a sense, improve on His creation.

Gardening never ends. You've constantly got to keep fighting the weeds, the bugs, the varmints, the pests, the rot, the fungus, the mold, the blights, and all kinds of the Devil's attacks. God's garden is constantly fighting with the Devil's garden. The Devil's garden is hellish, and the Devil is trying to transfer it to earth. He's trying to create hell on earth. His whole idea is to try to defeat God's plan by overrunning and destroying God's garden, but he's not going to succeed.

Life is like one big garden and we've all got a lot to learn about it. No gardener knows everything. Only God, the Creator of the garden, knows everything. Like every gardener, the rest of us have to study and learn from other gardeners and from God, the owner and the head of the estate. There's plenty to learn and plenty of work to keep us busy from now to eternity!

God's love knows no boundaries.

GOD'S LOVE IS SO GREAT that it will descend to any depth to save, go to any length to rescue. He can love man in his lowest state and save him in his hour of need from his most pitiful plight. For God there is no stopping place, no limit to which He will not go to save a poor lost soul with His infinite love and mercy. He stoops to the level of our need.

> The love of God is greater far
> Than tongue or pen can ever tell;
> It goes beyond the highest star,
> And even to the lowest hell.[1]

Look at the mercy of Christ: He even went down into the bowels of the earth in order to preach the Gospel of deliverance to the spirits that were in prison there (Matthew 12:40; 1 Peter 3:18–20).

"Where can I go from Your Spirit? Or where can I flee from Your presence? If I ascend into Heaven, You are there; if I make my bed in Hell, behold, You are there. If I take the wings of the morning, and dwell in the uttermost parts of the sea, even there Your hand shall lead me, and Your right hand shall hold me" (Psalm 139:7–10).

[1] Frederick M. Lehman (1868–1953).

We cannot hold a torch to light another's path without brightening our own.

NEVER UNDERESTIMATE THE POWER OF PERSONAL WITNESSING to not only win people to Jesus, but also to inspire and encourage your own heart and keep you alive spiritually. "The generous soul will be made rich, and he who waters will also be watered himself" (Proverbs 11:25). Witnessing in itself is a form of reward. It will inspire your own heart as you watch the Lord work. It will not only be worth it all when you see Jesus, but it will be worth it all right now when you see the wonderful, thrilling, and satisfying results of your labors.

Everyone you witness to, you're wooing in the Spirit—wooing and loving and sowing the seed of God's Word in the Spirit. You can't win them all, but those you do win are worth it all! Like the shepherd who rejoiced at finding his one lost sheep, and the angels of Heaven who rejoice over one lost sinner who finds forgiveness, others' happiness becomes your happiness and their victories your own.

Seldom can a heart be lonely,
If it seeks a lonelier still—
Self-forgetting, seeking only,
Emptier cups of love to fill.[1]

[1] Frances Ridley Havergal (1836–1879).

Honest, open-minded scientists throughout history have acknowledged the existence of God.

TRUE SCIENCE POINTS TO THE FACT that there had to be something, somebody, some planner, some designer behind the creation of the universe.

James Clerk Maxwell (1831–1879), the Scottish mathematician and physicist who did revolutionary work on electromagnetic fields and the electromagnetic theory of light, said, "Science is incompetent to reason upon the creation of matter itself out of nothing."

Lord William Thomson Kelvin (1824–1907), another Scottish mathematician and physicist who devised the absolute scale of temperature, declared, "We must pause, face to face, with the mystery and miracle of the creation of living creatures."

Sir William Herschel (1738–1822), the German-born English astronomer and discoverer of the planet Uranus, said, "All human discoveries seem to be made only for the purpose of confirming more and more strongly the truth contained in the Bible."

Today God is giving man more and more evidence of His existence through the marvels of His creation, and all that we see teaches us to trust the Creator for all we have not seen!

Nothing is more important to your spiritual life and health than the Word.

THERE IS A SAYING ABOUT HEALTH: You *are* what you *eat*." That's true in the physical sense, but it's also true of our spirits. We are spiritually what our minds and spirits take in. There is plenty to take in these days through the mass media, advertising, and the Internet, but most of it is spiritual junk food—or worse yet, spiritual poison.

That's why it's so important to make sure you're getting the right spiritual food—the good, wholesome, nourishing, faith-building, uplifting, encouraging, inspiring, truth of the Word of God. Jesus said, "The Words that I speak to you are spirit, and they are life" (John 6:63). The prophet Jeremiah said, "Your Words were found, and I ate them, and Your Word was to me the joy and rejoicing of my heart" (Jeremiah 15:16). Job said, "I have treasured the Words of His mouth more than my necessary food" (Job 23:12). The apostle Peter admonished, "Desire the pure milk of the Word, that you may grow thereby" (1 Peter 2:2).

Just like you have to eat in order to stay alive and have physical strength, you have to feed from the Word to stay alive spiritually and have the spiritual strength to overcome the problems of life. A balanced diet of God's Word is essential if you are to grow and stay healthy spiritually.

A baby illustrates faith.

HOW DO WE RECEIVE THE SPIRITUAL NOURISHMENT WE NEED FROM GOD?—It's simple: We just have to have the faith of a little baby.

When a baby is crying to be fed, he knows his mother wouldn't think of refusing him. God put it in that baby to know that if he calls, she will answer. He expects the answer and he gets it. Likewise, if we, as children of our heavenly Father, ask for milk, He's surely not going to give us a serpent or something else (Luke 11:10–13).

What is it that brings the milk out of the mother's breast? When the baby sucks, he creates a vacuum inside his mouth, which pulls the milk out. Prayer is creating a vacuum, an empty space inside our hearts, which God fills.

When the baby is very young, his mother has to bring the nourishment to him and show him where it is. But as he gets older, he automatically knows where to find the milk and he can reach out for it himself. Likewise, the more we practice receiving nourishment from God, the better we know where to find it. And as long as we keep sucking, we'll get more, because God has unlimited capacity to give!

Jesus is the Word of God.

THE GOSPEL OF JOHN begins with one of the most profound statements in the entire Bible: "In the beginning was the Word, and the Word was with God, and the Word was God. The same was in the beginning with God. All things were made by Him; and without Him was not anything made that was made" (John 1:1–3 KJV). That's one of the deepest truths in the Bible—that Jesus is the Word of God, the *expression* of God, as well as the *Son* of God.

What is a word? It's a means of communication. When God wanted to communicate His love to the world, what did He do? You can't see love and you can't see God, so He sent His Word. He said it in Jesus. He showed it in Jesus. He expressed it in Jesus. He communicated it in Jesus. Jesus was all of that. He was the expression of God's love. He was the meaning of God's love. He was the communication of God's love. He said God's love. He showed God's love. He symbolized God's love. He manifested God's love. He was and *is* God's own message of love to us!

Anybody can find love if they have love.

IF YOU SHOW PEOPLE REAL LOVE, you won't have a hard time winning friends. If you're sincerely concerned about others and you show them love, they'll be concerned about you and show you love. Love begets love. If you sow love, you're going to reap love. If you sow friendship, you're going to reap friendship (Galatians 6:7). It's a two-way street.

Love cannot fail. It makes no difference where it is bestowed, it always brings in big returns. You can't give without getting, you can't show true love and concern without receiving love in return—and the more you give, the more you get.

Many others around you are just as lonely and longing for love as much as you are. They're probably just waiting for you to make the first move. Step out and try to make someone else happy, and you'll find a whole new world of love you've only dreamed of.

If you *give* love, you'll *get* love! That's God's system; that's God's rule. God will make you happy if you make others happy. It's that simple!

"By your patience possess your souls" (Luke 21:19).

HURRY IS THE DEVIL'S BUSINESS. He's always trying to make people rushed because he knows that then they'll be more apt to make mistakes.

We should never rush ahead of the Lord or try to push things through in our own strength. When the wandering children of Israel thirsted in the wilderness, God told Moses He would give them an abundant supply of water out of solid rock if Moses would just speak to the rock. But Moses was so upset with all the people's complaining that he violently smote the rock twice with his rod. Moses did the right thing but in the wrong way, and God was so angry that He told Moses, "Because you did not believe Me"—angry impatience shows a of lack of faith—"to hallow Me in the eyes of the children of Israel"—to show more faith and be a better example of God's own infinite loving patience with His people—"therefore you shall not bring this assembly into the land which I have given them" (Numbers 20:1–12).

(Prayer:) Lord, we ask that You teach us patience and faith, which takes time. Teach us never to get in a hurry or push too hard, as though we had to do things in our own strength. Amen.

The Devil wants to get you under pressure, but Jesus wants to be your pressure release valve.

YOUR SPIRITUAL ENEMY, the Devil, will use anything he can to come between you and Jesus, and one of his favorite tricks is to cause you to feel under pressure. He tries to accentuate the stress you already feel by telling you that you're not accomplishing enough or doing it well enough, or by getting you to look at what's left undone. He knows that if he can get you under pressure, you are more likely to skip your times with the Lord, praying, reading the Word, and resting in Him, as well as your times of physical rest and relaxation, all of which are important to your overall well-being. Stress also makes you irritable and harder to work with or even be around. It can really take the joy out of life!

The key to overcoming this ploy of the Devil is in asking Jesus to help you learn your limits and live within them. Pray and ask Jesus to help you know your limits, reassess your priorities, and organize your time and work, and then take things one at a time. You'll be amazed at how involved the Lord wants to be in your daily planning and work, and how specific He will be in His instructions to you. Jesus can relieve the pressure and give you peace of mind in its place.

Hasn't everyone been a prodigal son?

You may be a stray sheep or a prodigal son, but God still loves you and always has hope for you, no matter how far you've strayed.[1]

God's plan for you is not going to fail. You're His child and sooner or later you're going to wake up to that and come running back to the Father's house as fast as you can. Salvation will prove much stronger in its pull than the pull of the mud and the mire of the swine pit on your feet. You'll run back home—back to the joy of the Holy Spirit and back to the food and plenty and warmth and fellowship of the home hearth.

It's never too late. Even if you've squandered your entire inheritance, the Father still loves you and will receive you with open arms. He'll take you to Himself, to His bosom of love, and give you a new garment of righteousness, a beautiful new golden ring of reward that you don't even deserve, and spread a feast of thanksgiving and celebration that this His son, though he were dead, is now alive and home again. Can you hear the Father's voice calling, "Please come home"?

[1] See the parable of the prodigal son in Luke 15:11–32.

You can change the world!

IF SOMETIMES YOU'RE DISCOURAGED with the world and the way it is, don't give up! You can accomplish some real good in this poor, sad, old world by helping people find joy and happiness, salvation and Jesus, and something to live for.

You, personally, can start to change the world by planting the seeds of God's love one by one, in heart by heart, day by day, wherever you may be, and God will cause those seeds to grow. They may seem only like tiny little buds at first, just insignificant little green shoots. What is that to the forest that's needed? Well, it's the beginning of the miracle of new life.

So why not try it? If you have changed one life by the power of God's love, you have changed a part of the world. If one life can be changed, it shows that it's possible for more lives to be changed, and that means the world can be changed—starting with just one person!

And who knows, you may live to see the day when the world *is* changed and was changed, in part, through you—all because you shared the love of God with others!

Warning! Please refer to the Maker's Manual before operating your machine.

ANY THINKING PERSON thoroughly studies the instructions to a valuable piece of equipment before they attempt to operate it. As a result, they save themselves a lot of time and trouble and possible permanent damage to their equipment. But those who are too impatient to read the instruction booklet first, those who think they already know it all, and those who think they can figure it out on their own usually have nothing but trouble.

When God fashioned our bodies, minds, and spirits and then put them all together to make you, He created an amazing but delicate piece of "equipment." You are a marvel of His design, but you won't last long or be very useful unless you take care of your equipment.

That's why your Manufacturer, God, had some men of His write a maker's instruction manual, the Bible, with definite diagrams and clearly stated specifications for the complicated business of living. You could waste an awful lot of time and do an awful lot of damage to yourself and others by not taking time to read the Book first. Don't take chances. Read and follow the Book!

"God will wipe away every tear from their eyes" (Revelation 21:4).

THE BIBLE DOESN'T SAY THERE AREN'T GOING TO BE ANY TEARS IN HEAVEN. When we get to Heaven and face God, we will no doubt all have a few tears to shed for mistakes we made and opportunities we missed. We'll have a few tears when we think about all that we could have done but failed to do—all the unfinished work we left behind and loved ones that we'll wish we'd loved more and been kinder to. We will all have something to be sorry about and ashamed of then.

But isn't God wonderfully loving and merciful? He says He's going to wipe away all those tears. He's going to wipe away all memory of those evil years and then there will be no more pain, death, sorrow, or tears—only wonderful eternal happiness, joy, and paradise forever and ever. He'll make up for all of our mistakes and lacks somehow.

Just a little more sorrow and a little more crying, just a little more pain, and then these things of time shall be no more. We shall forget the sorrows of the past for the glories of the future.

We're gloriously saved, and wonderfully and completely delivered.

WE HAVE BEEN SAVED AS BRANCHES PULLED FROM THE FIRE (Zechariah 3:2), and as wayward lambs snatched from the Enemy's clutches. We should be very thankful! We have come from the darkness into Jesus' glorious light (Matthew 4:16). We who were in darkness have become enlightened (Ephesians 5:8).

The Lord had to break the chains; we couldn't deliver ourselves. He had to purge and purify and cleanse us. We're all clean now, no longer under the power of the Devil. He can't harm us anymore. We're the Lord's possession now, and the Devil can't have us. We're the Lord's *forever*. We have been born again, like a newborn baby, into a whole new world and have been given a clean heart, a pure mind, and a new regenerated spirit.

> The memory of evil years,
> Burned like a flame within my breast.
> And though I sought relief in tears,
> I found it not; I could not rest.
> My yesterday, so dark with shame,
> Christ has forgiven! Oh, praise His name![1]

[1] Author unknown.

"I desire mercy and not sacrifice" (Matthew 9:13).

W‌HEN JESUS SAID HE DESIRED MERCY AND NOT SACRIFICE, He meant He would rather see us have love than a dutiful adherence to the law and performance of duties. He would rather we give love to somebody than to try to be so righteous and perfect.

The drunks and the harlots and the sinners came to Jesus for love and mercy, and He treated them tenderly, kindly. He forgave them and gave them the hope, love, and strength they needed to change for the better. Those sinners didn't go to the harsh, rigid, self-righteous, unyielding, unforgiving, critical, condemning religious leaders who told them to be perfect or go to Hell, but they came to Jesus for His love and mercy, forgiveness, encouragement, and patience.

Love throws a veil over countless sins (1 Peter 4:8). But some people are so self-righteous they think they never make mistakes. Remembering what sinners we are and how many mistakes we've made greatly helps to keep us humble and to avoid that spirit of self-righteous pride that causes us to criticize and condemn others. When you realize that you need a lot of forgiveness and mercy, it really helps you to extend it to others. "Blessed are the merciful, for they shall obtain mercy" (Matthew 5:7)—so be merciful!

Peace on earth will soon be a reality!

GOD'S CHILDREN ARE SUPPOSED TO BE PEACEMAKERS who try to bring peace to men's hearts and minds and spirits and bodies and countries (Matthew 5:9). We'll never have total peace on earth, though, till God gets rid of the evil hearts that make war. But that's exactly what's going to happen, thank God, when Jesus returns soon to "destroy those that destroy the earth" with their wars, waste, wickedness, and wanton destruction (Revelation 11:18).

Then at last shall the men of peace and the God of peace and the Prince of Peace rule and reign and bring peace on earth (Luke 2:14)—peace that will never end, under the righteous reign of Jesus Christ, the Son of God. Then at last there will be no more wars, no more horrible havoc, no more destruction, no more cruel, senseless, diabolical, murderous loss of life, no more suffering, no more dead and dying, no more noise and confusion.

"They shall not hurt nor destroy in all My holy kingdom" (Isaiah 11:9). There will be no evil in God's kingdom on earth— only a heaven-on-earth rule by Jesus and His children.

> There will be love and laughter and peace ever after
> Tomorrow—in God's tomorrow—when the world is free of wars.[1]

[1] Nat Burton, "The White Cliffs of Dover," paraphrased.

God waits for us to be humbled and pray for help.

THE HOLY SPIRIT GENTLY DESCENDS AND CAN BE EASILY SHOOED AWAY. It doesn't land where it's not wanted. God goes where there are open and receptive hearts that are hungry for truth. He seeks the lowly, the humble, and the contrite heart, but He resists the proud. He gives grace to the humble (1 Peter 5:5). So as long as you're calling for help, you can expect God to answer. As long as you're seeking, God will show the way. As long as you're empty, He will fill you (Luke 1:53).

It works the same way as salvation: It's not until you recognize you're a sinner that you're desperate enough to seek salvation. But when you realize that you're a sinner and need forgiveness and help, then you ask God to save you and He answers and comes to your rescue. He says, "And you will seek Me and find Me, when you search for Me with all your heart" (Jeremiah 29:13). When you cry out desperately to Him with a hungry, empty heart, asking Him to fill it, He will.

Jesus doesn't force Himself on anyone. He waits lovingly and meekly for you. God puts the responsibility on *you*. So call on Him for help and He will fulfill His promise to "show you great and mighty things, which you do not know" (Jeremiah 33:3).

Even while the world goes to pieces, God's Word stands firm!

SOMEDAY THE ONLY WORD OF GOD YOU MAY HAVE IS WHAT YOU KNOW BY HEART. That's why it is so important to memorize His Word faithfully, that you may be kept by the power of God and comforted in difficult times, now and in the future.

How firm a foundation, ye saints of the Lord,
Is laid for your faith in His excellent Word!
What more can He say than to you He hath said,
You, who for refuge to Jesus have fled?

Fear not, I am with thee, O be not dismayed,
For I am thy God and will still give thee aid;
I'll strengthen thee and help thee, and cause thee to stand
Upheld by My righteous omnipotent hand.[1]

That's an old hymn, and a wonderful one for these Last Days when you really need to stand on the firm foundation of His Word. "Lo, I am with you alway, even unto the end of the world" (Matthew 28:20 KJV). He's with you in His Word, and His Word is with you, and you can stand firmly on this as a foundation that cannot fail, for He's promised to keep you (Isaiah 41:10; 43:2).

[1] John Rippon, *A Selection of Hymns from the Best Authors*, 1787.

Because we love God, He makes even "bad" things work in our favor.

"ALL THINGS WORK TOGETHER FOR GOOD TO THOSE WHO LOVE GOD" (Romans 8:28). This is His promise to us, and as we learn to hold fast to this simple truth, we will see the promised results.

We need to try to look for the good in every situation, no matter how bad it may first appear. That takes conscious effort and prayer and doesn't come overnight, but it will make all the difference in the world when we are faced with problems and setbacks. On the other hand, if we fail to view our disappointments, hurts, tests, illnesses, and other problems from the perspective that Romans 8:28 gives us, we will tragically miss many of the valuable lessons that the Lord is trying to teach us, and we will rob ourselves of the peace that comes from trusting in this important promise and principle.

"Trials equal good." Understanding and believing this simple equation can make your life richer, more meaningful, and happier. It makes all the difference in the world whether you look at problems and challenges just waiting for the worst to happen, or if you look at them with excitement, waiting to discover all the good the Lord can bring out of them.

God's love is the reason and purpose for all things.

WHY DID GOD MAKE THIS WONDERFUL WORLD FOR YOU TO ENJOY?—So you'd know that He loves you. Why did He want you to know He loves you?—Because He wants you to love Him. God made you to love because He needed someone to love.

What is the whole duty of man?—Solomon says it in Ecclesiastes: "Let us hear the conclusion of the whole matter: Fear God, and keep His commandments: for this is the whole duty of man" (Ecclesiastes 12:13 KJV). But Jesus boiled it down to something even simpler: "Love the Lord your God with all your heart" and "love your neighbor as yourself" (Matthew 22:37–39). Jesus made it a more personal loving relationship between Him and you and others. Instead of "fear God," He said, "love the Lord." Instead of just "keep the commandments," He said, "love your neighbor as yourself." In this is fulfilled "all the Law and the Prophets" (Matthew 22:40).

You'll never be able to enjoy life to the full without Him, because He has created your heart with a vacancy, a hollowness, an emptiness, an aching void that only He can fill. He saved one spot in your heart, the very core of your life, for Himself. He created you to love Him. You're His creation, you're His child, and He wants you!

Every product of genius must be a product of inspiration.

You'll be amazed at what you and the Lord can come up with if you will pray. The Bible says, "If any of you lacks wisdom, let him ask of God, who gives to all liberally and without reproach, and it will be given to him. But let him ask in faith, with no doubting, for he who doubts is like a wave of the sea driven and tossed by the wind. For let not that man suppose that he will receive anything from the Lord" (James 1:5–7). Of course, we always lack wisdom, so we should always ask the Lord!

You can pray and get answers immediately, but if you lean on your own understanding and your own wisdom, you're apt to make some sad mistakes. If you do things in your own strength, relying on your own talents, your own knowledge, or your own supposed wisdom out of pride, it will come to naught. But if you "in all your ways acknowledge Him, He shall direct your paths" (Proverbs 3:6) … "and your thoughts will be established" (Proverbs 16:3).

No matter how small or incapable you are, there's a very big, capable God waiting to help you. So ask the Lord. Lean on the Lord. He's greater than you'll ever be, and if He inspires and guides you, whatever you do will be the greatest.

"According to *your* faith"—not someone else's—"be it unto you" (Matthew 9:29 KJV).

WHEN PETER AND JOHN HEALED THE LAME BEGGAR AT THE GATE OF THE TEMPLE, Peter said, "Look at us"—and immediately the man was healed (Acts 3:1–9). His faith was in *their* faith, and God honored it. But God expects more from those of us who are familiar with the promises in His Word and understand how faith works. He expects us to make direct, personal contact with Him, and to demonstrate our faith by claiming those promises ourselves. He wants us to learn to put our faith in Him alone, and not to depend on someone else's faith or prayers or connection with Him.

There are times, of course, when we should ask others to pray *with* us, but that's different from leaning on their faith. Sometimes we need to avail ourselves of the extra power that comes from united prayer (Matthew 18:19), or to demonstrate our faith by meeting certain conditions He has set down in His Word, such as asking others to pray for our healing (James 5:14–16). God doesn't hear and answer others' prayers more than our own, and the power isn't in the elders' hands—"the *prayer of faith* will save the sick." It's *our* faith that God rewards with the answer, and He does that for us because we have demonstrated that faith by putting feet to our prayers.

We need to understand the difference between the conviction of the Holy Spirit and the condemnation of the Devil.

NOT EVERYTHING THAT GOES WRONG IS NECESSARILY YOUR OWN FAULT or a result of your mistakes and sins, and not all trials are because God is punishing you. Sometimes these things are attacks of the Devil, who is trying to defeat you, trying to belittle, trying to accuse, trying to get you down and discouraged. He tries to convince you that you've made too many mistakes and failed too many times, so you might as well quit.

But God always has hope for you. Even when He has to correct you, He does so in love. His dealings are a proof of His love (Hebrews 12:5–6). He sometimes scolds and applies the rod, but He always adds love's healing balm afterwards to soothe, encourage, comfort, and give you hope of recovery and redemption. His encouragement after His correction is like the sun after a storm.

So don't give up the fight, especially when the Enemy of your soul is doing his best to discourage you and depress you. God will forgive you for past errors, and He can still mightily use you. Simply acknowledge and confess your sin, accept God's forgiveness, and get on with living for His honor and glory.

Our main job is to help God make people rich spiritually.

PART OF OUR DUTY AS CHRISTIANS is to show the world a social gospel, as well as a personal gospel. Jesus Himself nearly always ministered to people's physical needs before He ministered to their minds and hearts and spiritual needs. By His example of kindness, His example of love and concern for the people, they knew that He had something real.

You can't preach the Gospel to a man with a hungry stomach, but the main thing is to preach the Gospel. Visit the sick and the imprisoned, clothe the naked, and feed the hungry, but don't forget to feed their souls most of all.

God's greatest concern is saving their souls, and then He will save their bodies. The greatest thing we can give them is the key to success, the key to good health, the solution to poverty, and that's faith in God that leads to salvation. If they receive Jesus, then they're God's children. Then *He's* responsible to take care of them, and He will. God never fails to care for His own. He's the key to all their needs.

Thank God for tears, which wash our hearts and clear our minds.

THE ANCIENT GREEKS CALLED IT CATHARSIS—an emotional purging or purifying. In Greek tragic dramas, the audience was made to experience intense feelings of sorrow, pity and fear, which according to Aristotle, brought about a purifying of the emotions that turned people to the true values of life. Sorrow was an edifying experience.

Thank God that He and His service are not all sorrow and tragedy, but He does give us a few trials and a few tests and a few hard things to go through to bring out the sweetness and the best in us. Like a giant hand squeezing a honeycomb, God puts the squeeze on us and out comes the honey. Like a beautiful flower that is pressed and crushed, God applies the pressure and out comes the perfume. Like the beautiful music that comes from the throat of a bird—almost as though in pain, yet it comes forth with song. We learn a lot through sorrow, and some of the most precious lessons in life come out of deep dark experiences.

> O Joy that seekest me through pain,
> I cannot close my heart to thee;
> I trace the rainbow through the rain,
> And feel the promise not in vain,
> That morn shall tearless be.[1]

[1] George Matheson (1842–1906).

The world is your parish.

We need to go back to the original plan that Jesus gave His first followers, which they demonstrated in the book of Acts and which He stated so simply: "Go into all the world and preach the Good News to everyone, everywhere" (Mark 16:15 TLB). That and John 3:16 are all we need to know to preach the Gospel.

Jesus alone saves, but He can't save you alone. He wants to save the whole world and some day He will, but He needs you to tell others about His love. He wants you to give His love and message of salvation to your part of "all the world."

If you love Jesus and are serious about pleasing Him, you have a responsibility. He has given you a commission, a job to do for Him, and you need to do it. "Preach the Word; be ready in season and out of season" (2 Timothy 4:2). Love and win souls. Spread the Word. Spread the message. Spread His love.

All He needs is you. The fields are already "white for harvest" (John 4:35), so "pray the Lord of the harvest to send out laborers into His harvest" (Matthew 9:38)—and the first one He will send is *you*.

"Children are a heritage from the Lord" (Psalm 127:3).

ONE OF THE MOST PRECIOUS GIFTS any of us could ever receive is God's love in the form of a little child, so sweet and beautiful. They're all *His* children, really, but He entrusts them to our care and wants us to love and train them. They're a gift of God but, like flowers in our garden, we've got to take care of them. It's a case of God's gift is also God's work.

If we "train up a child in the way he should go ... when he is old he will not depart from it" (Proverbs 22:6). If you will only teach, train, and lead your children right and set the right example, they will carry that all through life. "All your children shall be taught by the Lord, and great shall be the peace of your children" (Isaiah 54:13).

Another wonderful thing about your children is that you're going to have them forever. If you rear them right and do a good job of God's work with God's gift, you will be so thankful when you get to Heaven and see them rewarded for their love for Him and all they did for Him and others—and you will share in their rewards because you helped guide them there.

Why doesn't God put a stop to all the world's atrocities and man's inhumanity to man?

FREE CHOICE IS A BASIC PART OF GOD'S PLAN, from the Garden of Eden to the book of Revelation. He put us here to make choices between good and evil, between doing right or doing wrong, between serving God or ourselves or the Devil.

Free choice also shows what happens if people are allowed to have their own way and go their own way, without God. God didn't stop Adam and Eve when they made the wrong choice in the Garden of Eden, but He did punish them. To see the consequences of our choices and our actions, whether right or wrong, is a great lesson to us and the entire universe. This is why God is now allowing man, by his own hand, to bring the earth from the heaven on earth He created to a state of virtual hell on earth: to demonstrate what a horrible mess results when His creations rebel against Him.

So God has His reasons for allowing the world to get into such a state, and one of the main reasons is to give us a chance to choose. Are *you* choosing God's way, or your own?

The most uncomfortable place for a Christian is a comfortable place.

THE MINUTE YOU COME TO THE CONCLUSION that you have gone as far as you want to go and are satisfied with yourself and what you've accomplished, watch out! The minute you think you've arrived, that's as far as you'll get. God's law of progress is: If you don't keep on getting more, you'll lose what you've got. The minute you think you've attained and you sit down to enjoy it, that's when you lose it. "Therefore let him who thinks he stands take heed lest he fall" (1 Corinthians 10:12). When you come to the point that you just want to stand still, you're finished.

It is impossible to stand still in the Christian life. You are either making progress, going ahead, climbing a little further upward every day, giving more of yourself and accomplishing more, or you are slipping backward and on your way down.

Are you alive and going, or dead and settling? Don't settle down and vegetate and become like the rest of the bumps on the logs. Rise up and live! Move now with the life of God, or you'll be left behind in the death of this world.

Praise God for His faithfulness!

GOD LOVES YOU AND IS CONCERNED ABOUT EVERY LITTLE THING. There's nothing too small for God or too hard for Him. He takes a personal interest in you and wants to help you moment by moment and step by step.

You are His and He loves you and is doing His best for you. Stay close to Him, and He'll never let you down. "If we are faithless, He remains faithful; He cannot deny Himself" (2 Timothy 2:13). He cannot break the promises He has given you in His Word. "He who has begun a good work in you will complete it until the day of Jesus Christ" (Philippians 1:6).

(Prayer:) You've cast my lines in pleasant places, Lord, and given me exceeding abundantly above all that I could ask or think (Psalm 16:6; Ephesians 3:20). Even the little things You do are evidence of Your great love and faithfulness. You're so good to me. In spite of all my shortcomings, sins, mistakes, failures, and weaknesses, You have mercy and take care of me, protect, and supply for me. "Surely goodness and mercy shall follow me all the days of my life" (Psalm 23:6). How good You are to me!

You don't have to know all the answers.

I**T'S IMPOSSIBLE FOR YOU TO SOLVE YOUR PROBLEMS ON YOUR OWN.** You dare not depend on your own wisdom or trying to put two and two together. You must look for the supernatural, miraculous, and powerful leading and guidance of the Holy Spirit. God is the One who has got to lead, because only He can!

Look how the prophet Daniel prayed before he received those mighty revelations of God. In the short book of Daniel—only twelve chapters—two or three chapters recount how Daniel cried desperately to God in prayer. Daniel didn't have the answers, so he had to ask God. In chapter 2, for example, how could Daniel have possibly interpreted King Nebuchadnezzar's dream when Daniel didn't even know what the king had dreamed? God had to reveal the whole thing!

So when you don't know what to do, for God's sake, quit trying to figure things out yourself. Follow God—not yourself, not your own ideas! Ask the Lord. Get down on your prayer bones and get desperate in prayer before God. Ask Him to give you downright, outright, upright revelations—Heaven-right, straight from Him—to show you exactly what to do. Cry out to God and ask God for the solutions you need, and God will never fail.

Anywhere with Jesus we can safely go.

JESUS PROMISES TO BE WITH US "EVEN UNTO THE END OF THE WORLD" (Matthew 28:20 KJV). But before you go anywhere, be sure you pray and find God's will, because only He knows the *best* place for you. Ask Jesus to guide every step, every move, every direction, and He will never fail. He will do His part faster than you can do yours. He will always be ten jumps ahead of you. "When He brings out His own sheep, He goes before them" (John 10:4). He knows what's ahead, and He will lead. All you have to do is follow.

God may give you your choice, but He alone knows what's best, so be sure to seek Him and find that out. Then do your best to follow His leading. Are you ready? Are you able? God will always provide and make a way for you to do His will if you'll obey and do things His way. If Jesus goes with you, you can go *anywhere*.

> If Jesus goes with me, I'll go anywhere!
> 'Tis heaven to me where'er I may be, if He is there!
> I count it a privilege here, His cross to bear,
> If Jesus goes with me, I'll go anywhere![1]

[1] Charles Austin Miles (1868–1946).

If you witness, you always win!

Our NUMBER ONE JOB IS TO PREACH THE
GOSPEL, and our number two job is to try to win those to whom
we preach it. Winning souls is really God's job because He's the
only one that can work in people's hearts, by the Holy Spirit. But
He has to work though us. We have to be His channels, His
instruments. We have to give people the facts—the truth of
God's Word—show them God's love, and bring them to the point
of decision to either receive Jesus or reject Him. That's our part.

Of course, we hope to win people to Christ, but that's really the
work of the Holy Spirit and each one has to make a personal
decision. Even if we don't win the soul, we win the favor of God
by our obedience in witnessing and have done our job.

Witnessing is never wasted. You accomplish your purpose just
by showing the love of God and sharing His Word with others.
What they do with it is their responsibility. "Love never fails"
(1 Corinthians 13:8), so if you're motivated by God's love and
are loving in your presentation, you just can't lose. You're on
God's side, and He just doesn't lose! Eventually He always wins
somehow. Being a witness for Him is a business that cannot fail!

Play the part that God created you to play.

GOD TOLD KING SAUL THAT HE WOULD MAKE HIM ANOTHER MAN (1 Samuel 10:6). God also made David into another man; He turned him into something he wasn't. It's almost like playing a role, but when God has given you a role to play and you can put your heart into it and play it with divine enthusiasm and inspiration, you become that creation of God.

God has His own plan. God has His own ways. God knows what He's doing. So for God's sake find out what He's doing and let Him do it. Find out what He wants you to do and do that. What you don't want to do is miss His best, the thing God most wants you to do, the special place God has for you in His kingdom. If you're willing to be what God wants you to be—not what you are, but what God wants you to be—then He can mightily use you.

Are you willing, not to present your program to God for His signature or to be presented with God's program for your signature, but are you willing to sign a blank sheet of paper and let God fill it in, without your even knowing what His program is going to be?

Do you want a crown?

THE HEAVENLY CROWN THE LORD PROMISES US IS NOT OUR SALVATION. We *have* eternal life through His Son, which is the gift of God (John 3:36; Ephesians 2:8–9). The crown is our reward, given only to those who run and win the race (2 Timothy 4:7–8).

God's Word tells us to endure hardness as good soldiers of Jesus Christ, and to not entangle ourselves in the affairs of this world, that we may please Him who has called us to be soldiers (2 Timothy 2:3–4 KJV). If we fail the Lord, we will lose our reward and another will take the crown that God intended for us (Revelation 3:11).

So watch and pray that you do not enter into temptation that might lead you astray from the straight and narrow way that leads to a crown and great reward. Fight the good fight of faith (1 Timothy 6:12). Keep the faith, finish the course, and win the crown. Keep your eyes on the goal and your hand on the plow (Luke 9:62). "Blessed is the man who perseveres under trial, because when he has stood the test, he will receive the crown of life" (James 1:12 NIV). When this life is over, if what you did was right, you'll shine as the stars forever (Daniel 12:3).

May you invest your talents wisely and reap great reward.

THE PEOPLE WHO LOVE GOD THE MOST, serve Him the most faithfully, and sacrifice the most for Him are going to get the greatest rewards and the greatest blessings, here and now and in Heaven hereafter.

The more you *use* what you have, the more you give, the more God blesses and gives to you. The more you use what you've got, the more God will increase it. "He who sows sparingly will also reap sparingly, and he who sows bountifully will also reap bountifully" (2 Corinthians 9:6). As in the story Jesus told of the man who was given one talent,[1] the man who was given two talents, and the man who was given five: The thing that was important was not that one was given more than the other, but how they each chose to *use* what He had given (Matthew 25:14–30). It's not what you've *got* that determines the outcome, it's what you *do* with what you've got.

So "be steadfast, immovable, always abounding in the work of the Lord, knowing that your labor is not in vain in the Lord" (1 Corinthians 15:58). You will be rewarded!

[1] talent: a quantity of money in Bible times, with approximately the value of one ox.

Just think how much Jesus loves us!

GOD GAVE JESUS AN OPPORTUNITY TO QUIT. Jesus had a choice in the Garden of Gethsemane. He could have chosen to save Himself, but He chose to go ahead and suffer and die for you and me so we could be saved. Think of that! He said, "Father, if it is possible, let this cup of suffering pass from Me; nevertheless, not as I will, but as You will" (Matthew 26:39). Jesus could have taken the easy way out, but He didn't.

"Greater love has no one than this, than to lay down one's life for his friends" (John 15:13). Jesus was that friend. He took our punishment for us. God "made Him who knew no sin to be sin for us, that we might become the righteousness of God in Him" (2 Corinthians 5:21). To make us clean, Jesus had to get dirty. God's Word says He "bore our sins in His own body on the tree [cross]" (1 Peter 2:24).

Jesus even had to let God turn His back on Him. "My God, My God, why have You forsaken Me?" (Mark 15:34). Jesus suffered not only physically, but also spiritually—the death of the unsaved sinner—and was three days and three nights in Hell (Matthew 12:40).

He was willing to go through all that so we could be saved. Imagine!

Heaven is our home.

W E'RE HEADED FOR THE HEAVENLY CITY,
NEW JERUSALEM, which will come down from God out of Heaven
and dwell with men. This is the hope of all ages—that wonderful
crystal-golden city where we shall dwell with God forever. That
will be the thunderous climax of the symphony of God, and is
described in the grand finale of the Bible, the book of Revelation, chapters 21 and 22. Our eternal home will be a place of
such resplendent beauty that it is completely beyond the
imagination of man. "For here we have no continuing city, but
we seek the one to come" (Hebrews 13:14), "whose builder and
maker is God" (Hebrews 11:10).

The most stupendous things that you have never even dreamed
of are already in existence right now, in that wonderful heavenly
city, and our departed friends and loved ones are already there,
enjoying Heaven and all its thrills.

So keep your eyes ahead on the goal, like those in Hebrews 11,
the faith chapter. They were willing to go through all the trials
and tribulations and to be strangers and pilgrims here—people
without a city or country—because they knew they had a
heavenly one coming (Hebrews 11:13–16).

"I'll take the mountain!"

"AND SEEING THE MULTITUDES, Jesus went up on a mountain, and when He was seated His disciples came to Him" (Matthew 5:1). The greatest sermon ever preached, the Sermon on the Mount, was given to a handful of men on a mountain.

Mountain peaks are never crowded. Why?—Because getting there is hard work and dangerous. If you're going to climb a mountain, you have to be willing to brave the elements and really work to get to the top. Only pioneers climb mountains—people who want to go beyond what has already been accomplished. Pioneers must have vision to see what no one else can see, faith to believe things no one else believes, initiative to be the first one to try it, and the courage to see it through!

Sometimes the challenge God sets before you may seem insurmountable, but there are no alps to men and women of faith. So what are you waiting for? Start climbing! It may be a rugged climb, but the view from the summit is worth it—every rocky step of it! Look forward and up to the heights you're soon to attain and views you're soon to thrill to if you keep fighting, climbing, winning, and don't quit!

Your prayers can do mighty things.

ALTHOUGH GOD CAN DO ANYTHING, He has limited Himself to work through you and your prayers.

It's not how long you pray or how much you pray, it's how much you *believe*. Jesus said that if you have faith as a grain of mustard seed, you can move a whole mountain (Matthew 17:20). If you believe, every prayer is heard and answered. But if you don't pray or don't believe, it is not done. An awful lot depends on you. God said to Israel one time that bad things were happening because no man stirred himself to call upon God (Isaiah 64:7).

God leaves a lot up to us and our concern and prayer. If you only cry with half a heart, you only get half an answer. But if you cry with your whole heart, you get a wholehearted strong answer. He says, "You will seek Me and find Me, when you search for Me with all your heart" (Jeremiah 29:13).

When you determine you're going to pray more and then desperately cry out to God—*Boom! Boom! Boom!*—the Holy Spirit goes to work and it probably won't be long before you begin to see some results. God always answers when we stir ourselves to call upon Him with a whole heart. So pray!

God never stops loving you!

WHAT IS GOD LIKE? Some people picture Him as an angry God, some kind of monster with an all-seeing eye, carrying around a big stick, ready to clobber them—a cruel tyrant who is trying to frighten them into Hell. But actually, God is *love* (1 John 4:8). He is a loving God who is trying to love everyone into Heaven. He's so close, so intimate, so personal, so loving, so kind, so tender, so gentle, so concerned—and He's waiting with open arms. The only reason He follows us around is that He's hoping we'll turn around and meet Him with open arms.

God never rejects us or withdraws His love. He always has hope for us no matter how far we've strayed. So if you feel far from God, maybe it's because you haven't opened your heart to receive His love and forgiveness. You need not continue to feel condemned for your mistakes and sins; only be sorry, ask for God's forgiveness, and be forgiven (Isaiah 1:18; 1 John 1:9).

If you will even start going God's way—if you'll just turn toward Him and start trying to find your way Home—the Father will come running toward you and receive you with open arms of love (Luke 15:18–24).

OCTOBER 6

We can enjoy a foretaste of Heaven, here and now!

THOSE OF US WHO KNOW AND LOVE JESUS HAVE A LITTLE BIT OF HEAVEN ALREADY. In spite of all that's going on in the world today, we have peace in our hearts—wonderful peace, glorious peace, sweet peace, a special touch of God's love!

We are already experiencing a little bit of Heaven—heavenly hearts, heavenly homes, heavenly loved ones, and a heavenly work to do for the Lord in bringing the heaven of His love to others. We're already living in the kingdom of God—or rather, the kingdom of God is living in us. Jesus said, "Behold, the kingdom of God is within you" (Luke 17:21). But God's Word also tells us that this is just the earnest of our salvation—just a little sample (Ephesians 1:14). Well, if this is only a sample of what's coming, think what the *full* Heaven is going to be like!

You don't have to wait for Heaven to find out what it's going to be like. You can have Heaven in your heart and your life and your family and your home, right here and right now! Do you? If not, invite Jesus into your heart by receiving Him as your Savior.

When you get filled with the Holy Spirit, you have a much closer relationship with Jesus.

YOU NEED THE INFILLING, OR BAPTISM, OF THE HOLY SPIRIT not only so you'll have the boldness and power to share God's love with others, but also to help you in your personal communication with Jesus.

Jesus promised His disciples that He would send them a comforter, the Holy Spirit, to strengthen, empower, lead, and guide them in their spiritual lives and relationship with Him (John 14:16–18; 16:7,13–14). As long as Jesus was with His disciples bodily, they knew that He loved them and they loved Him. They enjoyed being in His presence and hearing the comforting sound of His voice, yet they didn't really know Him as they were to later in spirit. When the promise of the Holy Spirit was fulfilled on the Day of Pentecost, the disciples found out that even though His body was gone from them, through the Holy Spirit He was with them in greater power than ever before—and not just with them, but *in* them!

Like those first disciples, if you've been filled with the Holy Spirit, you can be closer to Jesus and understand His truth even better than they did when they were with Him physically and watched Him perform miracles, because you have His Spirit *within* you!

There is great power
in united prayer.

SOME PEOPLE ARE SHY ABOUT PRAYING WITH OTHERS, and sometimes they probably think about the passage of Scripture where Jesus said, "When you pray, go into your room, and when you have shut your door, pray to your Father who is in the secret place; and your Father who sees in secret will reward you openly" (Matthew 6:6). Well, there is a time for that, but there is also a time to pray together.

Sometimes it's important that you make your request known not only to God, but also to others. That way, they can join with you in prayer and manifest their faith and confess their dependence on the Lord along with you. Never hesitate to ask for prayer when you need it.

God loves to answer prayer and He *has* to answer when He sees we're united in love and prayer and purpose and mind and heart and spirit. "If two of you agree on earth concerning anything that they ask, it will be done for them by My Father in Heaven. For where two or three are gathered together in My name, I am there in the midst of them" (Matthew 18:19–20). God's dynamics of the spirit really operate amazingly! The Bible says that when God's Spirit empowers us, one can chase one thousand, but two can put ten thousand to flight (Deuteronomy 32:30).

Be like Jesus!

IF YOU HAVE RECEIVED JESUS AS YOUR SAVIOR AND HAVE THE LOVE OF GOD IN YOUR HEART, you're going to be like Jesus. And if you want to know what Jesus is like, read the Gospels.

Jesus went about everywhere doing good (Acts 10:38), striving to lead God's children back to true worship of the Father, His little lambs back into the one and only true fold of the Great Shepherd and the way of simple truth and love and peace, the true kingdom of God. Study the Gospels and see how Jesus did things. Study the master teacher who only taught and lived love and sharing, who came for love and lived in love and died for love that we might live and love forever.

The words of Jesus are the most beautiful, inspired, and encouraging part of the Bible. He was almost always the peacemaker. When people didn't like His message, He didn't force it on them. It was all voluntary, all "whoever desires" (Revelation 22:17). Jesus was patient, loving, kind, sympathetic, and forgiving, always leading and feeding and encouraging and strengthening His little lambs. He was the greatest of all examples of love, humility, and mercy. May Jesus help *us* to be like *Him*.

New Christians need prayer, love, the Word, Jesus, and fellowship.

Whenever you help people be "born again" by leading them to receive Jesus as their Savior, they're your babies. You're responsible for them, and you must not forget to pray for them and help meet their other spiritual needs.

If you neglect them, you're failing God by begetting poor little homeless, starving orphans. Though orphans usually survive, they often have a pretty hard childhood and many of them become bitter against God because nobody loved them.

There are five major things new Christians need: First of all, they need prayer. You need to ask God to help them overcome past problems and progress spiritually (James 5:16). Next they need love. In order to understand God's love, they need to experience His love through you (Ephesians 3:17– 19). Then they need to be fed the milk of God's life-giving Word (1 Peter 2:2). They also need Jesus. Jesus is in them as soon as they're saved, but then they have to get into Jesus (Colossians 2:6–7). And they need fellowship. They need your companionship as well as your love, encouragement, instruction, and prayers (1 John 1:7).

"Do you love Me?" Jesus asks. "Then feed My lambs" (John 21:15).

The Devil can't win for losing!

It is impossible for the Devil to defeat you unless you give in to him. "Jesus who is in you is greater than he who is in the world" (1 John 4:4). Jesus has already defeated the Devil (1 John 3:8). If you keep fighting, the Devil cannot win.

The Bible says, "Resist the Devil, and he will flee from you" (James 4:7). As long as you keep resisting, he'll keep fleeing, but if you stop resisting, he'll use his lies and doubts to try to persuade you to quit. He'll try to persuade you that you're a hopeless case, so you might as well surrender and leave the field to him. "It's no use," he says.

Don't listen to him! Get tough and fight back with the "sword of the Spirit, which is the Word of God" (Ephesians 6:17). Don't let the Devil say "boo" and scare you out of doing what God wants you to do. Stand up and fight, and he will flee from you!

Put your faith in the Lord and His Word, and you're bound to win. Put on the whole armor of God and go on the attack with the truth of God's Word (Ephesians 6:10–18). The victory is already yours. With Jesus on your side, you can't lose for winning as long as you keep fighting!

OCTOBER 12

Get ready for the greatest job in the world!

IF THE WHOLE PURPOSE OF OUR EXISTENCE IS TO GET SAVED, then why doesn't God take us home to Heaven the minute we get saved?—Because we have a job to do, and it's a big one! There are a lot of other people who need to know Jesus.

What then is the most important job in the world?—To tell others about God's love, to show them the love of Jesus. We're here to witness and win souls. His Great Commission to us is, "Go into all the world and preach the Good News to everyone, everywhere" (Mark 16:15 TLB).

Nothing is more important to God than immortal souls, so we should never let anything take the place of our concern for their eternal welfare. The souls that you win to Jesus will be your brothers and sisters in Heaven, and they'll be thankful to you for all eternity because you told them about Jesus and His love.

God allows opposition for a purpose.

If THERE WEREN'T AN OPPONENT, AN OPPOSING SIDE, God's people would never be tried and tested. So God allows Satan to rise up and lead the opposition, to try and test His people.

Opposition tests the faith, determination, and loyalty of those being opposed, to see who's really got it and who hasn't. It also causes those who are undecided about what or who to believe to reach a point of decision.

It's part of God's sifting process to separate the wheat from the chaff, the good grain from the weeds, the sheep from the goats (Matthew 13:24–30; 25:31–33). The true sheep know the voice of the Good Shepherd and follow Him, and they will not follow a stranger (John 10:4–5). They won't listen to or follow the voice of the enemies of truth.

Those who are not willing to suffer and endure opposition for their faith quit and lose by default, but the genuine faithful followers call on God, and God always ultimately defeats the Devil and wins the victory!

"Your patience and faith in all your persecutions and tribulations that you endure … is manifest evidence of the righteous judgment of God, that you may be counted worthy of the kingdom of God, for which you also suffer"
(2 Thessalonians 1:4–5).

John 3:16 was Jesus' part; 1 John 3:16 is ours.

"FOR GOD SO LOVED THE WORLD that He gave His only begotten Son, that whoever believes in Him should not perish but have everlasting life" (John 3:16). Jesus made the way for us to be saved when He climbed Mount Calvary and died alone for the sins of the world. That was a price that He alone could pay for you and me, but He did it!

"By this we know love, because Jesus laid down His life for us. And we also ought to lay down our lives for the brethren" (1 John 3:16). If we are saved and truly love Jesus and others, we're going to want to take others with us. We can't work for our own salvation, but we can work for the salvation of others. These works are not required for our salvation, but they will come as works of love for the Lord. They're a *manifestation* of salvation and your love for Jesus and others. Once we get saved, the most important job each of us has is to give our lives daily in loving concern and care for others. Jesus came to love the world, and He calls us to do likewise in every facet of our lives.

"Do this in remembrance of Me" (1 Corinthians 11:24).

COMMUNION IS A REENACTMENT of the ceremony Jesus conducted for His disciples the night before He was crucified. It's one of the few ceremonies that Jesus went through with them, and the only one He asked His followers to observe until He comes again, in remembrance of Him. He intended for it to be a symbol, a simple illustration that has a number of meanings. It is a remembrance, a thanksgiving, a witness, and a demonstration of unity.

Communion means remembering Him and the sacrifices He made for us—the breaking of His body for our healing (Isaiah 53:5) and the shedding of His blood for our salvation (1 John 1:7). It is a celebration of the salvation of the entire man.

It is a witness to the unsaved who watch, to remind them of what Jesus has done for us and wants to do for them. It's also a time for believers to unite in spirit, renew fellowship, confess sins, make things right, thank Jesus for His sacrifice, obtain healing, and witness to all His goodness. God will bless you as you do what He commanded. "For as often as you eat this bread and drink this cup, you proclaim the Lord's death till He comes" (1 Corinthians 11:26).

The Holy Spirit gives us joy in our labors and glory in our tasks.

IF YOU HAVE THE DIVINE ANOINTING OF THE HOLY SPIRIT, it makes every task wonderful. Anything you do, no matter what it is or how big or small, you can do it in the Spirit. But if you do it in the energy of your own flesh or out of duty to the letter of the law only, it drags you down and leaves you uninspired. "The letter kills, but the Spirit gives life" (2 Corinthians 3:6).

> You've gotta have a *glory* in the thing you do.
> Oh, you've gotta have that somethin'
> That thrills you through and through.
> Cooking taters, washing clothes,
> Or blowin' baby's nose,
> You need that certain somethin'
> That will carry you through![1]

Call it what you like—inspiration, charisma, talent, personality, or the Spirit—you've got to have something that brings you to life and spurs you to action.

Do *you* have the firepower of God's Spirit in all you do? You can!

[1] Author unknown.

If you've been born only once, you'll die twice; but if you've been born twice, you'll die only once!

IF YOU HAVE BEEN BORN TWICE—once when you were born physically and again when you were born of the Spirit by receiving Jesus as your Savior—you will die only once, physically. But if you have only been born once, only physically, you're going to die twice—first the natural physical death and then spiritually, "the second death" (Revelation 20:14).

Jesus' death was far worse than the physical agony that He suffered when He was crucified. He also suffered the spiritual agony of the lost sinner, dying for his sins, without salvation, without God. Only in Jesus' case He wasn't dying for His own sins, He was dying for the sins of the world. He felt the weight of all the sins of a world full of sinners, and He did that so we won't have to go through that horror of dying a sinner's lonely death!

Those who reject Christ's atonement have to suffer for their own sins, but those who receive Jesus now are completely forgiven and completely relieved from the punishment of sin. "For the blood of Jesus Christ cleanses us from all sin" (1 John 1:7).

Turn your natural weakness into spiritual strength.

YOU MAY SOMETIMES FEEL DUMB AND INCAPABLE, but that's not a weakness if it causes you to depend more on Jesus. That attitude will actually be a strength to you, because when you're depending on the Lord and turning to Him for the answers to everything—like you should and like He wants you to—then you'll be strong in Him. That's the strength of weakness—knowing that you need to turn to Jesus for the answers, and faithfully doing that.

Your first reaction should be to pray and ask the Lord about everything. That's the good kind of weakness—the kind that causes you to not be confident that you know what's best, and even when you think you know, you still ask the Lord about it and humbly follow His lead. That's good because then you're letting the Lord work through you to perform His will. You're letting Him have control. You're letting Him make the decisions and do things His way, and that's when your weakness becomes your strength.

You'll never go wrong by continually turning to Jesus in prayer, because the more you ask Him about things, the more He can work through you. The more you feel incapable in yourself, the better off you'll be!

If we don't have Jesus' righteousness, we have nothing.

THOSE WHO ARE SO PROUD of their own success and their own righteousness that they thank God they are "not like other men" (Luke 18:11) tend to look down on others and have no mercy, no compassion, no sympathy. But in God's sight, such self-righteous pride is one of the worst sins of all (Isaiah 64:6).

Some people have to go through a lot before they get humbled, like King David. David probably had a lot of pride and needed to be humbled before God could use him to lead His people, because look at the great things he did before that. As a boy he fought and killed a lion and a bear to protect his father's sheep, and then he killed Goliath, the giant champion of the attacking Philistines, and all Israel hailed him as a great hero (1 Samuel 17:34–37,49; 18:6–7). Apparently David then became proud, lost his fear of God, and committed some awful sins. Worst of all, he became a self-righteous sinner because he covered it up and pretended to be righteous. Finally the judgments of God fell and he lost everything (2 Samuel 11–12). But a marvelous change occurred in him after God humbled him.

We haven't got anybody's righteousness except Jesus', and He's the only One who can give it to us (Philippians 3:9).

Wouldn't it be wonderful if people would simply do what Jesus said to do?

JESUS GAVE US THE KEY TO HAPPINESS AND HARMONY WHEN HE SAID, "Love your neighbor as yourself" (Matthew 22:39). So when people don't treat others with much love, of course they're going to have problems—and they have. In fact, all of the evils in the world today can be traced back to people's lack of love for God and each other. The simple love of God and each other is still God's solution, even in such a highly complex and confused society as ours. If we love God, we can love each other, follow His rules of life, liberty, and the possession of happiness, and all will be well and happy in Him.

So ask God to help you love your neighbors with His love. And remember, "neighbor" doesn't only mean the one that lives next door. Your neighbor is anyone He brings across your path who needs your help.

A little love and understanding and tolerance and sharing could go such a long way in solving the world's problems. In fact, this should be the goal of every Christian: to love God and our neighbor as ourselves. Love will solve all *our* problems too.

You'll never walk alone if you have Jesus in your heart and your hand in His.

I<small>F YOU HAVE</small> J<small>ESUS</small>, you always have company and love. No matter where you are, you are in His hands and He'll take care of you. Jesus is the one possession you'll never have to give up, never have to leave behind, never lose. You can give Him away as much as you like but you'll always have Him. He'll always be near (Matthew 28:20; Hebrews 13:5).

He's always there. It's not Jesus that's not always there; it's we who are sometimes not there. We sometimes run off somewhere else and leave Him way behind. But He never leaves us behind unless we don't follow. It's that simple.

> Walk on through the wind,
> Walk on through the rain,
> Tho' your dreams be tossed and blown,
> Walk on, walk on,
> With hope in your heart,
> And you'll never walk alone.[1]

(Prayer:) Go with us, Lord. That's the best that we can possibly desire—that You go with us every step of the way and that we go with You every step of the way.

---

[1] Oscar Hammerstein II, *Carousel* (1895–1960).

A Christian is not perfect, but he is forgiven.

SOME PEOPLE SEEM TO THINK THAT EVERYONE HAS GOT TO BE GOOD OR BAD, black or white, and there's no gray. But the fact of the matter is that when it comes to our righteousness, there's no such thing as black or white; we're *all* gray. Nobody is all bad, and nobody is perfectly clean and white except by faith in the blood of Christ. Only Jesus is perfect and able to help us, which is why He had to come.

Nobody is ever good enough. We're all fallible, we all make mistakes, we all commit sins, and it's only by the grace of God that we are saved. It's only His love and mercy and His grace and His sacrifice on Calvary that saves us. Nothing else. Nothing!

Thank God salvation doesn't depend on how good we've been or even how good we are now. It only depends on our faith in the mercy and grace of Jesus Christ. In spite of all our sins and shortcomings, failures, mistakes, and unsaintliness, God still loves and forgives us. "He has not dealt with us according to our sins, nor punished us according to our iniquities. ... As far as the east is from the west, so far has He removed our transgressions from us" (Psalm 103:10,12).

"Your kingdom come. Your will be done on earth as it is in Heaven" (Matthew 6:10).

EVERY DAY, millions of Christians all over the world pray, "Your kingdom come. Your will be done on earth, as it is in Heaven," but most of them probably don't really appreciate the tremendous *reality* of that part of the Lord's Prayer, or how literally it is going to be fulfilled.

Jesus told His disciples, "The kingdom of God is within you" (Luke 17:21). This is true for all of us who know and love Jesus; we already have heaven on earth in our hearts. But during the coming thousand-year reign of Christ on earth, the Millennium, He's going to wipe away all this hell on earth and set up His kingdom of peace and righteousness and fairness and justice and goodness and mercy and love. It's not going to be Heaven, but the next best thing—Christ's kingdom on earth. His kingdom won't only be within us then, it will be all around us. And "none of them shall teach his neighbor, and none his brother, saying, 'Know the Lord,' for all shall know Me" (Hebrews 8:11).

> For the darkness shall turn to dawning,
> And the dawning to noonday bright;
> And Christ's great kingdom shall come on earth,
> The kingdom of love and light.[1]

---

[1] Henry Ernest Nichol (1862–1926).

Faith is ...

Faith is hearing the inaudible, seeing the invisible, believing the incredible, and receiving the impossible. Faith is often completely contrary to natural expectation and natural reasoning.

Faith is asking for what you need. Faith is creating a vacuum in your heart for God to fill. Faith is not only believing that God can, but that God will. Faith is the opposite of doubt and fear. Faith is not surprised at the answer. Faith expected it to happen.

Faith is tranquil when it's very stormy. Faith isn't bound by circumstances or conditions. When man says, "Tie up in port," faith says, "Launch out into the deep!" Faith is not passive; it acts out what it believes.

Faith is standing your ground when all others desert. Faith is burning your bridges so you can't turn back. Faith is being willing to pay any price. Faith is doing what God tells you to do today and believing Him for tomorrow. Faith is choosing God in spite of all other possibilities. Faith is standing on God's Word, not your feelings. Faith is being willing to die trusting. That's the kind of faith that works miracles!

Faith is like a muscle that grows strong and supple with exercise. Faith is built by faithful study of God's Word (Romans 10:17).

God's will allows for freedom of choice, within certain limitations.

Gᴏᴅ's ᴡɪʟʟ—what God wants us to do because He knows it will work out best for everyone else involved—is sort of like a tunnel. It confines us and restricts us to a certain area of movement and possibility, while still allowing us to make our own decisions and operate according to our own faith. He keeps us within certain bounds, but where we go in the tunnel, to the left or right, depends a lot on us and our choices. He gives us leeway as long as we stay within the bounds He has set. We are allowed to find our way through the tunnel, but we should be making forward progress with each step, not going backward.

The tunnel always leads in the right direction. It always has a goal, and of course there's always the best, most direct path within the tunnel. When we yield to God and let His choices become our choices, when our primary motive is to please God and do things His way, when we delight ourselves in Him, then we go His direction and stay in the *center* of His will; we stay focused on His guiding light at the end of the tunnel, and really make progress.

"Earth has no sorrow that Heaven cannot heal."[1]

GOD'S WORD IS ALWAYS A COMFORT and the voice of His Spirit is always an encouragement in the hour of greatest trial. The Bible says, "The sufferings of this present time are not worthy to be compared with the glory that shall be revealed in us" (Romans 8:18). When we think about that, it helps us bear some of the things we have to go through now.

"Weeping may endure for a night, but joy comes in the morning" (Psalm 30:5). We need to keep our eyes on Jesus and the end of life's road. "For our light affliction, which is but for a moment, is working for us a far more exceeding and eternal weight of glory" (2 Corinthians 4:17).

God's tomorrow is a beautiful place. We'll be with Jesus and all our loved ones, and "there shall be no more death, nor sorrow, nor crying" (Revelation 21:4). He will wipe away our tears, and the former things shall be forgotten in the glories of the ecstasies of the kingdom to come.

[1] Thomas Moore (1779–1852).

Sometimes we limit God by our little faith.

Because God loves us, He tries to be as good to us as possible. As long as we're doing our best to do what's right and what we're asking Him for is good for us, He will give it to us. "No good thing will He withhold from those who walk uprightly" (Psalm 84:11).

But sometimes, the Bible tells us, we have not because we ask not (James 4:2). So if you really need something, pray it in. Just be careful what you ask God to do for you, because He'll often take you literally; He will take you exactly at your word.

The story is told of a man who prayed, "Lord, I need a car. I'm *desperate* for a car! Please give me a car—*any old car!*"—And that's exactly what he got, a real clunker! So the next time he needed a car he prayed for a *good* one, and he got it!

God is very definite, so be definite with Him. He'll give you what you ask for and what you have the faith for (Matthew 7:7–8; 9:29). God will give you what you have faith for, and you should have faith for what you need. If the need is there, the answer must be there too, so look around and pray it in.

You can't be God's fair-weather friend.

MOST CHRISTIANS CAN HAVE FAITH IN USUAL SITUATIONS and under normal conditions for what they expect God to do. But when everything goes wrong and seems contrary to the Word and the usual, only those with great faith can say with Job, "Though He slay me, yet will I trust Him" (Job 13:15). What Job was saying was, "Even though it seems like God is breaking His own Word with me, even though God kills me contrary to all His promises, I'll *still* trust Him."

If you're only going to be willing to believe and obey God as long as everything goes right, you won't be believing or obeying very much, because a lot of things can seem to go wrong when you're serving the Lord. "Many are the afflictions of the righteous," the Bible tells us, "but the Lord delivers him out of them *all*" (Psalm 34:19).—No matter how many or what they may be. So keep trusting and praising and following God, no matter what.

> Trust in God, however dark your way,
> No matter what hard turns the road may take.
> Hold to His hand until the break of day,
> When in His likeness we shall then awake![1]

[1] Author unknown.

God is pictured in His Son.

NONE OF US CAN REALLY GRASP HOW GREAT GOD OUR FATHER IS. The Bible says that He is so great even the whole universe cannot contain Him. He's so beyond our comprehension that He had to make Someone who could show us His love, Someone who was within our realm, Someone we could see, Someone we could feel, Someone we could experience, Someone who would bring God down to the level of our comprehension, one Man who was like Himself, whom He called His Son.

God stooped to send His Son, Jesus Christ, to be an example of what God Himself is like. Jesus is God's most outstanding means of communication with us, communicating to us His own love by means of His own Son.

Jesus is like the tip of the iceberg, the part we can see. The greatest part of the iceberg, God, is out of sight. Even though we can't see the rest of the iceberg, we can get an idea of what it is like from the part that shows, the part that's in our realm. The Bible says that God is love (1 John 4:8), and we know that is true because of the loving part of Him that we can see in Jesus!

No matter what else you're doing, you can always be praying.

In everything you do, you ought to be praying and looking unto Jesus, the author and finisher of your faith (Hebrews 12:2).

Prayer should be like breathing—just breathing the Holy Spirit all the time. Stay in constant communication with Jesus, constantly thinking about Him and asking Him about whatever it is you're doing, and you will be anointed and Spirit-led in everything you do. If you're praying and asking God for wisdom, He has promised to give it to you (James 1:5).

Jesus can save you a lot of trouble and a lot of time if you'll pray before you start any job. Ask Him to lead you and help you, even if your prayer is just a few words. You can pray in a split second and get the answer back quick, but if you don't take the time to pray, and you lean on your own understanding and your own wisdom, you're apt to make a sad mistake (Proverbs 3:5–7).

So ask Jesus about everything—every undertaking, every problem, every decision—and make sure you're doing what He wants you to do, the way He wants it done.

The Word of God is the foundation of faith.

How do you get faith?—It's a gift of God and is available to anyone who wants it. The problem is, most people don't want it until they need it, and then they suddenly find they don't have the faith they need because they have no background of faith in God's Word, no foundation. After all, how can they have faith in something they know little or nothing about?

As no good building is without a good foundation, there is no solid basis for faith without the Word; faith in God is built on His Word. So if you feel like you're weak in faith, there's a simple cure: God's Word will increase your faith.

Faith comes, it grows, by hearing the Word of God (Romans 10:17). As you faithfully read and study the Word, as you meditate on it and even memorize it, every word will inspire, strengthen, and increase your faith. Fill your mind and heart with positive, encouraging, strengthening, faith-building thoughts from His Word and you'll soon be amazed at the faith you'll have—true faith, the kind that can stand any test, the kind that works miracles, the kind that lasts, built on the solid rock foundation of His truth!

Does your Christianity reach down into your pockets?

KING DAVID ONCE SAID that he would not give to the Lord that which cost him nothing (2 Samuel 24:24). It doesn't really count until it costs you something to give, until you are sacrificing and can say, "The love of Christ compels me" (2 Corinthians 5:14).

Remember the widow who gave her last two mites? When Jesus saw that, He said she had given even more than the rich who had only cast in a little of their abundance. Although a mite was the smallest of all coins—only part of a penny—those two mites were all she had, so the Lord gave her more credit than He did the rich. She gave even more than it seemed she should, and Jesus honored her for it (Mark 12:42–44).

"Give, and it will be given to you" (Luke 6:38). That promise has never failed. That is a law of God, more sure than the law of gravity. You can even give everything you've got and still not hurt because God will bless you for it. If your motive is right, God will bless you for giving by giving you more.

Take one step for Jesus, and He will come through for you.

ARE YOU READING THE WORD? Are you obeying the Word? Are you taking time with Jesus? Are you praying and praising and listening to Him? Are you taking time to love Him, most of all? If you're doing these things, Jesus will never fail you. He *can't* fail you, because He has promised in His Word that if you will meet those conditions, He will bless and care for you.

If you will take these small steps, He will take the bigger steps— the steps that help you overcome obstacles and get you over the mountains of problems you face. But until you take those small steps, He can't take the bigger steps for you. If you just stand there and expect the Lord to do everything without demonstrating any faith or obedience, then you're not going to get very far. He will do what you can't do, but you have to do your part first.

> Take one step for Jesus, and He'll take one for you,
> Then take another step for Jesus; He'll take two for you.
> Then take another step for Jesus; He'll come through for you.
> Then take another step for Jesus; He'll get you over that mountain.

It's never too late for love.

T HE SIMPLE LOVE OF GOD AND EACH OTHER CAN SOLVE ALL OF OUR PROBLEMS. His love is the answer to everything: It saves souls, forgives sins, satisfies hearts, purifies minds, redeems bodies, wins friends, and makes life worth living. It can survive almost any difficulty, difference, weakness, shortcoming, failure, fault, sin, or obstacle. It's the only truth, the only way, and the only peace.

Love even has creative power, because God is love and He is the Creator (1 John 4:8). His love can change wrecks of lives into wonderful, productive, happy, warm, glowing sons and daughters of God. It can do *anything*. Nothing can resist the power of God's love. Whatever it touches it changes. It's so beautiful! There's nothing like it. It can heal every disease and cleanse every stain. It's all-powerful.

Love knows no hours or days. Love is *always*, for love is God and God is always. It's like a stream, a river that just keeps flowing no matter what, because of the dew of Heaven, Jesus.

> Ah, love, you've found me at last
> In my heart is a song!
> I dreamed of love in the past
> I have waited for you so long!
> Oh, love everlasting,
> Now all my dreams will come true.[1]

[1] Paul Francis Webster (1907–1984).

Faithfulness in little things is a great thing.

NEVER BELITTLE ANY TASK THAT THE LORD HAS GIVEN YOU, because even things that may seem little are important to Him. You may think that what you're doing now isn't very important, but you just might be in school for something that's more important than you realize. The Lord tests you first with little things, and the more He finds He can trust you with, the more He gives you. He knows that if you'll do little things diligently, faithfully, and well, then He can trust you with big things. Jesus said, "He that is faithful in what is least is faithful also in much" (Luke 16:10).

Little things are big in God's eyes. God runs the whole world on small things, and He judges us by small things. The world and the entire universe and God's kingdom are made up of small things. Without the small things, none of the big things would be here.

(Prayer:) Help us, Lord, to learn how important the little things are, and help us not to fail in even the least of them. Your Word says, "It is required in stewards, that a man be found faithful" (1 Corinthians 4:2)—full of faith and faithful at their tasks. Help us to be faithful in all things, small and great.

"Be not weary nor faint in your mind" (Hebrews 12:3).

It CAN BE A STRUGGLE TO LIVE. It takes faith and courage and a lot of fight! The trouble with some of us is that we stop trying in trying times. Some people faint in their minds. They give up mentally and they give up spiritually.

But God says, "Men ought always to pray and *not* to faint" (Luke 18:1 KJV), and, "Be not weary in well doing, for in due season ye shall reap if you faint not" (Galatians 6:9).

The will is powerful! "The spirit of a man will sustain him ... but who can bear a broken spirit?" (Proverbs 18:14). Strong faith and a strong will have many times overcome seemingly insurmountable handicaps!

When you're weak and incapable and insufficient, then God has a chance to be strong and capable and sufficient in you. So don't give up too soon; don't get rescued prematurely; don't quit just before the victory. Anything wonderful can happen in that little margin of time when you do not give up, but keep on believing and keep on praying! You'll never be sorry you trusted Him. You'll be glad throughout all eternity that you held on and kept on keeping on for Jesus!

After the darkest night in world history, we are going to have the brightest dawn!

THE FAST APPROACHING NIGHT IS GOING TO BE THE NIGHTMARE OF THE GREAT TRIBULATION, and the day, the coming of Christ.

Things have got to get worse before they can get better, but in spite of the horrors of the growing darkness of this world, we know that it's all going to work out right in the end. The darkest hour is just before dawn!—And the faster it gets worse, the sooner it's going to get better! So keep looking up!

We have to go through a dark place of trials and tribulations, but then we're going to come out into the sunshine on the other side and all these things will be blotted out like an evil dream! One of these days Jesus is going to stop the world and we're going to get off, away from all this worldly confusion and into the peace and the quiet and the beauty and the love and the wonder of that wonderland beyond in heavenly places with Him! Just a little longer, then dawns His glorious morn!

It's wonderful to hear from Heaven yourself.

GOD EXPECTS HIS CHILDREN—those WHO know Him personally and know His will and His Word—to make a direct, personal contact, rather than relying on somebody else's faith or prayers. That's why the most important thing that any Christian can learn—and each new Christian has to learn it himself—is how to follow God and hear from Heaven fresh every day.

You can hear from Heaven every day, and you *should*. Most of what you receive will probably come from Jesus because He is our link with the Father, our Mediator (1 Timothy 2:5). He doesn't always speak in an audible voice. You may just hear that "still small voice" inside of you (1 Kings 19:12), and sometimes He may not even use words. He doesn't have to communicate in words; He can just give you an impression or a picture or an idea.

If you really believe and ask Jesus, you won't be disappointed, and that which you see or hear with the eyes or ears of your spirit, that's the Lord. It will be such a comfort to you! If you really want to hear Him, He'll talk to you. You just have to have faith. Jesus speaks anytime and anywhere, if you believe!

Are you on the spot? Turn around and put God on the spot!

God LOVES TO PRECIPITATE A CRISIS! He sometimes lets things happen to make us pray and believe Him for the answer. He wants us to take a definite step of faith by making specific requests and expecting specific answers. Specific prayer puts both God and us on the spot, but it is also a sign of our faith, which pleases God.

Some people are afraid to ask God for definite answers to prayer for fear they won't get them—and that might be a reflection on their spirituality, or even hurt God's reputation! "What if He doesn't answer prayer? What will people think of our faith and our God?" So they just generalize in order not to be pinned down, in case they don't get an answer.

But God loves to be put on the spot because He knows He'll never fail. He'll never fail as long as we meet the conditions, exercise our faith in prayer, and obey His Word. And when He answers, it will be a testimony to His Word and His faithfulness, as well as to our faith in expecting a specific answer. So tell Him exactly what you need or want done, and He won't fail!

Does your heart break for the world?

CAN YOU REMEMBER WHEN YOU WERE LOST AND LONELY without Jesus and there seemed to be no love, no hope? It ought to break your heart and make you pray and do everything you can to try to reach others with the solution to their loneliness and other problems: Jesus and His love.

You need to hear the heartcry of the world. To love is to weep with them that weep, to suffer with them that suffer, and to feel the agony of heart with them whose hearts are broken. Jesus wept for the multitude. He was weary and yet, when He looked upon the multitude, He had compassion on them. He was sorry for them and felt He had to do something about it; He had to help them (Mark 6:31–34).

(Prayer:) Jesus, make us the blessing You want us to be to all the lonely, hopeless, helpless hearts that need Your love. Your salvation brings the joy and the love and the balm that cleanses and heals every heart. Help us to reach them with Your precious love and the Good News of happiness and love that lasts forever. Break our hearts. Melt us. Make us compassionate. Make us long to help and encourage others, to point them to You so you can lift and heal them. Amen.

Children are a mission field in themselves.

WHAT SO MANY PEOPLE FAIL TO REALIZE is that the world of tomorrow is what the adults of today make it, according to what they choose to give or not give the next generation.

"Let the little children come to Me, and do not forbid them," Jesus said, "for of such is the kingdom of Heaven" (Matthew 19:14). Children are the most sincere people in the world. They're at the age where they're beginning to think seriously about life, and they sincerely want to know and follow the truth. They're at an age of malleability, an age of reaching out, an age of choice, an age of decision. It takes time and patience and understanding and lots of real love to reach them, but this age is actually when most people accept Jesus as their Savior.

"Train up a child in the way he should go," the Bible says, "and when he is old he will not depart from it" (Proverbs 22:6). We need to educate them and inspire them and encourage them, and most of all we need to point them to Jesus and build their faith in God's Word.

> Open the door for the children,
> Tenderly gather them in,
> In from the highways and hedges,
> In from the fields of sin.[1]

---

[1] E.O. Excell (1851–1905) and Mary A. Kidder (1820–1905).

Jesus renounced His citizenship in Heaven.

THOUGH JESUS WAS RICH, for our sakes He became poor, that we through His poverty might become rich. Jesus not only had to come down and live amongst us, but He had to be one of us. He had to become a member of the human community.

He came as a meek and quiet, weak and helpless baby. He not only adapted Himself to our bodily form, but also conformed to the human ways of life. He was human. He got tired. He got hungry. He got weary. He was subject to all these things, even as we are, yet without sin, that He might have compassion upon us, know how we feel, know when we're footsore and weary, know when we've had enough.

God sent Jesus to become a human being in order that He might better reach us with His Father's love, communicate with us on the lowly level of our own human understanding, and have more mercy and patience with us than God Himself. Think of that!

"He knows our frame; He remembers that we are dust" (Psalm 103:14), having worn that frame Himself, suffering in it, and dying in it for our sakes. He came down here to our level that He might take us with Him back up to His. What a miracle—all for our sakes!

"Christ in you, the hope of glory" (Colossians 1:27).

CHRISTIAN DENOMINATIONS HAVE VARIOUS DOCTRINES ABOUT GETTING THE VICTORY. Some say that everybody's got a "good" self and a "bad" self, and the only way to get the victory is to get the good self on top of the bad self and hold him down. They call it "the doctrine of suppression."

Others preach the doctrine of eradication: Yes, you've got a good self and a bad self, and the only way to get the victory is to have the bad self cut out, and throw it away like a cancer. "Now I'm *all* good!" Self-righteous and holier-than-thou is what they really are!

The true doctrine of the Holy Spirit is neither one! You will never get the victory by holding down that bad self or resisting that temptation or weakness in your own strength. Neither will you ever get the victory by thinking that you can have God cut out the bad self once and for all and leave only the good self. There is no such thing as *good* self! Even the apostle Paul said, "I know that in me (that is, in my flesh) nothing good dwells" (Romans 7:18).

True victory is not found in ourselves, but in Himself—Jesus. "Thanks be to God, who gives us the victory through our Lord Jesus Christ" (1 Corinthians 15:57). Only Jesus is good enough, but He's good enough for us all!

Why does God allow wars?

"**I**F THERE IS AN ALL-POWERFUL GOD BEHIND THE SCENES,**"** people often ask, "why would He allow such horrible wars? Why doesn't He put a stop to all that if He's in control?"

Although God hates war and its bloodthirsty perpetrators and *is* soon going to intervene, He hasn't yet because in so doing He would have had to put a stop to one of the basic aspects of His great design: man's choice.

Man brings all this evil upon himself through his own sins. He dies by his own hand because of his refusal to receive the truth, follow God, and obey His Word (James 4:1–3). If enough people would turn to the Lord, repent, and ask for His forgiveness, He would lift the curse and there would be no more wars—but they won't! So He has to let the wars come. He has to let man bring all these horrors upon himself, to show what a mess mankind is without Him.

"Blessed are the peacemakers: for they shall be called the children of God" (Matthew 5:9 KJV). Join the peacemakers and help bring peace to the hearts, minds, and souls of men through the Prince of Peace, Jesus, who will soon take over and set things right!

Thank God for the oil of His Spirit that makes everything run smoothly and quietly, without friction.

Hardly anything mechanical in this world can function well without some kind of oil or lubrication. Where moving parts rub together, they create friction. Friction creates heat, heat creates fire, and fire causes parts of the machine to burn up, consume. But oil that's poured on parts of a mechanism that are squeaking makes those parts run quietly and smoothly, without complaint.

Our spirits, like machinery, need cleaning and oiling. If we didn't have the oil of the Holy Spirit, we would get rusty and break down or overheat from the friction, seize up, and come to a dead stop. Without proper maintenance and lubrication, there would soon be no useful motion and we'd be fit only for the junk pile.

But thank God, His Holy Spirit oils everything—our heads, our hearts, our spirits, our tongues, and even our feet so we'll go and preach the Gospel. He pours in the Holy Spirit, fills us from top to bottom, and covers every part. Instead of growling and howling, our machine hums with love, joy, peace, longsuffering, gentleness, goodness, faith, meekness, temperance, and other good things (Galatians 5:22–23).

"Unless you ... become as little children, you will by no means enter the kingdom of Heaven" (Matthew 18:3).

IT PAYS TO BE AS A LITTLE CHILD. In fact, Jesus said, "Let the little children come to Me, and do not forbid them; for of such is the kingdom of God" (Mark 10:14). We're to be like little children—loving, sweet, simple believers, in childlike faith believing and receiving all that the Lord has for us.

Children are samples of the citizenry of Heaven, like little angels dropped from the sky. They're so fresh from Heaven that they understand prayer and other spiritual matters better than most adults. They talk to God and He talks to them. It's that simple. They have no problem at all getting His ear with their pure, simple, childlike faith. It is given to children to be rich in faith. Faith just comes naturally to them. They have faith to believe anything God says, and with them nothing is impossible.

The problem with many grown-ups is that they know too much. They've been educated out of their childlike faith. But there are others of trusting childlike faith who are daily doing things that doubting intellectuals say can't be done. So be like a little child, and anything wonderful can happen!

The world has abandoned faith in God for the teaching of evolution, and the result is total chaos.

By ABANDONING GOD, the Bible, and Christianity and putting nothing in its place except the animalistic religion of evolution, the world is plunging itself into total anarchy and total confusion. There cannot be any kind of order without some moral basis, a code of conduct, a sense of right and wrong, good and evil.

The logic of evolution is, if you're just a beast, then live like one. After all, if there's no planner, then there's no plan. If there's no ruler, then there are no rules. If there's no judge, then there's no judgment. If there's no God, then there's no right or wrong. If life is only "the survival of the fittest," then there are no crimes (Romans 1:28).

To abandon the Ruler, God, they had to throw away all the rules, and the result is total anarchy. To abandon the One who gives the orders, they had to abandon order, and the result is total chaos. To get rid of God, they had to get rid of the absolutes, the right and the wrong, the meaning and the reason for things, and the result is total insanity, madness, that has the world hell-bent for destruction! "They sow the wind, and reap the whirlwind" (Hosea 8:7).

God will use everything you've got, if you'll let Him.

" THE GIFTS AND THE CALLING OF GOD ARE IRREVOCABLE" (Romans 11:29). God doesn't change His mind when He passes out the talents. He knows who to give them to, and since God was preparing you for His service even before you were saved, He's undoubtedly going to use every talent He's given you sooner or later if you'll be patient and faithful.

God needs you and would surely like to use you to help other people. There's much work to be done, and God needs every ounce of talent that you've got. You would be wise to ask God what He wants you to do. Size up the situation: "This is my calling, but not that. These are my talents, but not those. This is what God wants me to do—this, but not that." Don't miss the blessings God has in store for you by missing the job He's gifted you for. Invest your talents wisely and well, and you will reap great reward.

(Prayer:) Lord, You know what's best. Show me Your place for me, the job and place in Your kingdom for which I'm best suited, and then give me the faith and courage and determination to *do* it.

"Those that seek Me early shall find Me" (Proverbs 8:17 KJV).

You ought to try a little prayer time every day, early in the morning before beginning your day's work, asking Jesus to help you, lead you, and guide you. When you first wake up, before you do anything else, talk to Jesus. Get your orders from Him for the day. You'll be amazed at how He'll solve a lot of your problems before the day even starts, if you will simply listen to what He has to say.

But if you go plunging into your day's work without stopping to talk to Jesus and get your directions from Him, you'll be like a musician who decided to have his concert first and then tune his instrument. Begin the day with the Word of God and prayer, and get in harmony with Him first of all.

Don't ever think that it's too hard to pray or you haven't got time to pray. The busier your day, the more reason you have to pray and the longer you ought to pray. If you'll just spend a little more time praying, you will find that you'll spend a lot less time working to get things done later. If your day is hemmed with prayer, it is less likely to unravel. It's just that simple!

"He will reward every man according to his works"
(Matthew 16:27).

W E CAN'T EARN OR WORK FOR SALVATION; IT'S A GIFT. But we *can* earn special praise and special commendation from the Lord and we can work for rewards. God is no respecter of persons when it comes to salvation (Acts 10:34), but when it comes to works and accomplishing something for Him and His kingdom, He is a great respecter of persons.

Heaven is not going to be a classless society. In Heaven, there will be all kinds of grades and levels of reward, just like there will be all kinds of grades and levels of punishment for the unsaved. Each person will shine with a different glory, depending on how much they did for the Lord. Some of the Christian heroes of the faith who were living saints in giving their lives in love so others could be saved will be where they deserve to be, at the top, near the Lord's court. But some Christians who ignored His call to service and lived selfishly all their lives will be rewarded poorly.

Are you accomplishing all you can for God? Will He say to you, "Well done, good and faithful servant; you were faithful over a few things, I will make you ruler over many things. Enter into the joy of your Lord"? (Matthew 25:21).

The safest place in the world is in the center of God's will.

No matter where you are, or how you are, or what you are, or what's against you, God will keep you safe if you are in the center of His will. It's a charmed circle where you live a charmed life. "The name of the Lord is a strong tower; the righteous run to it and are safe" (Proverbs 18:10). "He who dwells in the secret place of the Most High shall abide under the shadow of the Almighty" (Psalm 91:1).

Don't run outside that circle of God's will and protection, or God may allow Satan to give you problems. We can suffer sometimes for our sins of carelessness, prayerlessness, haste, and disobedience to the Lord. God is bound by His own rules and laws, and He can't protect you when you violate the rules. When you're out of His will, He may even allow you to fall prey to the snares of the Devil.

(Prayer:) Help us to stay close to You, Lord, in the center of Your will. Then we know we have nothing to fear because we're also in the center of Your provision and protection and blessing, and can trust You utterly because we know we're being obedient and doing Your will. Amen.

"One's life does not consist in the abundance of the things he possesses" (Luke 12:15).

LIVING, THE REAL THING, doesn't consist of things at all, because things cannot truly satisfy. They may temporarily satisfy the body, but they can never satisfy the soul or the spirit of man that cries out to God its Father for the joy and happiness and eternal fulfillment that only He can give.

If you think that things will ever satisfy you, look at the unsaved rich. They've got everything, yet something's missing; the things of this world will never satisfy their souls. It can satisfy their bodies, but not their hearts. And when they do satisfy their flesh, they're not happy for very long, because the flesh can never get enough. The more they get, the more they want, because this world doesn't satisfy the needs of the spirit. Only God can do that.

"Life," Jesus says, "is more than things." It doesn't really matter how few or how many things you have. It's what's inside that really counts—love and joy and true happiness in your heart, and peace of mind. The greatest of all riches are yours for the asking. The most valuable thing you can possibly have is Jesus, and He's the key to all the rest (Romans 8:32).

The way to be happy is to make others happy.

ALL OF US HAVE BEEN GUILTY OF GETTING DOWN IN THE DUMPS. It's a terrible state to be in, especially because we can never be down in the dumps alone. We always drag somebody down with us. We can't keep our problems and our draggy spirits to ourselves. Others can just take one look at us and know that we're in the dumps. We can't hide a bad spirit that radiates gloom and doom any more than we can hide a good spirit that radiates happiness and light.

When we're down in the dumps, we want everybody to be miserable with us; we want everybody to sympathize and be sad with us. That's human nature. But it's *godly* nature to try to encourage and cheer up others, even when we need cheering up ourselves.

Happiness is what you make it. It's a spiritual law of God, just as sure as the law of gravity, that we don't get happy by trying to make ourselves happy or by trying to get somebody else to make us happy. We don't find happiness by chasing it. We get happiness by trying to give it to *other* people. If we go around trying to make others happy, then happiness will find us. Sooner or later it will catch up with us, and we'll find we're happy too.

God waits for you to command the situation.

You're in God's hands, but in a way He's also in yours. If you're doing your best to obey Him and be in His will, and desiring those things that please and glorify Him; if you're doing the right thing, love Him, and have faith in His Word, then He's already promised to answer prayer (Psalm 37:4; 84:11; Matthew 7:7–8; John 15:7).

So much of what God does depends on what and how you pray. He has limited Himself and His operations to your faith and your requests. "You do not have, because you do not ask" (James 4:2). He's just waiting on you to command the situation.

God's overall plan has never changed, but in certain details you can change His mind, otherwise there would never be any point in praying. If prayer doesn't change things, why pray? Prayer moves the hand and heart of God. He enjoys using us. He enjoys putting the majesty and the power of His omnipotence in the hands of frail men and women. So pray!

Who do you trust for your salvation—yourself or God?

MANY PEOPLE ASK, "How can you say that *you* have the truth? There are hundreds and hundreds of religions in the world and all of them think that theirs is the only right one. Who's to say which of them is the right one?" Well, people are wrong about there being hundreds of religions. Actually there are really only two. Granted, within these two religions there are many different sects and differences of opinion, but there are, in fact, only two.

One religion consists of all faiths that believe that they can earn their own salvation by doing good deeds and keeping various religious laws and commandments. This comprises most of the faiths of the world. The other religion consists of those who know they are incapable of saving themselves and look to God alone to save them. It all comes down to one simple question: Do you think you can save yourself by earning your salvation by being good, or do you realize that you need a Savior to rescue you from your sins and shortcomings? If you know you need help from above to make it, then Jesus is for you.

> My hope is built on nothing less,
> Than Jesus' blood and righteousness.
> On Christ the solid Rock I stand,
> All other ground is sinking sand.[1]

[1] Edward Mote (1797–1874).

We owe Jesus everything.

JESUS WAS WILLING TO DIE FOR US TO SAVE US, and He wants us to be willing to sacrifice to help Him save others (1 John 3:16). He bought and paid for us with His own blood. We're His property; we belong to Him now. Jesus saved our souls for eternity, so of course we should do what He asks of us, which is to try to win as many others as we can.

Jesus didn't go halfway to the cross for us, or almost all the way; He went all the way and gave His whole life for us. The main job He came to do was to die on that cross, and so the main job we've got to do is to bear *our* cross. He said, "If anyone desires to come after Me, let him deny himself, and take up his cross daily, and follow Me. For whoever desires to save his life will lose it, but whoever loses his life for My sake will save it" (Luke 9:23–24).

We can only find the fullness of faith that we seek in the path of complete obedience, when we're really willing to take up our cross and deny ourselves, yielding our pride and our will to follow Jesus. Then He will give us the power to follow as we surrender to Him.

God's will for you is what He made you for.

BELIEVE IT OR NOT, God has a special and unique calling for you—something that only you can do. He is the One who designs both the jobs and the tools to get those jobs done. He knows what kind of tool you are. He knows which job you're best suited for and what He wants to use you for, so you'd better do what He knows you can do best. Find the job that God has gifted you for, and then stick to it.

If everybody would only be willing and satisfied to fulfill their calling and not want any more or any less, God could greatly use them and make them very happy. But we sometimes make ourselves unhappy by being dissatisfied with what God has given us to do for Him because we haven't learned, as the apostle Paul did, to be content in whatever state we're in (Philippians 4:11). We all need to learn to be satisfied and thankful for the place and ministry God has given us.

"Make your calling and election sure. For if you do these things, you will never fall" (2 Peter 1:10 NIV).

God loves us with a perfect love.

IT'S A DIFFICULT THING, trying to describe God's love. Human words and expressions fall short. It's remarkable, astonishing! I'd say it's unbelievable, but I do believe it because I've seen it and experienced it.

God doesn't love us because of who we are, or because of our accomplishments. He doesn't even love us because we love Him. He just loves us because He loves us! He made us, He knows everything about us, and yet He loves us so!

If people could just understand the magnitude of the Lord's love, how truly unconditional it is, how vast and deep and wide and unending it is, it would solve so many of their problems. They would find freedom from so many of their fears and worries and condemnation. When we are secure in His love, we know that He is going to cause everything to work together for our good, because He is in control of every detail and His hand on our lives is so perfectly loving.

It's sad when people don't realize or believe how much God loves them. They miss that wonderful strength, comfort, peace, and whole different perspective on life that they would have if they would only believe His love, accept it by faith, and love Him in return.

One of Satan's favorite wiles is "wait awhile!"

PROCRASTINATION IS THE DEVIL'S OWN TOOL to get people to put things off until later. It's one of his cleverest weapons. If he sees he can't stop us, he tries to delay us. If he can't discourage us from doing something, he just gets us to postpone it. "All that is necessary for the triumph of evil is that good men do nothing."[1]

We need to remind ourselves constantly that the most precious thing we have outside of our souls is our time. Time wasted is gone forever, and though it is easy to waste, it can be pretty expensive. Time well spent may cost a lot in effort and strength and sacrifice and love, but it pays eternal dividends.

If you put off the job the Lord has given you until everything else is done, it will never get done, because everything else is never done.

> The clock of life is wound but once,
> And no man has the power
> To tell just where the hands will stop,
> At late or early hour.
> The present only is our own,
> Live, love and toil with a will;
> Place no faith in "tomorrow"—
> For the clock may then be still.[2]

[1] Edmund Burke (1729–1797).
[2] Robert H. Smith (1879–1950).

Why does God allow evil in the world?

GOD'S WHOLE CREATION IS THE STRUGGLE BETWEEN GOOD AND EVIL, and He did that for a reason: to show the difference. If there was no darkness, we wouldn't appreciate the light. If we didn't have the Devil, we wouldn't appreciate God and Jesus. There has to be evil in order to understand good.

In the Garden of Eden, God had to let Adam and Eve eat the fruit of the tree of the knowledge of good and evil so they would know the difference. They already had all the *good* but may not have understood what good was or *how* good it was, because they didn't have anything to compare it with; it was all good. They never really appreciated the Garden until they lost it.

There has to be a little evil and a little bad to help us appreciate the good things. If we didn't have a few troubles, we wouldn't thank God for all the good things. If we didn't have problems, we wouldn't appreciate the solutions He gives us. God allows the bad things to help us be more thankful when things are good, and especially to help us appreciate *Him*—the good of all goods!

Be an instant Christian.

WE HAVE AN INSTANT SALVATION. Anyone can receive Jesus right this instant, right this second, and be instantly saved. And then they can instantly start to witness and instantly start obeying Jesus. They don't have to wait; they can do it right that instant!

"Preach the Word! Be ready in season and out of season" (2 Timothy 4:2)—but better *in* season. Try to avoid that out of season business! Instantly obey, instantly witness, continue instant in prayer, and instantly serve the Lord every instant (Romans 12:12 KJV). Be always busy witnessing and always preaching the Gospel and leading others to Jesus, always showing Jesus' love wherever you go, wherever you are. Love and serve the Lord with all your heart, all your strength, all your mind, everything you've got, right up to the instant that Jesus returns to whisk you away to Heaven in an instant, in a twinkling of an eye. Then in an instant, with one sudden, supernatural, miraculous, mighty wave of His wand of power—presto! You and all the others who belong to Jesus will be instantly changed and raised to be with Him forever (1 Corinthians 15:52).

Constant spiritual victory
means constant battle.

OUR PRESENT LIVES FOR THE LORD are not something about which we can ever say, "I've won the war! Now I can settle down and enjoy life," because there are some battles we will have to keep fighting our whole lives, until our dying day.

It's a battle every day—especially with our besetting sins that so easily ensnare us (Hebrews 12:1). Some people seem to think they can get the victory over a particular weakness once and for all, and that they'll never have another battle with that. In reality, we can expect the Devil to test us the most on our weak spot, our Achilles heel, our besetting sin, our greatest temptation. But Jesus always has the victory for us if we'll keep going to Him for help. He says, "My grace is sufficient for you, for My strength is made perfect in weakness" (2 Corinthians 12:9).

It's thrilling to look back and see our own progress—to look back down that rugged mountain road we've just come over and to see we're really getting somewhere—but it's even more exciting to look forward and up to heights we're soon to attain and views we're soon to thrill to if we keep fighting, climbing, winning, and don't quit!

DECEMBER 2

"To obey is better than sacrifice" (1 Samuel 15:22).

A LOT OF PEOPLE TRY TO GO AHEAD IN THEIR OWN STRENGTH and their own wisdom and do what they think is God's will and God's work, but we can't *serve* God unless we *obey* God. We can't just do what we think is right, no matter how good it might be. Our best isn't good enough; it takes God to really do the job right. Our best, your own human strength or supposed wisdom, is not sufficient.

Do exactly what the Lord tells you—no more and no less. King Saul thought he could do better than that, and he lost his job. He had God's anointing and blessing as long as he obeyed and waited on the Lord, but when he started going his own way and disobeying, he lost it (1 Samuel 15:1–23).

There's no "little" disobedience to God. Any disobedience is a big one. Nothing short of right is right. It's either all or nothing at all with God. You're either obedient or disobedient. God's Word says, "Whoever therefore breaks one of the least of these commandments, and teaches men so, shall be called least in the kingdom of Heaven" (Matthew 5:19).

Wait and obey. That's one of the most valuable lessons you can ever learn about serving the Lord!

337

Why should certain prayers take longer to be answered than others?

GOD ALWAYS ANSWERS OUR PRAYERS, but not always right away or in just the way we expect Him to. Sometimes He says "yes," sometimes He says "no," and sometimes He says "wait."

When we pray for others, there are a number of factors that affect the whole process, including our will and our condition, God and His will, and the condition of those for whom we are praying. We don't control the outcome of our prayers completely, others don't control it completely, and God has specifically limited Himself not to control it completely, which is, of course, one reason why we don't always get the answer right away. The trouble may be with us, or it may not be God's time to act or move, or the trouble may be at the other end, with those for whom we are praying. But when the conditions are ready for the result God knows is best, He *will* answer.

When God doesn't grant our request right away, it tests our faith and draws us closer to Him, but His delays are not denials (James 1:3). Never doubt for a moment that God is going to come through, and He will—He has to. Trust Him, and thank Him for answering your prayer, even if you don't see that answer immediately.

Pride doesn't pay.

THERE IS NO ASPECT OF GOD'S WORK WHERE PRIDE PAYS. In fact, the biggest failures in the Bible were the supposed big shots that thought they could do things in their own strength or natural wisdom, and fell flat on their faces. Samuel told Saul, "When you were little in your own eyes, were you not head of the tribes of Israel? And did not the Lord anoint you king over Israel?" (1 Samuel 15:17). But when Saul became proud and started depending on his own wisdom and his own arm of flesh instead of the Lord, the Lord had to abase him.

"Pride goes before destruction, and a haughty spirit before a fall" (Proverbs 16:18). Success often precedes failure, because if we let that success go to our heads, we're setting ourselves up for humiliation.

(Prayer:) Deliver us, Jesus, from the spirit of pride that causes us to think that we are something great when we're not (Galatians 6:3). If we would only remind ourselves how nothing we are without You, we'd never entertain the sort of thoughts that lead to that spirit. Help us not to strive to be big shots that have too big a shot of our own egos, but rather to have a good shot of You and the Holy Spirit. Keep us close to You, Jesus, in that sweet place of humble serenity and surrender in Your arms. Amen.

God will confirm His Word and your witness with wonders!

GOD IS STILL THE GOD OF MIRACLES, and what He's done before He can do again if you need it and have faith for it. "Jesus Christ is the same yesterday, today, and forever" (Hebrews 13:8).

Do you know what the word "miracle" means? It comes from the Latin word *miraculum*, "object of wonder," which comes from *mirari*, "to wonder at," which comes from *mirus*, "wonderful." The purpose of miracles is to attract attention to the message. God often performs miraculous healings and other miracles to publicize His message.

When Peter and John met the lame man at the Temple gate, God picked somebody that everybody in town knew had been lame since birth. Peter and John prayed in the name of Jesus for the man to be healed, and he was—and all who saw or heard of it were filled with wonder. They wondered what was going on, and Peter was ready to tell them. He took advantage of the opportunity to preach the Gospel, and over 5,000 people received Jesus (Acts chapter 3; 4:4).

As long as the love of Christ compels you (2 Corinthians 5:14), as long as that's your motivation, then God will inspire you and confirm your witness with signs and wonders and miracles (Mark 16:17–18,20).

DECEMBER 6

"We have this treasure in earthen vessels, that the excellence of the power may be of God and not of us" (2 Corinthians 4:7).

BEFORE I WAS FILLED WITH THE HOLY SPIRIT, I was so very shy and timid that I could hardly do anything. But when I was 19 years old, I prayed very earnestly and asked God to fill me with His Holy Spirit. Immediately I had new boldness—a sort of fearlessness, a God-given courage. It no longer mattered to me what others thought about me, as long as I knew I was right and doing the right things and saying the right things. As long as I knew I was in the will of God and doing what He wanted me to do, then the Spirit of God gave me this boldness. I didn't care about myself anymore. *I* just didn't matter! I was no longer self-conscious; I was *Christ*-conscious.

When the disciples were filled with the Holy Spirit on the Day of Pentecost, they boldly preached to the people (Acts chapter 2). Peter had been so afraid when Jesus was under arrest that he denied Him three times. But right after being filled with the Holy Spirit, Peter preached fearlessly to the multitudes. Peter's transformation showed that whatever got accomplished wasn't due to any greatness of his own, but because the power of Christ was in him.

341

"When the enemy comes in like a flood, the Spirit of the Lord will lift up a standard against him" (Isaiah 59:19).

SOMETIMES LIVING FOR THE LORD IS A REAL FIGHT, but the Devil can't prevail against you if you resist him with the Word of God. The Bible is God's standard, like a banner or flag that we can wave in front of the Devil's sharp pointed nose to make him flee (James 4:7). He can't take the Word.

When the Devil tempts you, what's the first thing you should do?—Ask the Lord for a Scripture to answer the Devil's lie. That's what Jesus did. He just quoted the Scriptures. Of course, the Devil also tried quoting Scripture to Jesus, but he twisted them and took them out of context. So Jesus just fired Scriptures back at him the way they *should* have been applied: "It is *written*" (Luke 4:1–13). And the Devil fled!

The best way to stop an attack is to counterattack. The best defense is an offense. Wage a militant warfare against the Devil. Pray. Memorize and quote God's promises to the Devil, as well as to yourself, to bolster your faith. Put the Devil out of action with the Word. Bury him in a flood of the truth!

When we see God's glorious creation, we know everything is under His perfect control.

THE HEAVENLY SPHERES THAT GOD MADE OPERATE WITH PERFECT PRECISION, like the wheels of a great clock. They have moved in their courses, virtually unchanged in direction or speed, for thousands of years since God first created them. There's not a thing out of time or out of sync or off its bearings in any way, and all of that is going to endure as long as His throne, which is forever (Psalm 89:36–37).

Think of what marvelous control systems God must be using to control the universe and everything in it, material and spiritual. It all operates within certain limitations set by God and is controlled by His Spirit and marvelous spiritual controls that guide and influence the Earth and the Sun and the Moon, the other planets of our solar system, the other stars of the Milky Way galaxy and their planetary systems, and the entire universe.

So why should we worry when God's creation keeps right on going? It just faithfully goes about doing what God created it to do, never questioning, never worrying, and never faltering, knowing that God is in complete control.

You have to follow God to find out what to do.

GOD HAS ALREADY TOLD US THE BASICS OF WHAT HE WANTS US TO DO: love Him and love our neighbor as ourselves (Matthew 22:37–39), and "preach the Good News to everyone, everywhere" (Mark 16:15 TLB). But if you don't know where to start or how to do it, just get started right where you are and He will lead you. If you obey what you know God wants you to do, then He will show you what to do next; and when you obey that, He'll give you a little more. Step by step as you follow Him, He will show you more and more. But if you don't go, He can't show. If you don't obey, He can't make a way.

Follow God as though everything depends on Him, which it does! Do what the Holy Spirit leads you to and you'll stay on the right track, know where you're going, and get there.

> He leadeth me. O blessed thought!
> O words with heavenly comfort fraught!
> Whatever I do, wherever I be,
> 'Tis God's hand that leadeth me![1]

(Prayer:) Lord, please help us to follow closely, moment by moment. Help us to obey the leadings of Your Holy Spirit in every step we make, because if we do that, we'll never go wrong. Amen.

[1] Joseph H. Gilmore (1834–1918).

Hold on!

SOMETIMES WE QUESTION GOD about why He puts us through the trials and breakings He does. Well, there are some things that God can't reveal to us in advance because we're not yet ready. He's got to let us go through them without our knowing why or what the future holds, to see if we'll turn to Him and depend on Him, to see how loyal and faithful we are, to see how spiritually strong we are, to see if we will be willing to do whatever He asks. If He told us the end from the beginning, that would be too easy—like giving you the answers to a test in advance. That wouldn't be a test.

Although it hurts Him to see us suffer, He loves to watch us make it in spite of all the tests and trials. He loves to watch us run and win the race, endure the affliction, and fight through to victory.

If you can stand and pass the test, God will probably use you for something greater than you've done before. In fact, that's one of His main reasons for allowing the tests and trials in the first place: to prepare you for the special job He has for you. So don't settle for anything less than His best. It's just around the corner and worth it (Revelation 3:11). Hold on!

Everything must be judged from the standpoint of love.

WHEN JESUS CAME, He put an end to all the religious laws of the Old Testament by giving one law that fulfills them all—love for God and fellow man: "'You shall love the Lord your God with all your heart, with all your soul, and with all your mind.' This is the first and great commandment. And the second is like it: 'You shall love your neighbor as yourself'" (Matthew 22:37–39). Jesus' law of love is all encompassing and goes above and beyond all of the other laws put together.

God's only law is now love. As long as something is done in love—unselfish, sacrificial love, God's love—then it is lawful in God's eyes. We are not judged by how well we keep the endless, legalistic commandments of the old Mosaic Law (Galatians 2:16); we are now judged only by how much love we have and how much we let love guide our actions.

The rule we must go by now in every case is this: Is it done in love? If you know you're acting in God's love, then you can go ahead by faith, according to God's Word.

The easy way is to believe the truth, God's Word; then you don't have to learn the hard way.

GOD GIVES US THE OPPORTUNITY TO LEARN THE EASY WAY by obeying what we're told, even if we don't always know why. But if we insist on learning the hard way, God is a good Father and in His love and wisdom He will let us learn by our mistakes.

God allowed Adam and Eve to go ahead and disobey so they would learn by bitter experience what they wouldn't learn the easy way, by being told, by the Word. When they went ahead and ate the fruit of the forbidden tree, God had to apply the rod—and we've been suffering for it ever since (Genesis chapter 3; Romans 5:12). But through Adam and Eve's bitter experience, all their descendants, including us, have learned the rewards of obedience and the consequences of disobedience.

"All things work together for good to those who love God" (Romans 8:28). Even our mistakes are profitable as long as we learn from them. We don't very easily forget the lessons we learn that way, but how much easier and better to follow the path of obedience to the truth of God's Word!

A crown of life is even more than a reward.

JESUS HAS PROMISED, "Be faithful until death, and I will give you the crown of life" (Revelation 2:10). He's not talking about your salvation there. Salvation is a *gift* of God (Romans 6:23). You don't work for it or earn it at all, but your *crown* is your *reward* and even more. It's not only a reward but also recognition before all of a job well done. Once we receive Jesus, we're saved whether we endure to the end or not, but we'll be given special rewards and special honor if we are a special blessing while here (Daniel 12:3; 2 Timothy 4:7–8; James 1:12).

Of course, you're going to fall down before Jesus and cast your crown before His throne like the 24 elders in Revelation 4:10. Every time you start praising the Lord you're going to forget all about that crown and it's going to tumble off right at His feet, but you'd better pick it up again and put it on and wear it proudly, because that's why He gave it to you. That's what's going to show what you have done for Him, and He wants the world to see it—your badge of faithfulness, a crown of life!

Keep the Gospel simple.

GOD'S MERCY DOESN'T HANG ON THEOLOGI-CAL TECHNICALITIES. Jesus said, "Unless you are converted and become as little children, you will by no means enter the kingdom of Heaven" (Matthew 18:3). You've got to be a baby, and babies don't waste their time arguing over theoretical theological doctrinal shibboleths.

If, as Daniel Webster[1] once argued, the Bible was intended for the instruction and conversion of the whole world, why should God cover its true meaning in such mystery and doubt that none but theologians and philosophers can discover it? It's the Devil who is the author of confusion (1 Corinthians 14:33). He tries to make salvation seem so complicated or so difficult that people can't understand it.

Don't be led away from the simplicity of the Good News of God's love in Jesus (2 Corinthians 11:3). Not everyone can understand strong doctrine or complicated theological interpretations, but everyone understands love. So stay on the main line and stick to the most important points: Jesus and His love and His salvation. Let's not argue over doctrine; let's get souls saved.

---

[1] Daniel Webster (1782–1852), U.S. lawyer, politician, and orator.

Work together, unite together, stick together, win together!

WE ARE MEANT TO BE THE LOYAL ARMY OF THE LORD, the true King and rightful Heir of Heaven and earth. We're fighting against a usurper, an impostor king, the Devil. Our goal and commission is to rescue the masses from the morasses of satanic power and the grip of the Devil on their souls, and to help restore the kingdom to the King of kings, Jesus Christ.

We must work together hand in hand in the service of the Lord, against the common enemy. The Devil's own tactic all through the ages has been to divide and conquer. If he can get God's own people fighting amongst themselves, it eventually weakens them to the point that they're unable to fight the real enemy, and down they go. So let's not allow the Devil to divide and conquer us, but rather, let's conquer him and his forces.

Things shall grow worse and worse until the end comes, so we'll need to work more and more together in greater strength and unity to overcome the Devil (2 Timothy 3:13; Ephesians 4:3). For God's sake, let's plead with God to help us be melted together in the white-hot love of His Spirit, fighting together against the foe!

Jesus came to try to make it as easy for us as He could.

JESUS TRIED TO MAKE THE CHRISTIAN LIFE SO EASY THAT ANYBODY COULD LIVE IT. He walked those dusty roads and talked to the simple fishermen and the tax collectors and the drunks and harlots to show them that God loved them all and that they could all love God, they could all be Christians, they could all love each other and serve each other and serve the world with the Gospel.

God changed His whole system when it was proven that we couldn't keep His laws. He made a way of escape, a way of mercy, a way of forgiveness and grace: salvation. Now nobody has any excuse for blaming their problems on God, because He has made a way out, a way to get the victory, a way to overcome our sins and faults and shortcomings and problems and weaknesses, whatever they may be. Jesus is the Way, the Truth, and the Life (John 14:6). He paid the price, made the way, and gave us the truth, and He alone can help us to live the kind of life we ought to live.

He never asks of any of us a standard that is beyond our individual reach. Whatever He asks, we can do with His help and by His grace, and through His power and His love we can attain it (Philippians 4:13).

"This is the condemnation, that the light has come into the world, and men loved darkness rather than light" (John 3:19).

WHY WOULD ANYONE CHOOSE DARKNESS?—Because darkness seems easier. The light is blinding and burns out all the darkness. A lot of people are not willing to let the light destroy their old ways.

When people reject the truth, God allows them to believe a lie, because after they reject the truth there's nothing left to believe but a lie. When they reject God, there's no god left for them but Satan. It's like Adam and Eve in the Garden: When they believed Satan's lies over what God had told them, they ate the forbidden fruit of the tree of the knowledge of good and evil (Genesis chapter 3). Their greatest sin was not eating the fruit, but rejecting God's truth and believing the Devil's lie instead. Those who want to believe the Devil's lies will do so, but the Holy Spirit will show the Lord's children what's true and what isn't.

Thank God for His Word, which has brought us out of the darkness of this world into His glorious light and the freedom of the true Gospel of Jesus Christ. "For you were once darkness, but now you are light in the Lord. Walk as children of light" (Ephesians 5:8).

Don't let the Devil sidetrack you into anything less than God's best.

Did you know that the Devil sometimes tempts us to do *GOOD* things? Not all opportunities are of God. Some of them can be tricks of the Devil—decoys, blind alleys, red herrings, sidetracks, and downright disasters put there by the Devil to try to distract you. If he can't stop you, he'll try to keep you from doing the *best* thing; he'll try to sidetrack you into wasting your time on something that he makes you think is good, and sometimes it is. He tries to distract your attention from the things you should be most concerned about so that you become busy with a little here and a little there until the opportunity to do the most important thing is gone.

How do you tell the difference between the voice of God and the voice of the Devil? Well, if the voice tells you to do something bad, you know it's the Devil. If it tells you to do something good, you can be pretty sure it is God. It could be a trick of the Devil, though, so always ask God for a confirmation. If the first voice was the Devil, God will tell you to do something that will prove better in the end.

Let Jesus be your "first love," and always keep Him in that place (Revelation 2:4).

F OR CHRIST TO BE VALUED AT ALL, He must be valued above all. You must seek first the King and His kingdom, and to seek first means foremost and above all—before everything else, above everything else, beyond everything else, and more than anything else. The *first* place must belong to Him.

What Jesus values most from us is our time. To neglect your fellowship with the King of kings because you're so busy with the affairs of the kingdom can be disastrous to your spiritual life and communion with the Lord. "You shall have no other gods before Me" (Exodus 20:3)—not even His service or lost souls. So it behooves you to give Jesus time, and you should give Him some time every single day.

If you'll just put Jesus first and delight yourself in Him most of all, then He can trust you with other things, because they will not come between you and Him. They will not supersede nor distract, but they will augment your service to Him and "all these things shall be added to you" in His time (Psalm 37:4; Matthew 6:33).

Desperate prayer means crying out to God with a whole heart.

ALL OF OUR LITTLE PRAYERS ARE WELL AND GOOD. God hears them and knows they're sincere, and He answers accordingly. But there should also be times when we are not satisfied with the usual run of things, when we really get desperate with God in prayer and seek Him for a needed change, pouring out our hearts to Him.

God never fails. He always answers when we stir ourselves to call upon Him with a whole heart. He says, "You will seek Me and find Me, when you search for Me with all your heart" (Jeremiah 29:13). Wholehearted means getting in the Spirit, really focusing on the object of your prayer, and praying with a whole soul.

Desperate prayer is good for your own spiritual condition. It's good to know that you have really poured out your heart to the Lord. When do you really pray? When do *you* really get in the Spirit? When was the last time you really poured out your heart in prayer, beseeching God for some particularly serious situation or interceding for someone else? You should!

DECEMBER 21

Don't let the Devil
get you down.

DISCOURAGEMENT IS ONE OF THE DEVIL'S FAVORITE WEAPONS. He tries to get us looking at our own mistakes, sins, weaknesses, and failures. The Devil, the accuser of the saints, picks on all the little things, all our tiny faults. If he can't discourage us any other way, he tries to belittle us and belittle what we're doing. He whispers the lies that are the most easily believed, either about us or about other people.

But the Bible doesn't say to look at yourself or others. It doesn't say to look at all the problems and troubles either. It says, "Look to Jesus" (Hebrews 12:2).

What does it mean to be discouraged?—It means to not be encouraged, to be without courage, or when courage is at a low ebb. Discouragement is really a loss of faith.

"Faith comes by hearing the Word of God" (Romans 10:17), so when you get discouraged, the quickest remedy is to start praying and reading the Word and quoting Scriptures and telling the Devil he's a liar. That's how your faith will grow, and as it does, the doubts will flee and you'll be on the road to victory again. So when things look darkest, don't look down, look up! Start praising the Lord and you'll often praise your way right out of the pit into which the Devil is trying to cast you!

The Word is our guide, our standard whereby we measure all things, even the Words that God gives us today.

SOME PEOPLE THINK THAT THE LAST TIME GOD EVER SPOKE was to Saint John on the Isle of Patmos, when John received the book of Revelation, the final book of the Bible, and that God hasn't spoken since. But aren't you glad that God still speaks to His children today? Once you're a growing, maturing Christian, you can get the guidance and instructions you need for your present circumstances directly from the Lord Himself.

But how do you know that what you hear is really the voice of God? How do you test your inspiration? Scripture is the yard-stick; it's the final authority by which you can measure anything that's said. The Lord may give you new details or clarification, like filling in the gaps, but true revelations will never contradict the basic principles of the Bible.

Revelations usually come like a quick flash, but then you have to see if there is a scriptural precedent where such a thing could have happened before. Look for a similar situation in the Word. Measure it with the yardstick of the Scriptures. Weigh it in the balances. Check it out with the Department of Weights and Measures, the Bible.

"We who have believed do enter that rest" (Hebrews 4:3).

If you know that God loves you and is going to look after you no matter what happens, you can have perfect peace and rest in the Lord, knowing He's going to take care of everything (Isaiah 26:3). But if you're confused and worrying and fretting and fuming, you're not trusting. You don't yet have the faith you ought to have.

The secret of calm and peace, rest and patience, faith and love is resting in the Lord. Trusting is a picture of complete rest and peace of mind, heart, and spirit. Put Him first each day by taking time to bask in His spiritual sunshine, rest in His arms, drink deeply of His Word, and inhale of His Spirit. Then even when you may be busy and your body in motion, your attitude and spirit will remain restful and calm.

> There is a place of quiet rest,
> Near to the heart of God.
> A place where sin cannot molest,
> Near to the heart of God.
>
> O Jesus, blessed Redeemer,
> Sent from the heart of God,
> Hold us who wait before Thee
> Near to the heart of God![1]

[1] Cleland Boyd McAfee (1866–1944).

DECEMBER 24

Tonight we commemorate Your birth, Jesus.

 A PRAYER FOR CHRISTMAS EVE:

Thank You, Jesus, for this time to celebrate Your birth. Every day is like Christmas for us because You're so good to us every day, but this time is extra special because You pour out Your love in extra measure. We feel Your love from loved ones, acquaintances, and even strangers. There's just something about Your birthday that turns people's hearts and minds to peace and love and goodwill. It brings out the best in everyone because it brings *You* out, and You're the best!

We thank You most of all for the greatest gift ever—Yourself. Thank You for coming to earth and living like one of us so we could understand Your Father's love, and then for dying for us so we could experience His mercy and forgiveness. Thank You for all that went into giving us salvation and eternal life. You did all that for our sakes! Help us to return Your love by helping to keep the spirit of Christmas alive throughout the coming year as we share You and Your love with those You bring our way. Amen.

> O Holy Child of Bethlehem,
> Descend to us we pray.
> Cast out our sin and enter in,
> Be born in us today.[1]

---

[1] Phillips Brooks (1835–1893), "O Little Town of Bethlehem."

Jesus came for love and lived in love and died for love that we might live and love forever!

Jesus DIDN'T JUST COME TO EARTH AND LIVE AMONG US; He had to temporarily renounce His citizenship in Heaven to become one of us (Philippians 2:6–7).

He came as a meek and quiet, weak and helpless baby, and conformed Himself to our human ways of life. He was human. He got tired, He got hungry, He got weary. He was subject to all these things, even as we are, that He might better reach us with His Father's love and communicate with us on the lowly level of our own human understanding (Hebrews 4:15).

In the end, He suffered for us at terrific price, because of His love. He was spat upon, cursed, condemned as a criminal, and despised in death. But as He hung on the cross in disgrace and agony, dying for the sins of the very ones who were crucifying Him, He was showing love to the whole world. "Greater love has no one than this, than to lay down one's life for his friends" (John 15:13). Jesus is the friend who loved us enough to lay down His life that we might be saved—and it all started with a tiny babe in a manger!

> Out of the ivory palaces,
> Into this world of woe,
> Only His great eternal love
> Made my Savior go.[1]

[1] Henry Barraclough (1891–1983).

With God's help you can do anything, go anywhere, and be anybody He wants you to be!

GOD DOESN'T WANT YOU TO TRY OR PRETEND TO BE SOMETHING YOU'RE NOT and couldn't possibly be. However, He teaches in His Word that almost anybody can be almost anything if they have faith and it's according to His will.

Too many Christians have been taught two conflicting doctrines: first, that they can't be saintly and perfect; second, that unless they are, they can't be saved. Both are the Devil's own doctrines! It's no wonder that a lot of Christians give up trying to be or do anything for the Lord! But the wonderful truth of the matter is that you can do anything with Jesus' help. "I can do all things through Christ who strengthens me" (Philippians 4:13).

So whenever the Devil lies to you and tries to convince you that you're nothing and nobody and could never do anything for the Lord, slap him in the face with Scriptures. "It is no longer I who live, but Christ lives in me; and the life which I now live in the flesh I live by faith in the Son of God, who loved me and gave Himself for me" (Galatians 2:20). Where sin and human faults and failings abound, God's grace does more abound (Romans 5:20). That's what it's all about!

"His banner over me is love"
(Song of Solomon 2:4 NIV).

THE BIBLE TELLS US THAT "GOD IS LOVE" (1 John 4:8), so we know that the converse is also true—that love is God. Jesus said the greatest commandment is to love (Matthew 22:36–40). To love God and our neighbors as ourselves should be what we teach and preach—our message, our life, our goal, our everything.

Love is an emotion, something that causes us to move into action to do something good. Then we can move others into motion by the loving power of God's Holy Spirit.

So step out by faith and talk to others today about God's love, and try to make them happy. There are wonders of love that you yourself can enjoy along with some other lonely soul if you will only try. If you give love, you'll get love. It multiplies and grows like the bread and the fish or the cruse of oil and the barrel of meal (Matthew 14:15–21; 1 Kings 17:11–16; 2 Kings 4:2–6). The more you give, the more you get, and you give and give and give, and you get and get and get!

> Love wasn't put in your heart to stay.
> Love isn't love till you give it away![1]

[1] Author unknown.

Love, the Lord, the real values in life—how worthless everything else is!

ONLY JESUS CAN REALLY SATISFY YOUR HEART. He is the answer. But as long as you're still looking for the things of this world to satisfy and make you happy, you won't find the truth (1 John 2:15–17).

God's Word warns us "not to be haughty, nor to trust in uncertain riches" (1 Timothy 6:17). Don't be like the rich man in the Bible who wanted to build bigger barns to hoard his goods rather than share them with others (Luke 12:15–21). His own soul became barney and materialistic, and he was deluded by "the deceitfulness of riches" (Matthew 13:22). If God blesses you with money, don't trust in money or love it (1 Timothy 6:10), but trust "in the living God, who gives us richly all things to enjoy" (1 Timothy 6:17).

> You can have your earthly treasure,
> Your silver and your gold,
> But the Spirit, it's the Spirit,
> That can never yet be sold!

(Prayer:) May we desire, love, and hunger for Your Spirit, love, and simplicity—the realities, Lord, not the things of this world that are soon to pass away. "For the things which are seen are temporary, but the things which are not seen are eternal" (2 Corinthians 4:18).

God engineers everything.

G OD HAS THE WHOLE WORLD TO THINK ABOUT, yet somehow He manages to keep everything under perfect control and ultimately going the direction He wants it to go. Everything is planned; everything is ordered in "decency and in order" (1 Corinthians 14:40), and nothing can happen without His will. Whatever happens is what ought to happen or what God allows to happen for a reason. Everything is in His hands and nothing happens without His will, especially to His children whom He loves and to whom He wants to be good.

God engineers every situation and has a good purpose for everything—even our troubles. "We know that *all* things work together for good to those who love God" (Romans 8:28). So the next time you find yourself in a situation that doesn't look so good to you, take another look. It may not be immediately apparent, but sooner or later God will turn your "bad" to good!

(Prayer:) Thank You for always working everything out for our good, because we love You and You love us, and because You promised to. Help us to see Your hand in everything, and help us to hold tight to Your hand through everything, knowing that You know best and want only the best for us. Amen.

We're in a hurry!

TIME IS SHORT AND GETTING SHORTER ALL THE TIME. The end is not far away, so we'd better get as much done as we can, and get it done fast! The main thing that we're short of is time. If we could see things as God does, we'd no doubt decide that a lot of the things we place such importance on now can wait till we get to Heaven. We'll have all eternity to enjoy those things, but right now we are living in time and we've got very little of it left.

We should thank the Lord for each day He gives us the opportunity to serve Him and help spread the Gospel. Every day is precious. We'd better make hay while the sun shines. We'd better put our best into what is best and make it count. The hour is late and we have to do the works of Him who sent us while it is day, because the night is coming when no one can work—at least not like we can now (John 9:4). It's late and the days are evil, so we've got to redeem the time (Ephesians 5:16). We need to make every day count and really try to finish the job He has given us to do.

Goodbye, past!
Hello, future!

As the year comes to a close, before the New Year comes in, it's good to sit down and ask yourself, "What have I accomplished this past year? Have I done my best for Jesus, when He has done so much for me?" Has it truly been His year, lived for Him, by His power, His strength, and His guidance? Was it spent doing His will? Did it bear the fruits of His Spirit and the fruits of His Word? Has it been a year that you're thankful for because you're sure Jesus is pleased with it?

It's also a good time to count your blessings. What are you most thankful for during the past year? What prayer or hope do you have for the New Year? What promise from His Word do you claim for the New Year?

(Prayer:) Help us, Lord, as we start this New Year, to look forward with faith. Give us strength to do what You want. Lead and guide us, and keep us in Your will. Help it to be a year that we live to the fullest for You. Amen.

> Another year is dawning, dear Father, let it be
> In working or in waiting, another year with Thee.[1]

[1] Frances Ridley Havergal (1836–1879).

About the Author

David Brandt Berg (1919–1994) and his back-to-the-basics approach to Christianity started a worldwide missionary movement.

Berg's parents were both Christian pastors and evangelists, and his early years were spent traveling with them in evangelistic work. In 1941 he nearly died of pneumonia, shortly after joining the U.S. Army. After determining to rededicate his life to Christian service, he experienced a miraculous healing.

For most of the next 27 years he worked as a pastor and in various evangelistic endeavors until, in 1968, he received God's call to take the Gospel to the hippies of southern California. There he and his then teenaged children began a ministry to the youth that grew and eventually became known as The Family International. Today, members of The Family International engage in missionary and humanitarian work in over 100 countries worldwide.

Berg called on his followers to devote their full time to spreading the message of Christ's love and salvation as far and wide as possible, unfettered by convention or tradition, and to teach others to do the same.

Berg also decried the de-Christianization and decay in values of Western society. He viewed the trend toward a New World Order as setting the stage for the rise of the Antichrist, a godless world dictator whom the Bible predicts will rule the world in the last days before Christ's return.

Berg's lively, down-to-earth, and often unconventional approach to heavenly matters makes his writings an important and unique contribution to Christian literature.

INDEX

Communion

Conviction / Compromise

Creation / Evolution

Death / Afterlife

Devil's Devices

Disasters (see **God's Plan**)

Discipleship

Faithfulness

Fear, Freedom from

Fellowship (see **Unity**)

Forgiveness and Mercy

Giving

God

God, Dependence on

(See also **Hearing from Heaven; Righteousness / Self-Righteousness; Strength and Power**)

God, Seek First

God's Care and Protection

(See also **Comfort and Hope; God's Love; God's Supply**)

God's Love

God's Plan

God's Supply

God's Way vs. Man's Way (see **Righteousness / Self-Righteousness**)

Good Example

Grace vs. Law

Happiness and Joy

Haste (see **Patience**)

Healing and Health

Hearing from Heaven

Heaven

Holidays and Special Days

Holy Spirit

Humility / Pride

Inspiration and Enthusiasm

Jesus

Jesus' Return and the Millennium

Little People and Little Things

Love

Love for the Lost

Love One Another

Marriage

Miracles

Missionaries

Music

Obedience to God

Old Age

Patience

Peace/War

Persecution

Pleasure and Enjoyment (see **Happiness and Joy**)

Positiveness

Praise

Prayer

Reading and Viewing

Relations with Others

Simplicity

Sin and Repentance

Spiritual Growth and Maturity

Thankfulness (see **Praise; Positiveness**)

Time, Redeeming the

Unbelief

Unity

Vision and Goals

War (see Peace / War)

Wealth and Materialism

Will of God

Wisdom

Witnessing

Word of God

Yieldedness